BACK FROM THE DEAD

Piia Wirsu with Mick Doleman

based on the award-winning ABC podcast

EXPANSE

ABC
BOOKS

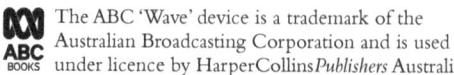 The ABC 'Wave' device is a trademark of the Australian Broadcasting Corporation and is used under licence by HarperCollins*Publishers* Australia

HarperCollins*Publishers*
Australia • Brazil • Canada • France • Germany • Holland • India
Italy • Japan • Mexico • New Zealand • Poland • Spain • Sweden
Switzerland • United Kingdom • United States of America

HarperCollins acknowledges the Traditional Custodians of the lands upon which we live and work, and pays respect to Elders past and present.

First published on Gadigal Country in Australia in 2025
by HarperCollins*Publishers* Australia Pty Limited
ABN 36 009 913 517
harpercollins.com.au

Copyright © Piia Wirsu 2025

The right of Piia Wirsu to be identified as the author of this work has been asserted by her in accordance with the *Copyright Act 1968*.

All rights reserved. Apart from any use as permitted under the *Copyright Act 1968*, no part may be reproduced, copied, scanned, stored in a retrieval system, recorded, or transmitted, in any form or by any means, without the prior written permission of the publisher. Without limiting the exclusive rights of any author, contributor, or the publisher of this publication, any unauthorised use of this publication to train generative artificial intelligence (AI) technologies is expressly prohibited. HarperCollins also exercises its rights under Article 4(3) of the Digital Single Market Directive 2019/790 and expressly reserves this publication from the text and data-mining exception.

HarperCollins*Publishers*
Macken House, 39/40 Mayor Street Upper
Dublin 1, D01 C9W8, Ireland

A catalogue record for this book is available from the National Library of Australia

ISBN 978 0 7333 4380 3 (paperback)
ISBN 978 1 4607 1828 5 (ebook)

Cover design by Michelle Zaiter, HarperCollins Design Studio, based on a design by Isabel Muldoon, Senior Design Creative, ABC
Front cover image: *Blythe Star* by Rex Cox
Back cover images (from left to right): Tasmanian Archives (LPIC33-1-132); Mick Doleman; Piia Wirsu
Author photographs by (from top to bottom): Edith Roley and Unity Bank
Maps by John Frith
Typeset in Sabon LT Std by Kirby Jones
Printed and bound by CPI Group (UK) Ltd, Croydon, CR0 4YY

*Dedicated to my wife of 50 years, Joanie,
who has been my rock.*

*And to all seafarers and the International Transport
Workers' Federation that keeps them safe – MD*

*For Harry, Pip, Ollie and Henry.
The world is yours – PW*

CONTENTS

Map of Tasmania		viii
Map of Deep Glen Bay		ix
Preface		1
Prologue		3
Chapter 1	Seafaring in the Blood	11
Chapter 2	All a Bit Mad	30
Chapter 3	One In, All In	47
Chapter 4	A Final Glimpse	55
Chapter 5	Sinking Realisation	73
Chapter 6	In the Shit	83
Chapter 7	We've Lost a Ship	102
Chapter 8	The Search that Wasn't	118
Chapter 9	Headless Chickens	131
Chapter 10	Losing Time	147
Chapter 11	Bickering and Delay	160
Chapter 12	Goodbye	175
Chapter 13	A Last Push	192
Chapter 14	The Best of Them	207
Chapter 15	It's Over	229
Chapter 16	You're All Dead	248
Chapter 17	Someone's Playing a Horrible Joke	266
Chapter 18	Welcome Home	290
Chapter 19	Who's to Answer?	298
Chapter 20	Not Just a Shipwreck Survivor	317
Epilogue		329
Acknowledgements		333
Timeline		335
Glossary		339

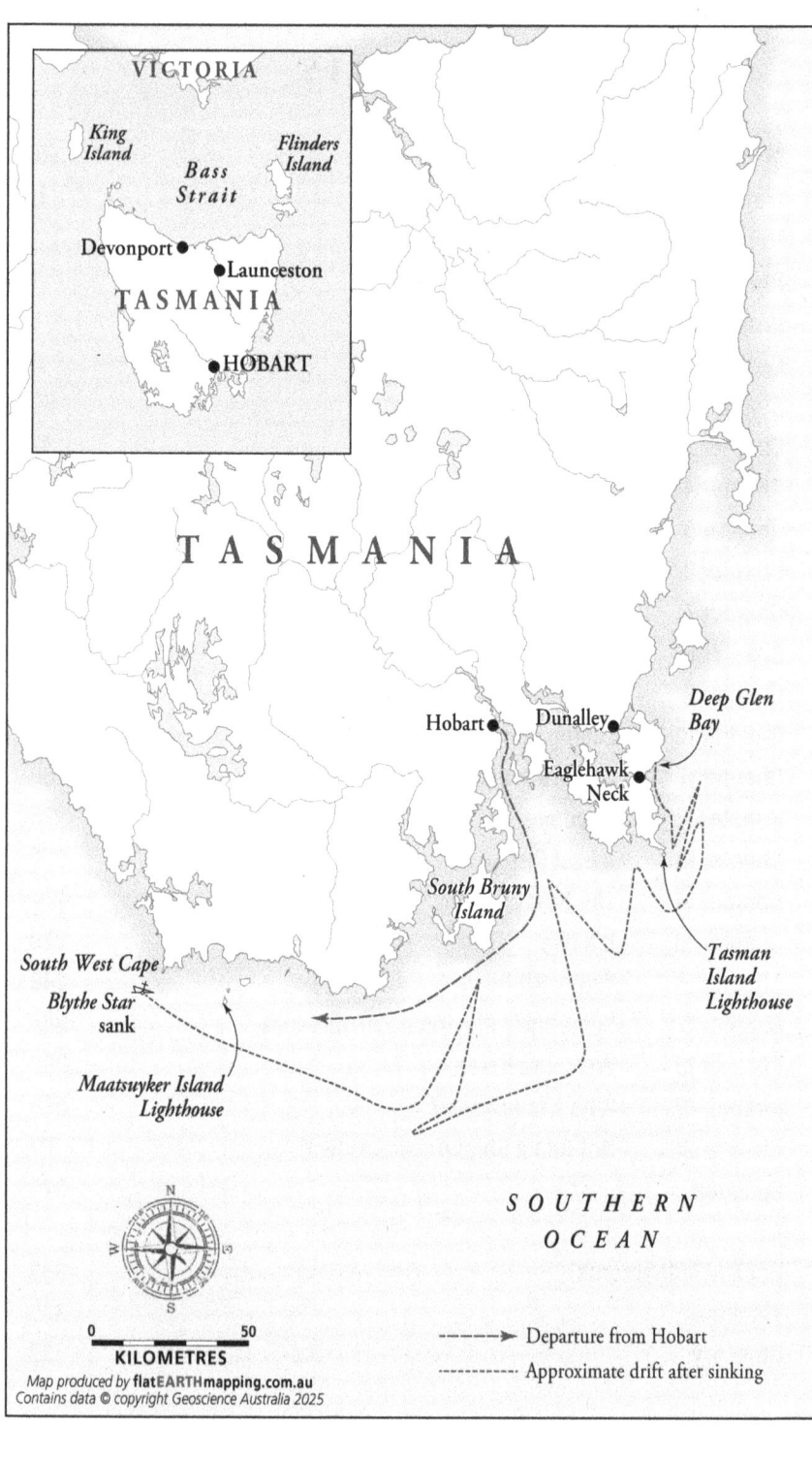

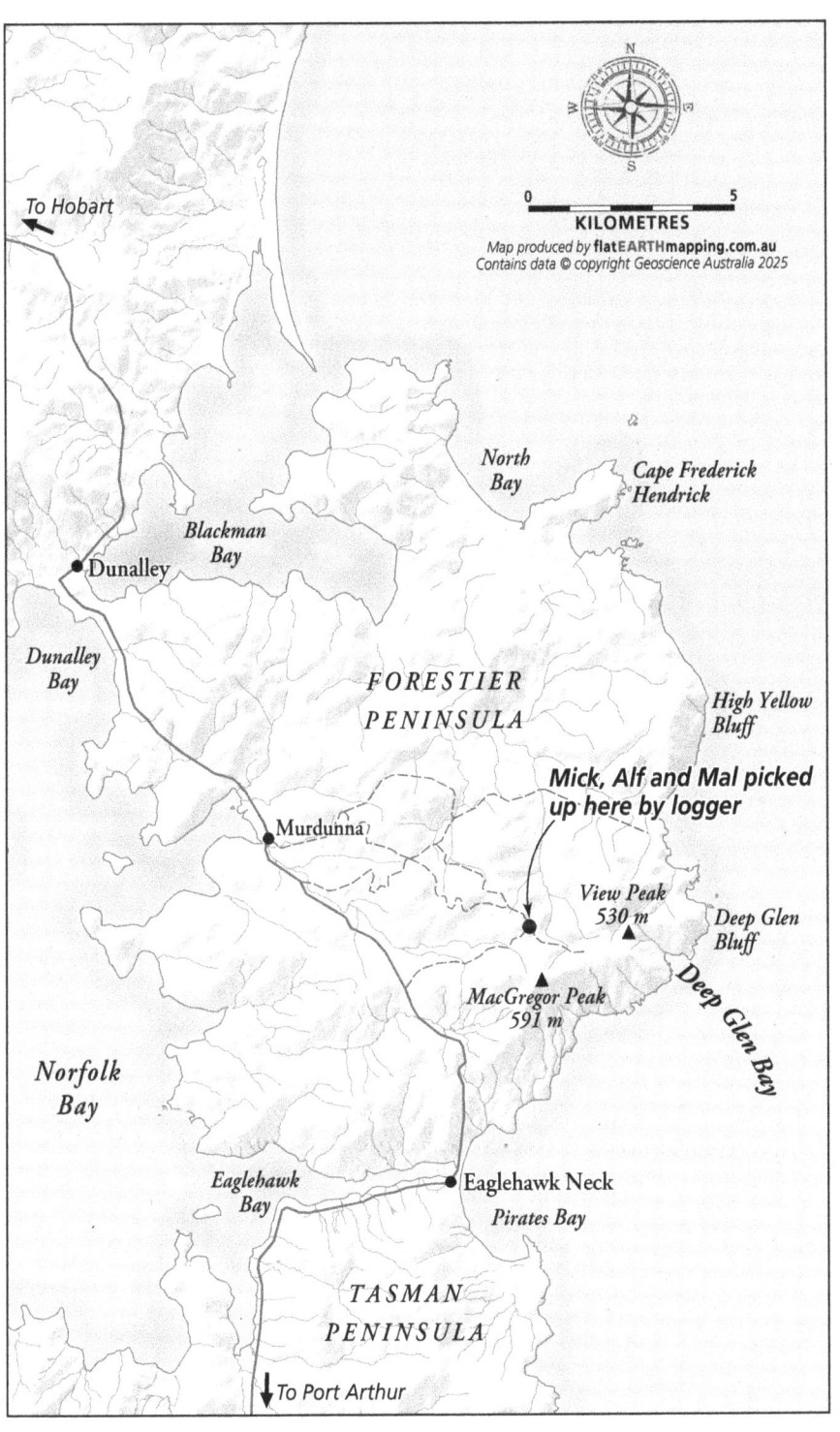

Preface

The story of the sinking of the *Blythe Star* in 1973 was largely untold for more than four decades despite being the largest sea and air search in Australia's history at the time. Mick Doleman is the last remaining survivor and was only 18 years old when disaster unfolded around him. He realised that if he didn't talk about what happened aboard the *Blythe Star* and the following days as the ten-man crew fought for survival, then this story would be lost to history.

In 2023, Mick sat down for an extended interview for the ABC podcast *Expanse. Back From the Dead* is inspired by this podcast series and has been informed by extensive interviews with the key people who remain to tell the story, by archival news reports, interviews and accounts, and by the transcripts of the Marine Court of Inquiry that followed the miraculous survival of some of the crew. Dialogue has either been directly quoted from historical sources or from the memories of people who were there.

The story of the *Blythe Star* and its crew is so incredible it needs little embellishment.

Prologue

17 October 1973

The waves were hungry. They towered as high as telegraph poles, powered by some of the wildest winds in the world which had worked themselves into a fury over thousands of kilometres without touching land. Known as the Roaring Forties, they feel vindictive and make the Southern Ocean one of the fiercest places on earth.

In the middle of this heaving, desolate world tossed a small orange life raft. Eighteen-year-old Mick Doleman gritted his teeth against the churning swell. How the hell had he found himself here? He'd never wanted to join the *Blythe Star* supply ship on its two-day voyage around Tasmania to King Island. If he'd known what was coming nothing would have dragged him aboard, because now he was at the whim of nature in a tiny life raft with nine other crew.

Nothing could have prepared Mick for the moment, days earlier, when he'd been thrown from his bunk, biting cold water rushing into his cabin along with the realisation that the ship was sinking. This happened in movies – it didn't happen to blokes like him. Except it was.

In the confusion, as the men had scrambled to get off the deck before the *Blythe Star* sank silently in front of their eyes, they'd had to put their lives in each other's hands. Now, here they all were, five days later, sardined inside a domed orange life raft the size of a children's paddling pool, while the malevolent Southern Ocean impressed upon them that they were only human.

Salt crusted around the crevices on Mick's face, leaching the moisture from his swollen lips and the air felt sharp. A swill of seawater stewed around his legs, causing the skin on his pale feet to soften until it seemed as though it might fall away. Mick's bare torso rubbed against the side of the raft, the salt water chafing against his skin. For the thousandth time he wished he was wearing more than just his jocks, which were wholly inadequate in the freezing conditions. It had been hours since Mick's last drink of water. Funny thing how, when you know you can't have something, it's all you want. It consumes your thoughts. Although in honesty he would happily neck a beer too, if it were on offer.

A gravelly voice interrupted his thoughts. 'My missus is going to go crook I lost her new kitchen mixer,' Ken Jones said. Ken was the first mate of their doomed ship. He was tall and handsome, years of working at sea giving him the muscles to fill out a suit in just the right way to draw the eyes of unattached young ladies.

Mick laughed. 'I'd give anything for my cassette player. Give me something to pass the time. Mind you, Joanie will be stoked. She bloody hates my music.'

Talking of home made it seem closer somehow. Otherwise it was too easy to forget that a world beyond this cramped raft existed. Mick would find his mind drifting away on spirals of thought, as though he no longer controlled its meanderings. And when he'd stir from his reverie, he'd feel stung by reality – ripped forcibly from the soft cocoon of memory and daydream into a savage present that was more fantastical than anything his mind could have conjured.

Somehow, in all his dreams of seafaring, he had never imagined this; endless days in an emergency life raft the size of a three-man tent with nine other men he barely knew. They sat with their backs propped against the circle of rubber that was their only protection, their legs thrown together in the centre like some warped game of Hokey Pokey. Clinging to soggy hope, they were blind to the world outside the cramped confines of the raft. No one had spoken for a minute, or an hour. It was hard to tell as time melted with the rhythm of the waves. Up, down. Up, down.

They longed for homes and loved ones they might never see again. Did anybody know where they were? Did anybody even know they were missing?

Mick looked across at a sorry figure curled on the other side of the raft. They had heard nothing from the captain since the day the *Blythe Star* had lifted its bow into the air and slipped without fanfare below the inky blue. Not a striking man to begin with, after five days in a raft, Cruikshank's frame seemed to have fallen in on itself. And still he said nothing, even as the light faded under the weight of dark clouds and the wind started to howl a warning as it tore over the waves. The weather was changing.

'I think things are about to get a bit curly, lads,' Ken Jones said.

The crew shared apprehensive glances, and Mick's eyes slid over to John Sloan. He was asleep, his chest rising and falling rapidly. No one said anything – they didn't have to. They all knew John was in no fit state to be taking on a storm after his medication disappeared with the ship.

Apprehension built as the minutes ticked to God knows where and there was a distant roll of thunder. A storm is different on the ocean. It whips itself into a frenzy, picking up the waves and hurling them, unleashing a fury untamed by land. The roiling grey of the tempestuous ocean reflected in the sky. If Mick had been able to stand and poke his head out of the raft cover, all he would have seen was a wall of white-flecked grey water towering over him. But standing was definitely out. In fact, just about anything other than gritting their teeth and hanging on was out.

Night came suddenly, the usual creeping dusk engulfed by the brewing storm. The blackness was complete. Mick could sense the others around him, but his eyes might as well have been sewn closed. The waves were still building with no regard for the men huddled inside the flimsy speck of orange.

Mick could hear occasional curses and grunts from the rest of the crew as they tried to keep themselves upright in a world that had become liquid. Everything moved. There was not a single solid point of reference. The body stew that had sloshed around their feet for days was thrown into the air, mixing with the gaspingly cold water hurled by spiteful winds. The ever-present numbing cold had become biting.

'Where's the can opener?' Ken asked.

'I've got it.' Cook Alf Simpson replied.

'Make sure you keep tight bloody hold of it,' Mick growled.

They'd long since pitched overboard the fishing hooks they'd discovered in the emergency kit, the needle point too risky on the flimsy rubber that was keeping them afloat. But they needed the can opener.

Mick's muscles screamed as his whole body tensed against the inevitable heave of the next wave, his fingers scrabbling for something to cling to. 'You right, lad?' Ken asked Mick, leaning toward him to be heard.

Mick couldn't say he was all that chipper, but didn't like to be the one to say so. 'Yep,' he replied. Luckily, Ken couldn't see the fear in his eyes.

'We're not going to let this beat us,' Ken said. It was a statement of fact, and Ken's certainty injected a kernel of strength into Mick.

Fucking oath, thought Mick. He was a fighter used to coming out of scraps and be buggered if he'd let some weather get the better of him. But his fists were no use out here.

The next wave built under them. Curling fingers of water picked up the raft and hoisted it metres into the air until it perched on the crest. Then, with a flick, they were crashing down its back, flying with the speed of a show ride. As the raft smashed into the trough it collapsed in on itself. Mick felt himself being flung into the air by the force and for a moment he was airborne, hoping the raft would be there to catch him as he fell. An elbow he couldn't see smashed into him, the thud lost in the fury of the storm. Somewhere in the black, the tins of water they had been so carefully rationing were flying like metal missiles around the heaving mass of bodies.

As the raft flattened back out on its way up the next wave, they all scrambled to untangle their limbs and find purchase on the slick rubber floor. But already they were hurtling down again, the two sides of the raft snapping together at the bottom, hurling them into each other once more. They were like socks in a washing machine. Only socks don't have bones that break.

Mick listened desperately for the shriek of tearing rubber, certain the floor of the raft would be torn free, that it couldn't endure this pummelling. The darkness was a stage for his fears to perform on. In his mind's eye he saw the wet, flapping canvas slapping against the waves as the raft deflated in pathetic capitulation. He saw the men being thrown into the bitter waves and imagined the water-like needles piercing his skin with cold. He felt the minutes he'd have to survive before his organs shut down from the shock of the cold. Then the sharks, cocooned from the raging world above, coming for his body as the life drained from it. Their screams and cries silenced as the storm mauled the sea.

Mick's breath was shallow and fast. He held his arms over his head as he was thrown again and again into the maelstrom of limbs. They were no longer individual men, but a single heaving tangle of bruised and broken body parts, each just trying to protect what they could of themselves in this rolling, violent world of motion.

The ocean no longer felt like just an expanse of water. It felt mean, menacing, something to be feared, something cruel in its indifference. It didn't care if he lived or died. As the storm dragged them moment by excruciating moment, he began to wonder. Forget getting out of this raft and finding help. Could he even make it through the night?

CHAPTER 1

Seafaring in the Blood

1960s

Mick Doleman grew up on a street where every house was one of three designs, all constructed with prefabricated concrete. The Housing Commission houses were designed to go up quickly, not look flash. Most were bursting at the seams, with children practically hanging from the rafters.

His childhood was one of long Australian summers, where the heat baked the air. If you could have stilled the incessant whine of cicadas and the distant drone of a lazy lawn mower, you could probably hear the brown lawn crackling as it shrivelled under the sun. The sun would rise early and didn't chase the children home until late. Long days were all skinned knees, adventures on bikes with rusted paint and bombies in the local pool.

Mick shared a room with his three brothers. Self-described maniacs, to a man they were dirty on the fact their sister had a room of her own. So, the brothers implemented a coordinated program of haunting, trying to convince her she was being visited by people passed. But growing up in a family of four brothers bred a certain cynicism, and Mick's sister wasn't fooled.

Doveton, Victoria, now a far-flung suburb of Melbourne, was built on the sweat of migrant workers. Every other family was called McCoy, Ryan or Fitzpatrick. Fathers would head off on foot in the morning to take their place on the line in the factory in exchange for a weekly pay cheque while their children ran a little wild. Footy was like a religion, and practically everyone who could played for the local club.

Young Mick once asked the priest who coached his football team why the team hadn't won a game if God was on their side. Mick was deadly serious – the fact God couldn't swing one single victory for his team was proof enough in his young mind that religion wasn't for him.

The priest didn't appreciate Mick's enquiring mind and not long after the back of Mick's calves were aching from a strapping.

Mick's house was 100 metres from the abattoir, and when the wind blew a certain way the smell of freshly slaughtered meat would drift through an open window, catching on the lace curtains. At the slaughterhouse, accents from every corner of the globe could be heard; occasionally, the abattoir would see an outbreak of fighting between those of different nationalities or loyalties. Break time on shift would see big, burly men striding down Mick's street to the local shops, blood and gore clinging to their clothes and scaring the living bejesus out of half the residents.

Mick knew that whenever he got home the front door would be open – there was no point locking up, as no one had much to steal. But more than that, people in Doveton were loyal to their community. You'd never do something that would hurt your neighbours or friends. Everyone was in it together. And if someone popped around, they'd always be welcome to stay for a cuppa.

Poverty isn't a word Mick likes, but growing up he knew what it was like to live from meal to meal. One day, his mother chivvied Mick out the door to the butcher's to get some sausages for tea. Just put it on the family tab, she said.

Slipping through the busy shop to stand before the big, glass bays displaying the day's meat, Mick ordered the sausages. 'Mum said she'll fix you up later,' he told the butcher.

'No. You haven't paid for the last lot yet,' a booming voice replied. 'You're not getting them, so nick off.'

As Mick made his way back to the door empty-handed, his cheeks stinging with embarrassment, he felt the burning gaze of other shoppers. The butcher was only saved a brick through his window that night because Mick's conscience got the better of him, but he never forgot that day and how it made him feel.

* * *

Life in Doveton could be rough. People spoke with their fists as much as words, and there was a raw honesty to things. People tended to be tough as guts, but more often than not with a heart of gold. They wouldn't take bullshit from anyone and welcomed a straight shooter with a warmth that lit the belly. Mick's father, Thomas, was a man like that.

Thomas was a baptised Catholic, but you wouldn't say he was a devoutly religious man. Still, the family went to church from time to time, where the brutal Father Fitzpatrick presided over his somewhat wayward flock. That is, until one Sunday.

Mick and his four siblings, hair neatly combed and dressed in their school uniforms, found themselves fidgeting in the pew beside their parents.

Father Fitzpatrick's sermon washed over Mick, his young legs itching to be outside and moving. Then he noticed his father's face – it was dark as a summer thunderstorm.

Oblivious, Father Fitzpatrick continued on with his diatribe about the evils of contraception. 'There'll be no such thing in my parish,' he bellowed, his voice echoing in the brick church and beating down on the heads of his parishioners.

'It's a sin! God does not accept it, and neither do I ...'

But people weren't looking at the priest anymore. To Mick's horror, they were looking at him and his family.

Mick's dad was on his feet, contempt in his face. 'Get up! We're getting out of here,' Thomas said to his family.

See, in Doveton, half the people started their life somewhere else. The kids had the arse out of their pants from wear, and they didn't have a penny loose in their pockets.

Thomas might not have been an educated man, but he knew right from wrong. And telling people living from meal to meal with five hungry kids already at the table that they couldn't use contraception? Well, he knew that was wrong. And he wasn't going to sit there and cop that from anyone. Even a minister of God.

So Mick, his mum and siblings all stood up and walked right out of the Catholic church behind his dad.

'We're never going back there again,' Thomas said to his family.

Mick might have been embarrassed at the scene his dad caused, but he couldn't help but think, *That was a bloody good decision, Dad. Don't know what you done it for, but good one.*

Mick was no stranger to the punishments doled out by the priests and religious sisters. With a streak of rebel in him, he'd regularly butt heads with Sister Clements.

Dressed in what he called her 'scarecrow clothing', the sister kept a leather strap in the pouch of her black habit. It'd come out when she called Mick to the front of the class and crack as it made contact with his hands.

She would only stop when you said, 'Thank you, Sister.'

With every strap, Mick hated the church even more. So he was delighted when, true to his word, his dad severed all ties. The children found themselves out of the Catholic school and headed to the local public school.

Up until then, when Mick and his Catholic school mates walked to school every day they had to walk past the so-called

'Protestants' from the public school. Whenever the Catholics and 'Proddies' crossed paths, it was on. Fists flew and insults were hurled. Now, Mick found himself on the other side in that little fracas – in with the Protestants, fists flying at the Catholics. Fickle world.

Thomas's sense of right and wrong must have been genetic because Mick had it too. He couldn't stand a bully. He didn't give a shit how many honorifics came before your name – if you took advantage of other people, stood over them or pushed them around, he had no time for it.

* * *

For as long as he could remember, the sea had been calling to Mick. His head was filled with ideas of a life on the waves. As he puts it, 'I could eat a ship – loved them.'

Mick's dad was a seafarer. Originally from Glasgow, Scotland, Thomas had a lust for adventure. As a young man he'd signed up to become a policeman in the Middle East. Then adventure had called again, and Thomas boarded a ship to Australia. He'd gone on to spend the rest of his working life at sea.

As a boy, Mick would head down to the docks when his dad's ship was in port and the sea breeze would blow dreams of a seafaring life into his head. But life in a family with five children doesn't leave much room for daydreaming. When Thomas's ship was in port it would be time for Mick and his siblings to have a rendezvous with the cook. A big man with a rounded belly, the cook owned bowls and scissors, which perfectly qualified him for the job of Doleman family hairdresser.

Mick's family would traipse up the gangway onto the Mobil tanker and make their way to the galley. Then, one by one, each unwilling boy would perch on a chair and the cook would clap a cooking bowl on his head. The cook would then whiz around the bowl with the scissors before whipping it off and shaving the rest underneath.

Considering it nothing less than juvenile torture, Mick would be squirming, wanting to be away. But enduring the haircut did come with perks. Once they were all done and curious eyes were looking the other way, they'd all stuff as much food as they could into their clothing. Tins of pineapple and peaches clanked as they shuffled back down the gangway to the shore, their father having recruited them into his little heist. It meant food on the table that night.

Whatever Mick's dreams, his dad had other ideas. Thomas decided that seafaring wasn't going to be Mick's life and was determined to shake Mick's dream loose. So he packed up his 13-year-old son and headed for the docks. Mick was about to become a stowaway – or 'ringbolt', as it's called in the merchant navy.

Once on board, Mick crept into his dad's cabin. Once they were heading for open ocean, the rise and crash of the bow was like an elixir to Mick, and the salt in the air like a drug for his young mind. Mick's father might have hoped the experience would put an end to Mick's plans, but it did anything but.

One morning, the tanker was forging through the swell, spray flying backwards with a hiss. Mick woke up on the little couch where he was bunking down in his dad's cabin. Throwing off the covers, he made his way to the porthole. He flung it wide open to let in the sharp, salty air, and stuck his head out to let the wind whip his recently bowl-styled hair back and feel the sting of the spray on his face. Suddenly, he noticed a flash in the water. Then another. A pod of four dolphins were swimming alongside the ship, dipping and surfacing and playing. Their small black eyes seemed to lock onto Mick's, apparently curious about the small face poking out.

Mick laughed. With the wildness and rawness of the heaving ocean just metres away, exhilaration flushed through him. It was heady fodder for his dreams.

Mick pulled his head back inside and yanked the porthole closed as the ship heaved and lurched. The weather wasn't being kind to Mick's first-time sea stomach, but there was no way he was going to miss out on breakfast.

Food was never in abundance at home and the weather meant the mess room was poorly populated. Mick dived into two rounds of bacon and eggs, happily ploughing into the grub left after others had had their fill.

It seemed like heaven; dolphins playing alongside, a full stomach of bacon and eggs. Despite his dad's best efforts to put him off, Mick's time as a ringbolt cemented it. Mick was going to sea at the earliest opportunity.

Which came when he was just 16. Mick packed a couple of pairs of jeans, some shirts and the bare necessities of toiletries in a little rucksack and jumped on a flight to the industrial town of Newcastle, on Australia's eastern seaboard. This was where his career as a seafarer would begin, at the Maritime Industry Deck Boy School.

A big, burly man, George Martindale might have been pushing 80 but he was well up to the task of teaching a rowdy bunch of tough young men about life on the open ocean. Mick sat alongside his contemporaries in the classroom on his first day, ready to realise his lifelong dream.

Lesson one began with George laying down the law in his English accent. 'Now, I'm telling you, lads, there'll be no drinking, no fighting.' He looked at them all fiercely. 'I've never been drunk a day in my life and if I catch any of you lads drinking there'll be hell to pay.'

As the boys would find out in time, George may have been being economical with the truth.

After school Mick and his classmates would head back to their lodgings in the Cross Keys Hotel across the road. Living above the pub was where their first real lesson in seafaring began. While weekdays would see them practising boatmanship, splicing ropes and tying knots, or learning to row around in lifeboats from the BHP ships, the weekends found them partaking in the convenience of the downstairs bar and getting into all sorts of strife.

One lazy Sunday afternoon, the boys were killing time in their rooms above the public bar, which was closed. Looking for something to do, they convinced the smallest boy in the class, Jamie, to clamber into the hotel's dumb waiter.

With hushed cackles they slid the doors closed and started lowering the dumb waiter, boy and all, down. He might have been the smallest, but the lower he got the heavier he got. Suddenly the rope got away from them, flying through their hands as Jamie went sailing down and smashed into the floor below.

Screaming blue murder, it was clear Jamie was crook about the outcome. But, ever the team players, Mick and the rest reminded him of his important role in their plan. 'Just open up the doors, Jamie, and we'll look after you.'

Jamie dragged himself out, helped himself to a selection from the bar and made his way back upstairs, where he partook in what were, surely, medicinal beverages. The boys enjoyed a delightful Sunday afternoon, even if Jamie walked a little gingerly into school the next morning.

After ten weeks, Mick was officially ready to join the ranks of a ship as a deck boy. The survival training they'd had was minimal, and most of it Mick filed away in a dusty recess of his brain. After all, he wasn't going to need it, right?

* * *

Standing on the wharf in Geelong, south of Melbourne, Mick was buzzing with anticipation. He was about to board his very first ship, the *Solen*, a sizeable Shell tanker.

A lifeboat pulled up at the wharf to collect him. Mick leapt in and introduced himself.

'Oh yeah, I knew your old man,' the bosun replied. 'He was on board when we sailed her out here.' The Doleman name was known and respected in maritime circles.

When they'd boarded the ship, the bosun showed Mick to his cabin. It was everything Mick had dreamed of. Up until that moment, Mick had spent most of his life sharing a room with his three brothers. Now he had an entire cabin all to himself.

'Get yourself settled down, then come up to the messroom,' the bosun said. 'Dinner will be on at five o'clock.'

Mick unpacked his few belongings, revelling in the space and quiet of his own berth, before heading to dinner. In the messroom, he hesitated, unsure of the protocol.

An older seafarer jumped in. 'Go through there, that's the pantry, and on the other side of that is the galley. There's a menu on the bulkhead and you just tell the cook what you want, right?'

Mick nodded his thanks and headed off, as directed.

'Am I allowed to have a steak?' he asked the cook, hopeful. He'd never had a steak before.

''Course you are. How do you want it?' the cook replied.

'What do you mean?'

'I mean,' the cook repeated, 'how do you want it?'

'I want it on my plate,' Mick replied, a bit lost.

The cook smiled. 'I mean, do you want it well done, rare, medium?'

'Oh, I dunno. How should I have it done?' Mick asked, never having faced this quandary before and not entirely sure what the difference was. Wasn't a steak a steak?

'Let's start with medium and see how we go,' the cook suggested.

Back in the mess, Mick sat down and devoured his steak alongside the friendly fellows he'd met earlier. In no time it had disappeared and he was down to the bone. He set to stripping off any skerrick of meat that was left.

'You can go back in there and get another,' the bloke sitting next to him said with an amused smile.

Barely able to believe his luck, Mick went back through to the galley and politely requested if he could have another steak.

'Sure. You've had medium, do you want to try rare or well done this time?' the cook suggested.

'Sure,' Mick replied, just delighted to have seconds.

The second steak also disappeared in no short order and Mick turned to the man beside him again.

'Do you think he'd go crook on me if I had another?'

'Nah, he's a good cook,' replied one of the now highly amused seafarers.

Sure enough, Mick went back and polished off his third steak. Delighted, Mick went into the galley to thank the cook. When he sat back down at the table in the mess, the others nodded approvingly.

'Make sure you always thank the cook,' the bosun said. 'Don't upset them unless you want to be eating nothing but Weet-Bix for the next five weeks!'

Mick laughed, but noted the advice. Shortly after, he staggered back to his cabin. He was better fed than he had ever been in his life. Lying curled up and cosy in his beautiful, large cabin, he was content. He had a full stomach and a day's work on a boat ahead of him the next day. Mick couldn't have been more content as he slipped into sleep.

Mick adjusted to life at sea well. He loved Doveton, but he also couldn't wait to leave and now he had his ticket out. He was young, earning and doing what he'd always dreamed of.

* * *

While Mick was finding his sea legs, enjoying his newfound freedom and single-berth cabins, dark-haired 16-year-old Joanie McGrath was working among the taffeta and lace in a bridal hire shop in Dandenong. It was one of three jobs hardworking Joanie juggled.

It had been two years since Mick left for Newcastle, and he'd been on and off ships since with trips home in between. Joanie knew Mick from way back. In Doveton everyone knew everyone else, and the Dolemans had always spent a bit of time with the McGrath family. When Joanie was a youngster and heard the Dolemans were coming around she'd run for cover, hiding in her bedroom from the boisterous lads. Mick had the manners and grace you might expect of a young boy bouncing along with three brothers. Which is to say, they played hard. They were all too rough for Joanie, who would stay safely hidden away in the refuge of her room. She had managed to largely avoid Mick for years, so long as she had enough warning of their impending visit.

Work was a social place for Joanie. People would pop in and out of the shop to say hi and exchange the latest gossip. One day, Joanie was whiling away a few quiet minutes in the shop chatting with Mick's young sister, Marree. 'How's Mick?' Joanie asked. 'I haven't seen him for such a long time.'

'He's good,' Marree replied. 'He's been at sea, but he's coming home soon.'

'Oh well, give him my regards,' Joanie said. The conversation moved on to other things, and she thought no more of Mick.

It wasn't unusual for people to ask after Mick – he was well known in Doveton. He played for the local footy team and had always been well liked and respected. At 18, Mick was strong-willed and determined, but the sort of person others gravitated to.

It hadn't been lost on Mick over the years that the McGrath girls, Joanie, Julie and Bernadette, thought he and his brothers were all a bit rough. Which is why it came as a surprise when his sister, Marree, casually dropped into conversation that Joanie McGrath had been asking after him.

At first, Mick filed this little morsel away, but a few months later he decided to act. It was a Friday morning. Mick gave his curly mullet a final comb, slung on his much-loved faded denim jacket and headed out of the bedroom he still shared with his three brothers. He made his way to Dandenong, found the bridal shop and pushed open the door. He was ready with a smile for Joanie, but it was wasted on a shop that was empty save for Joanie's boss.

'G'day,' Mick said, rallying. 'Is Joanie McGrath around?'

'No, sorry,' the manager replied. 'She's working in the city, but she should be back a bit later this arvo.'

Mick thanked the manager, and said he'd pop back in a bit.

At a loose end, and with a few hours to kill, Mick headed to the pub and ordered a VB beer. One beer turned into a few more, until Mick headed back to the bridal shop. Pushing his way through the door again, and looking wildly out of place, Mick peered hopefully around the frills and chiffon for Joanie. Again, it was only her manager to be seen.

'She's not back yet,' the manager said again. She repeated that Joanie was expected back in the shop later that afternoon. Not one to be so easily deterred, Mick headed back out to keep a seat warm at the pub while he waited – and sank a few more beers.

After several more trips between bridal shop and pub, Mick tried yet again. Finding the shop once again unattended by Joanie, and half-drunk from his hours of waiting, Mick said to the manager: 'Do you hire out gorilla suits?'

'What's wrong with the one you have on?' she laughed, by now well amused at the persistence of this cheeky and determined young man.

'Fair enough!' Mick laughed, before heading out once again to take up his waiting post.

An hour or so later, Mick traipsed the well-trodden path back to the shop once again. Finally, his persistence was rewarded by the sight of Joanie, cackling with laughter. Her manager had duly filled her in on Mick's exploits.

'G'day, Joanie,' Mick said, his ready smile lighting up his face.

They laughed about his day spent beating the pavement between pub and shop, before Mick said, 'Marree said you were asking about me.'

'Oh yes, well you know I haven't seen you in ages,' Joanie said.

If Mick had known the question he would ask next would change the course of his life, he might have felt more nervous. 'Um, well, I wouldn't mind taking you out. Would you like to go out with me?'

'Oh, gee I dunno about that, Mick.' Joanie was playing for time. 'I'll have to ask Mum. I'll get back to you.'

Sure, this 18-year-old Mick seemed more grown up than last time she'd seen him, but there were still those memories of hiding from the terrorising young Doleman lads during family get-togethers. Not to mention that this ploy meant Mick would have to come back to the shop to get her answer. Again.

That night after the shop lights clicked off and the door shut, Joanie headed home. 'Mum, Mick Doleman's asked me out,' she said to her mum, Carmen. 'What do you reckon, can he take me out?'

'I'll have to talk to the boys about this, Joanie,' Carmen replied. 'I mean, we all know Mick but he's a bit rough around the edges. I'm not sure.'

And so began a McGrath family debate. One older brother on each side, her Mum undecided in the middle.

'Absolutely not,' Peter said, the protective older brother taking over.

But then Joanie's other brother Buffy chipped in. 'Nah, come on, Mick will look after her. He's a good sort. He'll make sure nothing happens to her. I reckon it'll be right.'

Meanwhile, realising he couldn't do anything to change the outcome, Mick was doing what he did on the weekends to keep his mind occupied. He headed around to best mate Stevie Henwood's place and had a couple of drinks watching the footy replay, the disgruntled girlfriends enduring it until they all hit the social scene.

Down at the Dandenong Town Hall to catch a band, Mick waited for the great McGrath debate to be settled. He knew he was the subject of discussion and, not entirely confident he'd come up trumps, he figured the best thing he could do to help his chances was to keep out of the way and not put his foot in his mouth. As he laughed and joked with his mates, Mick could only guess the scrutiny his character was under.

Mick and his mates left the hall and headed to a burger joint just down the way, where they had a six-pack of beer stashed. By the time he'd washed down his burger with a stubby it had been decided in the McGrath house. Joanie's mum, Carmen, had made her ruling. Buffy had won out and Mick had his chance to impress Joanie. Now it was over to him to pass probation.

* * *

A few days later, dressed casually in jeans and a shirt, Mick knocked on Joanie's front door at seven o'clock. Joanie came to the door looking a million bucks and smiling shyly.

But Carmen had a few things to say before she just let her daughter go off into the night with Mick. 'I want her home by eleven o'clock, Mick,' she said in a voice that only the ignorant would pay no heed to.

'Sure thing, Carmen. I'll take good care of her,' Mick replied.

'So where are you taking her?' Carmen asked.

While Mick might have got a job, been to sea and learned about the world, there was one area he could have taken a few pointers on. Romance.

His great plan to win Joanie over was all set to start at … Pizza Hut. Mind you, this was the 1970s, when olive oil was still sold at the chemist and your standard Aussie fare was lamb chops and boiled vegetables. And, if Mick was strictly honest, a key drawcard for Pizza Hut was the waitresses. Not that Mick ever would have let on to Joanie about that. Tonight, his eyes were just for her.

Along with some of Mick's mates and their girlfriends, they chatted as they drove to the restaurant. It didn't take Joanie long to realise that there was a softer side to Mick that she hadn't seen before. And he was fun, so much fun.

That evening, Joanie tried her first ever slice of pizza. The night was full of chatter and laughter, and Mick always seemed to have just the right thing to say. Without even trying, Joanie realised she was having a ball.

True to his word, Mick had Joanie home by 11 o'clock with the promise of another date in his pocket.

As he headed off, he couldn't believe his luck. *How the hell did I jag her?* he asked himself delightedly. *Hope she doesn't wake up and come to her senses.*

CHAPTER 2

All a Bit Mad

1973

If there's one thing small towns do well, it's gossip. Had a bust up with a mate? You can bet your bottom dollar Shirley at the grocery store knows about it. New beau? You won't keep that secret for long. In no time at all it was well known that Mick and Joanie were an item.

Mick had passed probation and was regularly seen picking Joanie up in his pride and joy, a silver EH Holden he'd picked up cheap in Geelong. The first time he'd rolled up to the kerb in his newly acquired car to collect Joanie, he couldn't help but say with a proud swagger, 'What do you reckon? Pretty flash, hey?'

And it might have been, had he not made the mistake of turning the engine off. Joanie jumped in and, ready to impress, Mick turned the key. The engine gave him nothing. He tried the key a few more times, sweating under the pressure. Finally, Joanie jumped out and started pushing, with Mick inside, steering.

She pushed the car all the way to the hill where Mick clutch started it, the engine roaring into life as the car sailed downhill with Joanie running behind to catch up and hop in.

Geez, Mick thought to himself wryly, *I'm really running the risk of this girl giving me the arse.*

But it was clear to anyone who was anyone in Doveton that Mick and Joanie were smitten. Pizza Hut was clearly doing good business, and after they'd been going out six weeks Mick was planning something special. Joanie's 17th birthday was coming up and Mick knew just what to do. Of course, being Mick, it involved a boat. He booked two tickets on the *Argonaut*, a former sailing ship that had been transformed into a floating restaurant. Mick was going to treat Joanie to a meal and harbour cruise on the Yarra River.

It was going to be perfect. There was just one catch – Mick was on the top of the maritime roster. *Shouldn't be a problem*, he thought. Being at the top of the roster gave you first pick to take whatever job came up, but if you didn't want it, you could always offer it to the blokes below you on the roster. The only thing was, if no one else wanted that voyage you were compelled to take the job. That was called being 'shanghaied'. No ifs, no buts, and certainly no 'but I have a cruise booked'.

* * *

BACK FROM THE DEAD

Thursday, 11 October 1973 – Doveton

Mick showed up along with all the other seafarers at the pick-up to see if there were any jobs that needed filling. Sure enough, the MV *Blythe Star*, a small coastal freighter that did regular shipping runs supplying fertiliser to King Island in Bass Strait to the north-west of Tasmania, needed a bucko (a seafarer with a year's experience at sea). Mick passed the job on, but as each man on the roster was asked and turned it down Mick realised he'd have no choice. No one else wanted to sail on the *Blythe Star*.

The union said he had to sail, so he was going to sail.

Mick headed straight back home to pack his bags ready to head to the airport that afternoon. On the way, he called into another of Joanie's workplaces to break the news that he'd been shanghaied onto the *Blythe Star*. He would be throwing his things together and heading to Hobart, Tasmania. They would have to celebrate her birthday when he got back.

They had only been going out a couple of months, but Joanie knew she liked Mick. But she also knew that Mick wasn't Mick without seafaring – and this was part and parcel of the job. Neither of them thought to ask at the time why no one else wanted to take the job on the *Blythe Star*.

Saying goodbye, Joanie had a horrible feeling in her stomach, a tight, nauseating knot. It was the first time since they'd started dating that Mick would be headed to sea and she would miss seeing him around their family dinner table. In the past couple of months, Mick had become a constant in the McGrath household. Joanie knew she'd feel his absence for the next six weeks.

Mick packed his bag and flew to Tasmania, the island state that clings to the skirts of mainland Australia. Lovingly known for being a couple of decades behind the rest of the country, Tasmania in the 1970s was a welcoming place, although newcomers would be informed in short order that it'd be at least a generation before they could call themselves a local. It was the sort of place where someone called Beryl would pop around with a homemade casserole to welcome you to the street. A house in the capital, Hobart, went for a measly 15,000 dollars.

Hobart's streets were peppered with majestic buildings built of yellow sandstone blocks chiselled and laid by convicts 150 years ago. The hulking mass of kunanyi/Mount Wellington sits squat over the township, and the Derwent River cut a swathe through the city.

After landing at Hobart airport, Mick caught a taxi to Prince of Wales Bay, around 7 kilometres north of central Hobart, where the *Blythe Star* was waiting. Slinging his small rucksack over his shoulder, he climbed out of the taxi, thanked the driver and turned in the direction of the wharf, where he'd find his ship.

It had been a long day, and Mick was looking forward to finding his bunk on the *Blythe Star*. As he made his way along the wharf, he was expecting to see the welcoming glow of the ship's lights but all he could sense in the darkness was the sound of water lapping against the dock. *Where's the bloody*

The *Blythe Star* being loaded at Prince of Wales Bay the day before it set sail on its last fateful voyage. *(Courtesy of the Tasmanian Archives: NS3745-1-692)*

ship? he wondered. Finally, he saw it, a hulking shape in the inky blue, like a malignant growth on the docks.

I guess that's it, Mick thought to himself, unimpressed.

A 44-metre-long steel-hulled freighter, the *Blythe Star* was the latest acquisition of the Tasmanian Transport Commission, which came under the purview of the Tasmanian Government. The ship may have been a new addition to the fleet, but you wouldn't call it the jewel in the crown. Eighteen years old, the *Blythe Star* had previously run aground, and the bickering over its purchase was turning out to be a thorn in the side of the commission bureaucrats.

The commission had given the flick to the crew that came with the ship, insisting they could man the operation more cheaply. Negotiations with the union around crewing and working conditions were ongoing, although the union had agreed to supply crew while those details were ironed out.

Usually, when a ship was scheduled to sail the next day, there would be some activity underway. But the *Blythe Star* was quiet and in darkness.

Mick walked bag in hand up the small gangway and found his way to the mess. Inside the dark messroom, he made out a collection of figures from the gloom.

A voice emerged from the black. 'Hello, who've we got here?'

'Mick Doleman,' Mick replied. 'What the hell's going on? Why the bloody hell are you all sitting in the dark?'

Another voice came back from the shadowy figures huddled around a table. 'Someone chucked the power cord in the drink, so we pulled up stumps for the night.'

Mick might have been relatively new to this game, but he was taken aback by the scene. With the cord connecting the ship to shore power apparently on the floor of the bay, here were the crew sitting in darkness, without food, lights or entertainment. It seemed entirely mad.

Mick was tired, less than impressed and missing Joanie's birthday for this circus. Great. He felt a nagging unease in the pit of his stomach. But it was nothing a square meal and the light of day wouldn't put to rights. Pulling up a chair, Mick joined the crew and introduced himself.

There'd be ten crew sailing the *Blythe Star*. Captain George Cruikshank, aged in his 50s and master of the ship, had been working for the Transport Commission for two years – although he'd been at sea far longer. First mate Ken Jones, 42, was a personable second in charge. Chief engineer, John Eagles, and second engineer, John Sloan, were both in their 50s and had farming interests outside seafaring. Stanley 'Tas' Leary, who had served 25 years at sea, was the ship's bosun overseeing the equipment and crew.

Then there were the able seamen: 23-year-old Brenton Power, who everyone knew as Mick; Malcolm McCarroll, 33, who loved fishing at the shack and newspaper crosswords; and Cliff Langford, who at 53 still had an impish sense of humour and loved a practical joke. Keeping the hungry crew fed was the job of 43-year-old ship's cook, Alf Simpson.

The crew couldn't all fit in the mess at once, though, so Mick was only meeting a few of his shipmates. He'd heard of two of them before, but the rest were new acquaintances. At 18, he was easily the youngest crew member. Brought on board as an ordinary seaman, Mick was the 'bucko' of the crew.

They chatted and soon got down to important business; namely, what Australian Rules team you barracked for?

'Oh, there's only one answer to that, mate – Collingwood!' Mick replied to laughs and jeers from rival fans. This easy camaraderie was part of why Mick loved being at sea – men, young and old, drawn together and looking out for one another. He loved the banter and jokes but also how they relied on each other. There was no calling an ambulance or fire brigade once you'd left port – the crew had to pull together and rely on their collective wits to do whatever needed to be done.

Eventually, Mick was ready to turn in, and he headed to his small but comfortable cabin. He'd be sharing with Mick Power, who, with wavy dark hair to his shoulders, looked something like a 1970s rock star.

Mick hung his clothes in the small wardrobe and placed his much-loved cassette player on the chest of drawers for the morning.

Then, ready for bed, he heaved himself up into the top bunk – as the junior crewman on the ship he didn't get the pick of the bunk. Making himself comfortable in the narrow berth, he closed his eyes and slipped into sleep.

* * *

Friday, 12 October 1973 – *Blythe Star*

At around 7 am, Mick woke to a knock on the door by bosun Tas Leary. After climbing down from his bunk, he dressed then headed out to the mess.

Just as he was finishing his breakfast the captain swung by. A weather-beaten Scotsman, George Cruikshank was someone who, like Mick, had been called to the sea young and had never left. He once said it was all he'd ever known. That was where the similarities ended, however. The captain had the red, ruddy cheeks of a drinker, a lined, angular face with a thin mouth and nose and high cheekbones. His hair was neatly cut, but to Mick he seemed a diminutive figure. A taciturn man, he didn't seem to be part of the crew. He slept away from the ship when it was in port, heading back to his home in South Hobart, and he never joined in the chat and camaraderie.

'Come on, lad,' Captain Cruikshank growled in his Scottish brogue, 'we've got to get you to the office and get you signed on.'

Mick was surprised. The job of signing on new crew was normally left to the first mate. To this day, Mick has no recollection of any other captain taking on that particular job. Clearly things worked a bit differently on the *Blythe Star*.

As Mick stepped onto the deck, a cool breeze hit his face as he looked around to get his bearings. The sky was low and heavy and threatened rain. Divers were already in the water retrieving the drowned power cord. Wharfies and the rest of the crew were also up and at it, loading and stowing cargo.

First mate Ken Jones, a charismatic Liverpudlian, was overseeing the loading of the cargo, all the while keeping track of its weight, how it was distributed and calculating the ship's stability. Ken cut a dashing figure. Handsome, with broad shoulders and an easy smile that could melt hearts, he was the kind of person who inspired confidence when he walked into a room. Ken was something of a heartbreaker, but he was besotted with his three-year-old daughter, Susan, who was at home in St Kilda, Victoria. She'd turn four while he saw out this stint ferrying cargo back and forth from Hobart to King Island on the *Blythe Star*.

Ken had sat down the day before to pen a letter to Susan's mother and his de facto partner, Francis, talking about his hopes for their future. He had almost finished his Masters ticket that would allow him to exercise his natural leadership as captain of a ship. Ever eloquent with a pen, he'd been less than enamoured with the Tasmanian Transport Commission. The old saying 'couldn't organise their way out of a paper bag' came to mind. But a job was a job and it paid for the brand-new state-of-the-art Mixmaster he'd be taking home for Francis.

As Mick and Captain Cruikshank walked past Ken and onto the dock, pallets loaded with superphosphate fertiliser were being stowed in the hold. No one was going to forget the pallet of beer that also had a place aboard. They didn't

First mate Ken Jones inspired confidence from the outset. He took Mick under his wing. *(Courtesy of Susan McKenna)*

want to be the ones who would have to explain to the thirsty farmers on King Island that they hadn't brought a refreshing brew as requested.

Mick slid into the back of a taxi after Captain Cruikshank and they headed through the streets of Hobart to the Transport Commission offices in Collins Street. Once there, Mick signed his article of agreement. He was now officially signed on as Ordinary Seaman Doleman, working on the MV *Blythe Star*.

Formalities out of the way, Captain Cruikshank looked at his watch. 'We've got time for a quick drink,' he said.

They crossed the road to the nearest watering hole. As the door swung open, the stale smell of last night's cigarettes greeted them.

After taking a seat at the bar, Mick looked around. The place was a well-worn classic Tasmanian pub, with rustic brick walls and a big old fireplace that would roar on a winter's night.

It might have only been 10.30 in the morning, but it was five o'clock somewhere so they ordered a couple of drinks. George Cruikshank wasn't a naturally personable fellow and conversation didn't flow easily between Mick and the old Scotsman. Mick was relieved when, after polishing off a couple of whiskies, the skipper was ready to head off.

Back at Prince of Wales Bay, loading was well underway. Mick went aboard to pitch in. As the crew secured the cargo, George Cruikshank headed to the wharf-side office of Captain David Bond, superintendent of the Transport Commission.

As midday struck, the crew's minds and stomachs turned to lunch as they worked. Tas Leary watched as the deck cargo made its way aboard. Square-jawed and moustachioed, Leary had thick, wavy hair shot through with silver. He turned to the foreman of the wharf. 'How much is going on the decks?' he asked.

'Forty-eight pallets all up,' the foreman replied.

Tas queried what that was in weight, and on hearing it totalled about 54 tonnes, he raised his eyebrows. 'That's too much. Last time she was loaded up like that she wasn't in good shape.'

Just months earlier the ship, similarly loaded, had struggled in calm seas. It had corrected and continued sailing, but there had been advice that it shouldn't carry deck cargo as hefty again. It seemed that someone had forgotten to pass on the missive.

The foreman shrugged. 'Take it up with the mate. He and the skipper are happy with it.'

Tas wasn't the only one with raised eyebrows watching on as pallet after pallet swung aboard and they were stacked up into towering piles. Able seaman Cliff Langford reckoned it was the biggest deck cargo he'd ever seen.

'You'll be putting it in your cabins and everywhere else soon,' one of the wharfies joked to Mick Power, who was standing nearby.

Power peered over the edge of the ship, and called Mick across. 'Take a look, she's sitting low in the water,' he said.

Mick peered over, and saw that the water level was well up the ship's hull. But he was just the bucko and it was above his paygrade to be thinking about that. The captain and first mate would have all that in order. They did this all the time and they knew what they were doing.

Mick wandered off to start sealing the air vents to keep the water out of the hatches. As he worked, the banter continued.

'Where's your Plimsoll line? On the funnel?' quipped a stevedore. The Plimsoll line is a mark on the ship that shows the maximum depth it can sit in the water safely.

Mick laughed and kept at it.

While the crew were watching the cargo pile up with some scepticism, Captain Cruikshank was deciding the route they'd take up the Tasmanian coast to King Island. He and Captain Bond decided the ship would head south around the bottom tip of Tasmania then sail up the west coast.

Cruikshank left Captain Bond's office, where the unspoken message had been to get as much cargo up the coast as quickly as possible. So the towers of pallets on the deck continued to grow. Leaving first mate Ken Jones to ensure the cargo was stored safely, Cruikshank nipped into town to get a few bits before they sailed.

As the loading finished up, 350 tonnes of superphosphate and one tonne of beer had been packed away, covered in tarps and lashed down.

Ken Jones made his way around the cargo, testing the lashings and checking the chains were tight.

Not long after five o'clock, Power, Langford, Leary and McCarroll were in the mess room when Captain Cruikshank came in. He was back from buying a carton of cigarettes and some magazines.

'Which way are we going?' piped up McCarroll to the captain.

'We're headed west about,' Cruikshank replied. 'Captain Bond says there's only a slight southerly forecast and the weather conditions are all right. He wants us at King Island early Sunday morning so we can get out again for the *Straitsman*, which will come in Monday.'

Despite never having sailed the more treacherous route up Tasmania's punishing west coast, known for storms that will near strip the skin off your face, Captain Cruikshank had been convinced to take this shorter route. This route would also take them into the Southern Ocean to the south of Tasmania, a stretch of water known for strong currents, savage winds and intense and unpredictable storms.

After ten minutes, the captain headed back out and along to his cabin.

Dusk was creeping into the corners of the sky by the time the *Blythe Star* was ready to sail. The gangway was pulled away and Mick headed up to the bridge. Once there, he spotted the captain on the starboard side, just inside the door, leaning on the window sill and looking straight out at the still river that would take them out to sea. Ken Jones was there, too. He smiled at Mick, his engaging demeanour in stark contrast to the dour countenance of the captain.

Mick had the first shift steering. He'd be navigating the ship down the river under the captain's direction. He settled himself in the central helmsman's seat, which had a view through five large windows. Mick placed his hands on the wooden wheel, he could feel the notches in the timber under his rough hands.

The *Blythe Star* left the wharf and slipped out into the river. The captain pulled the telegraph, which sent signals from the bridge to the engine room, calling for full steam ahead. When nothing happened, he moved it again. 'What the bloody hell's going on down there?' he grumbled.

'Is the telegraph moving?' Ken asked.

''Course it's bloody moving. Ken, head down and find out what the story is,' the captain barked.

Ken did as he was told, leaving to root out the source of the trouble. Little did Mick know, this was the least of the trouble that was headed his way in the next 24 hours.

The stern of the *Blythe Star*, where the crew leapt to safety. The white, oblong box that can be seen was the stowed life raft that kept the men alive.
(Reproduced by permission of the Australian Broadcasting Corporation – Library Sales © 1973 ABC)

CHAPTER 3

One In, All In

Friday, 12 October 1973 – *Blythe Star*

The *Blythe Star* had scarcely cut a line through the water away from the wharf when raised voices emanated from the engine room.

John Eagles, chief engineer, had a red flush in his face. Like many on the *Blythe Star*, he was an ocean-going man through and through. He'd joined the merchant navy in World War II, but his ship had been bombed while moored alongside the wharf in Darwin. Covered in oil and trying to help those around him while navigating away from open flames, he'd escaped with his life – if not all his fellow shipmates. Recent times had found him taking up farming life, running a banana plantation in Coffs Harbour with his wife, Una, and three young sons.

John Eagles was a man of contradictions. He loved opera, but give him a few spare hours and he'd be stripping down an old Land Rover engine, polishing each individual part to a shine. He'd meticulously piece the vehicle back together so it'd turn over like a dream and run like a Swiss watch.

Life on the land is fickle and, recently, a glut in bananas had sent John Eagles back to sea to put food on the table. He'd joined the *Blythe Star* three weeks earlier. When Mick had met him earlier that day, he'd found John a bit aloof and they hadn't said much to each other beyond the pleasantries.

Right now, though, John Eagles was squaring up to Tas Leary. 'You put water down the funnel so the thing won't start,' he accused.

Tas was an old-style bosun who knew what he was doing. A personable man, he took affront at being accused of such a blatantly ludicrous act. There's no reason on God's good earth that someone would go to the effort of deliberately scaling the heights of the funnel, essentially the ship's exhaust, to throw water down. 'All right, if you have an accusation to make we'll go up and see the old man on the bridge,' Tas shouted, his blood running high. 'You can make the accusation in front of him and I'll have it put in the official logbook.' The logbook was the official record of events on the ship. To be written up in it was a big deal.

Tas turned on his heel and stormed out of the engine room. John strode along in his wake. As they approached the bridge, they passed Ken Jones, who was on his way down to see why the telegraph was being ignored. Seeing the two men who should have been on the other end of the telegraph barrelling past him, he followed them back to the bridge.

Tas Leary burst through the door, John close behind. Mick looked around and realised the two men were in the midst of a flaming row.

Tas strode up to Captain Cruikshank. 'I have just had a bit of a donny with the chief engineer and I want him to accuse me of what he has already accused me of in front of you, and I want it put in the logbook.'

'I want this man logged!' John Eagles shouted. 'He put water down the funnel onto the manifold.'

Stirred from his reverie, Captain Cruikshank turned sharply to face the two men. The colour in his face rose.

Mick looked on, bemused. He didn't take the accusation seriously. Why would anyone bother doing such a ludicrous thing? It just seemed like a pair of ratbags having a game.

But the captain took the bait. 'Don't be stupid!' the captain barked. 'Why would anyone do that? The logbook is mine and I am the only man aboard this ship that can log anyone.'

John Eagles stepped forward, gearing up to kick on. But Tas Leary was done. He walked off in disgust. Ken Jones followed, heading to his cabin for a kip before he took the next watch.

After a few minutes, John recognised the futility of his continued remonstrations and also turned to leave, retreating back to the confines of the engine room. However, Captain Cruikshank wasn't done and called him back. When it was clear that the chief engineer wasn't paying him any heed, the captain, a wobble in his step, turned back into the bridge.

'The chief engineer is an idiot,' he spat. Then he turned to start on Mick, the most junior member of the crew and the one there to take the brunt of the captain's wrath. 'I am the captain of this ship and I am the only one who does the logging,' he ranted, ruddy cheeks aflame and eyes red. 'When I log a man he stays logged. When you go down, you can tell your [union] boys that too.'

Mick stood at the wheel, letting the captain's words wash over him for ten minutes until Cruikshank finally exhausted himself and settled into a broody silence.

Growing up with a seafaring dad and with a few years at sea under his belt, Mick was no stranger to the unique relationship shipmates shared. They lived cheek by jowl for days on end, so tensions were bound to arise. The maritime industry in the 1970s wasn't for the faint-hearted. Some of the men at sea had stared down bombs, submarines and enemy soldiers in World War II, including some of the men aboard the *Blythe Star*.

Weakness had no place at sea, you didn't want to be seen to be soft. To hold your own you had to know how to talk with your fists and not back down. There was violence, and alcohol fuelled its share of disputes. But there was also a deep camaraderie. Mick would judge a good ship not by its size or how big his cabin was but by the crew. And to Mick, this crew seemed a bit mad, led by a skipper who left Mick uninspired and unimpressed. A man who seemed to have a more than a usual fondness for the drink. But it seemed everyone had moved on, even if the captain's silence had a frisson of anger.

Now making full steam, the ship headed down the river, Hobart lining the banks either side. Soon they'd make their way out toward Storm Bay, where they would head to the open ocean.

The captain had returned to his still, silent contemplation, but every now and then he would bark out a course adjustment to Mick, who would turn the wheel. The river slowly revealed itself, as gentle drizzle created a soft haze above the horizon.

Every few minutes, the captain would leave the bridge and head back to the chartroom to make contact with Harbour Control. After a while, though, Mick realised that Captain Cruikshank was no longer within cooee, it seemed he had gone further than the nearby chartroom this time. With just a few years at sea under his belt, Mick had total control of the ship.

The captain returned ten minutes later, but said nothing to mark or explain his absence. Mick noticed a looseness in his movements and a redness in his eyes that he put down to drunkenness.

Under Cruikshank's piloting, Mick steered the freighter under the Tasman Bridge, a daunting challenge even with a small ship like the *Blythe Star*. Just 15 months later, the helmsman of the *Lake Illawarra*, would make a momentous error, the steel carrier smashing into the bridge, bringing it down and killing 12. But on this evening, with night settled on his shoulders, Mick navigated the narrow channel between the bridge pylons, and the ship continued its low rumbling passage down the river.

At 7.30 pm, Mick asked Captain Cruikshank for permission to leave the bridge to call the next watch.

The captain nodded. 'All right,' he grunted.

Mick left his post at the wheel, and headed out the starboard door and down the stairs to the accommodation. He knocked on Malcolm McCarroll's door. 'Mate, time to get ready for your shift,' Mick said.

Once he got an answer from Mal, Mick headed back up to the bridge to resume his post at the wheel. He hadn't been gone more than five minutes so was surprised to find the captain not at the wheel steering the ship but still looking out the window, lost in some private contemplation.

Keeping his thoughts to himself, Mick took the wheel and checked their course against the compass bearing. He checked again. *This can't be right*, he thought. They were 15 degrees off course. Glancing at the captain again, Mick realised there had been no one at the wheel the entire time he was gone. Mick pulled the wheel around to bring the ship back on course, his confidence in the captain diminishing by the minute.

When Mal McCarroll popped his curly-haired head around the door and stepped onto the bridge, Mick was glad to leave the dour captain and his eccentricities behind. There was a shower and bed calling his name. He knew he'd be getting a knock at 1.30 the next morning for his next shift at the wheel.

As the warm water ran over him in the shower, he thought back over the day's events. He'd sailed with some jokers before, but this ship seemed in a different league. Turning into bed for the night he thought of Joanie. Tomorrow was her birthday. What he wouldn't give to be spending the evening with her, not tucked under a scratchy blanket in a narrow bed with a snoring seafarer in the bunk below.

Mick fell asleep as soon as his head hit the pillow. Meanwhile, up on the bridge Mal McCarroll overheard the captain making radio contact with a passing ship, the *Joseph Banks*. The two captains shot the breeze for a few minutes, talking about their schedules and sailings, George Cruikshank suggesting an anchorage Captain Trevor Roberts could use for the night. Then Cruikshank told Roberts he was planning on heading 'west about' up the coast.

Captain Cruikshank ended the call and switched off the set. It was the last time anyone would hear from the *Blythe Star*.

* * *

Saturday, 13 October 1973 – *Blythe Star*

By the wee hours of the morning, the *Blythe Star* was well on its way. Rolling gently, the incessant rhythmic shush of the waves against the hull amplified in the cool, damp air. The freighter had passed Tasmania's southernmost point and was headed west. Clouds, glowing silver under a full moon, scudded across the sky. Perhaps the full moon explained all the craziness of the day before?

Woken by a knock to wake him for his shift, Mick wiped the sleep from his eyes, splashed some water on his face, threw on an extra layer of clothing and headed up to the bridge, where he'd be on for the next two hours.

Mick was relieved to find that Ken Jones was on the bridge for this shift rather than the captain. One's patience can stretch only so far at two in the morning. As Mick kept the wheel steady, the bow rose and fell gently in the moderate swell. Alone in the vast expanse of the Southern Ocean, the *Blythe Star* sailed with her slumbering crew on into the black.

CHAPTER 4

A Final Glimpse

Saturday, 13 October 1973 – Maatsuyker Island

If you want to feel the wrath of Mother Nature, there are few places better to go than Maatsuyker Island, just two and a half kilometres on its longest axis. Maatsuyker might only be 10 kilometres off southern Tasmania, but it is situated in a desolate stretch of ocean at a latitude of around 43 degrees south, smack bang in the path of the wild westerly winds that tear across the Southern Ocean: The Roaring Forties.

The winds aren't called the Roaring Forties for nothing. They scream as they hurl themselves tempestuously at the island that has had such temerity as to stand in their way.

Maatsuyker is the home of seabirds, seals and just a few families crazy enough to work as lighthouse keepers in one of the wildest places in Australia. It's remote and beautiful. When the wind blows northerly the fetid smell of the seal colony is heavy on the air.

Maatsuyker was where an energetic and fit 25-year-old, Tony Parsey, found himself after giving up a job in the Postmaster General's Office in Hobart. In just two weeks he'd taken the job as lighthouse keeper, sold the family home, packed up their belongings and loaded his young family into an old, small fishing boat – the *Kathleen Del Mar*. The rustic little ship would take them from mainland Tasmania to the small wedge-shaped island that was to be their home and workplace.

They sailed at night, and the sea was rough and unwelcoming. The passengers were packed into the vessel, tucked safely below decks. If Tony, his wife, Robyn, and two young children didn't get sick from the journey then the salty, fishy tang that hung in the air would have done it. *My God, where have I come to? What on earth have I done?* Tony wondered as the waves crashed and swirled over the ship.

When they finally got to Maatsuyker and they shakily made their way above decks, they were greeted with cloud so low that it seemed the island started in the heaving ocean and disappeared up into heaven. Except the weather would undoubtedly be better in heaven.

Sick, soaking wet and wrung out, the family loaded their gear into a dinghy to get to the jetty, before hauling it up onto solid land at last. From there they piled their belongings into a trolley attached to a pulley which then disappeared up the steep rock into the clouds above.

During the months since that inauspicious landing, the family had settled into their new life. They had a small garden plot outside number-2 quarters, a cosy little place with a roaring combustion stove in the kitchen.

The isolation took some getting used to. They had no phone connection to the outside world and they hung out for the fortnightly boat deliveries that would bring mail – weather permitting. With no electricity on the island and only a small kerosene fridge, most food came canned or dehydrated. When they needed to restock, they'd radio Cape Bruny lighthouse to dictate their shopping list to the lighthouse keeper there, who would then call the lighthouse department who would gather the requested items to send back on the next mail boat.

Keeping in touch with family wasn't easy. Any communication would have to be relayed by radio to Cape Bruny lighthouse. That keeper would be on the phone to whichever loved one, and would relay the message and wait for a reply. They would then parrot that reply back into the radio to the Maatsuyker keeper. It was basically a game of broken telephone.

Tony had picked up the work of a lighthouse keeper quickly, even if he didn't much like the long night shifts. He and his family had arrived in March so hadn't had much time to settle in before winter made itself known with tearing winds and driving rain. Tony had mastered the art of crawling to work in the lighthouse on his hands and knees in poor weather. It was the only way to move about as the wind screamed over the top of him.

On the morning of Saturday, 13 October, the wind was mild and just the odd lazy sheet of drizzle whispered on the roof. At 2.30 am, Tony was woken by his alarm clock's shrill. Groaning, he rolled over to silence it before heaving himself out of bed.

Tony dressed quietly in the dark and then headed out to the kitchen, where he brewed a cuppa in the hope of raising some will to be awake at such an ungodly hour. Tony was due to start shift at the lighthouse at 3 am, and, much as he might hate the brutal call to arms at this time in the morning, the thought of leaving the lighthouse keeper on shift waiting beyond his scheduled knock-off time seemed like a far worse option.

Ten minutes later, Tony stepped outside and gently pulled the door closed behind him. Fingers of cool air scrabbled at his face. Pulling his collar higher, he walked the 300 metres down to the lighthouse. He would be relieving the chief lighthouse keeper, whose job it was every night to light the kerosene lantern that beamed out across the Southern Ocean. The lantern would sound a hissing roar, emitting the distinctive stink of kerosene as the mantle burned through the dark hours.

Tony's number-one job was to make sure the light kept burning. He dreaded the mantle collapsing; the fabric mesh that surrounded the light's flame was delicate and prone to tearing. The rush to burn a new mantle to keep the light burning – praying the blasted thing wouldn't collapse too – was fraught and stressful. The blowflies the summer would bring were enemy number one. A blowfly in the lantern room spelt disaster for the precious mantle.

This morning, he settled into his lighthouse routine. He took regular weather observations, noting them in the logbook, pumped up the pressure to the light to vaporise the fuel for burning, and took a spin around the balcony at the top of the lighthouse every half-hour. On a rough night this was a scary proposition. The entire lighthouse would shudder and vibrate in the face of gale-force winds that would rip into any crevice – air vents, hand rails – and scream in protest. But that morning the worst he had to contend with was the dampness in the air creeping down his collar.

As a gentle light started to creep into the clouds hanging over the scene laid out below, Tony was starting to think about putting the light out and knocking off. He decided to head out and around the lighthouse balcony one last time. Stepping out into the grey morning, Tony looked seaward. He noted a slight sea swell. Then, in the distance, he saw the unmistakable shape of a ship labouring through the roll of the ocean.

Pausing, he leaned against the balcony and focused on the ship. What he saw seared itself into his mind, where it would stay clear as cut crystal for half a century. A steel freight ship was making heavy work of it, forging through the swell with her bow barely clear of the water. As Tony watched, the swell rose and broke over the bow then travelled the full length down the deck, which was totally awash, before breaking around the wheelhouse at the back of the ship. The ship all but disappeared entirely beneath each swell for several long moments. *I wouldn't like to be working on that ship*, Tony thought to himself. *They're probably warm enough in the wheelhouse, though, I guess.*

Tony had never seen a ship as low in the water, and as he watched he thought it looked as much like a submarine as a ship. He ducked back into the tower and grabbed the station binoculars, putting them up to his eyes as he stepped back outside. He watched as swell after swell battered the ship, his eyes locked on the ship for ten minutes as it gradually moved further away.

Had he had a few more years of lighthouse keeping under his belt he might have done something differently, but with only eight months in the job he dismissed it. *They must know what they're doing*, he thought to himself.

Lowering the binoculars from his eyes, Tony glanced once more at the ship before heading back into the tower to shut down the light and wind up the night shift. He turned the kerosene off, watching as the flame died, then drew the curtains around the light room.

Heading down to the office room below, he sat down and pulled the logbook toward him. He scrawled a note with a description of the ship he had seen – remarking just how low in the water it had been. Flipping the book closed, he set aside his pen, gathered up his coat and headed down the spiral stairs. Stepping out into the morning, he wandered up to number-2 quarters, thinking of breakfast and the plans for the day ahead.

As he walked through the front door, he shrugged off his jacket. Relishing the warmth radiating from the wood stove, he checked to see if he needed to throw another coal briquette on it. Warming his hands, he started to get a cuppa and breakfast going.

As he went through his routine that morning, he stopped at one point and looked out the kitchen window which framed up a view across to Tasmania's south-west coast. He looked out across five hulking chunks of rock that were dotted like fallen pearls in the ocean to the south-west. Referred to as the Needles, these five rock islets are what the lighthouse would illuminate in the inky water each night to keep ships clear of their hungry sides.

Taking a moment to scan the skyline, Tony spotted the ship. It was now just a distant shape still toiling through the swell. 'Come and take a look at this, love,' he called to his wife, Robyn. 'See that little ship out there?'

Robyn peered out, but couldn't pick the hard lines of the ship from the water. Tony extended his arm, pointing it out to her while telling her that he had seen it earlier sitting remarkably low in the water. But as he was talking the weather closed in, a windy rain squall blurring the scene before obscuring it from view. When the weather lifted again Tony peered out again toward South West Cape. After a few minutes he realised the ship had gone and he turned away.

* * *

Saturday, 13 October 1973 – *Blythe Star*

While Tony had been standing, binoculars to his eyes, watching each swell roll along the length of a labouring freighter, Mick was tucked up and soundly sleeping in the upper berth of his cabin.

As it ticked over to 5.30 am, the *Blythe Star*'s cook, Alf Simpson, rumbled into wakefulness. A solid man with a mess of curly hair, Alf had one of those faces that looked like it was made for smiling. He liked a joke. One old crewmate remembered how he would load up your plate with food, and when you would protest at the amount he'd say reassuringly, 'Just leave what you can't manage.' But, should you return to the galley with any skerrick left on your plate he'd adopt an injured air, proclaiming, 'What, don't you like my cooking?'

Alf was firing up the stove in the galley as Cliff Langford was woken by a knock on his door, calling him for the 6 am shift. Cliff Langford may have been a quiet man, but he had a warm and kind heart with a mischievous sense of humour. On cold winter's nights at home, he'd sneak into his children's bedrooms and tie their pyjamas up in knots. When they ripped their clothes off and tried to yank on their pyjamas as quickly as possible before the cold could bite their bare skin, they'd find themselves in a knotted tangle. Cliff's cackle could be heard from the kitchen, where the children would find him in fits of laughter, an impish light dancing in his eyes.

At five minutes to six, now up and dressed, Cliff made his way onto the bridge to relieve Mal McCarroll. He noted that the captain, who was also due to clock on at 6 am, was still to emerge.

Cliff chatted briefly with Ken Jones, who, after the red-eye shifts, was ready to hit the pillow. But he had to wait until the captain showed up to relieve him. After another 15 minutes, Ken left Cliff at the wheel to go and call the captain again. It wasn't until a few minutes later that Captain Cruikshank eventually turned up on the bridge to relieve Jones, who was finally able to have a wash and turn in.

Two hours later, around the time lighthouse keeper Tony Parsey was getting breakfast in the kitchen at number-2 quarters, Cliff went down to call Mick Power for the next shift. Power hailed from Newcastle and came from a salt-of-the-earth family. Much like Mick, he'd knocked about with boisterous brothers and grew up tough.

Mick had joked with him the day before, Power's reputation having preceded him. 'Who's the best fighter in your family?' Mick had asked.

'Me mum,' Power replied, face straight and deadly serious. Despite his reputation, Power was a good bloke and Mick enjoyed having a laugh with him.

Getting up, Mick Power brushed his teeth and splashed water across his face. After pulling on his clothes, he went to see Alf in the galley.

'What do you want for breakfast?' Alf asked.

Power put in his request then took his food through to the mess. He sat down across from Tas Leary, who was revelling in a morning coffee. Tas had been up and at it by 7.30, and had already sounded the bilges. Letting a weighted rope down into each ballast tank to check the level of water in each, he had noted a slight list to starboard.

BACK FROM THE DEAD

The two men discussed the list as Power made short work of his breakfast.

Up on the bridge, Cliff Langford held the *Blythe Star* on course but also noticed her listing slightly as he looked out at the horizon.

'Bit of a list to starboard,' Captain Cruikshank observed.

Cliff wasn't concerned and made no reply. The sea was calm enough – Cliff reckoned you could row a dinghy out there.

Ten minutes later, at five minutes to eight, Mick Power came onto the bridge to relieve Cliff at the wheel. Captain Cruikshank marked up the new course on the blackboard and pointed at it to direct Power to change course by 5 degrees. Clearly conversation was beyond him at this time of the morning.

Power adjusted the wheel as the chief engineer, John Eagles, joined them on the bridge – now much calmer than the evening before, when he'd burst in on the tail of Tas.

'What's caused the list?' John asked the captain.

'I don't know, but there's nothing to worry about,' the captain responded, mildly puzzled but not alarmed. 'She's righted herself for now.'

'I'll shoot down below and look at the starboard tanks,' John said, meaning he'd check whether the ballast tanks – which can be filled with water to help a ship maintain stability – were full or empty.

Mick Power heard John Eagles head out. A moment later, he noticed the captain also go out the starboard door and realised he was alone – the captain must have followed John off the bridge. Power continued steering, holding the ship steady on its course. But after a few minutes he noticed the list was getting worse. The foaming sea washing over the starboard side of the decks wasn't cleared before the next swell began to surge over again. Power watched with growing apprehension as more and more water washed over the decks. He started worrying that the water wouldn't get away at all, which would spell disaster for the ship. Still alone on the bridge, without direction from the captain, he did the only thing he could in that instance: he held the wheel and tried to keep his rising panic at bay.

The crisp, strong wind grabbed the wisps of coffee-scent sneaking out of the *Blythe Star*'s galley. As the bow of the steel-grey freighter laboured through the swell, the wash foaming along the deck, Alf Simpson nodded good morning to Cliff Langford as he appeared in the galley for breakfast after shift changeover.

Tas Leary was still in the mess warming himself over his cuppa. When Cliff came in with some Cape Cod fish, Tas looked away – he wasn't all that fond of the stuff at any time of the day let alone at eight in the morning. 'She has a bit of a list in her,' Tas remarked as Cliff sat down.

'Yeah, she listed a while ago but she's come up pretty straight again,' Cliff said, tucking into his breakfast.

'She's still got a bit of a list to starboard,' Tas insisted.

'It's only light. I think she'll probably be right.'

Nodding, Tas heaved himself up and, returning to the galley, washed his cup up and placed it back onto the rack. Then he made his way to his cabin – checking the cargo on the way to make sure it was secure. Seeing it was all as it had been when they sailed, he continued on.

In the mess, Cliff picked up his empty breakfast plate and headed back to the galley to get a cup of tea. Suddenly a string of curses flew from Alf as his pots went crashing off the stove in an almighty din. Cliff flailed at the air as he was thrown across the galley, smashing his elbows on the door. He slammed onto the deck against the bulwarks. Down in his bunk, the sleeping Mick stirred as he felt gravity pull at him and push him up against the bulkhead wall.

Cliff grumbled as he picked himself up before heading back into the galley to get another cuppa. Alf's face was dark at the mess he now had to tidy. Cliff had just long enough for his cup of tea to steep when again the ship lurched to starboard. This time Alf and Cliff weren't caught so off guard, and managed to hold fast to stop themselves being thrown from the galley.

'Looks like she's going right over this time,' Cliff said, adrenaline starting to run through his bloodstream like fire. Striding out the port door, he passed the captain's accommodation and looked down onto the main deck. *That's not right*, he thought with a sharp inhale of breath. The starboard railing was just moments away from disappearing into the water. Cliff had seen a ship succumb to the hungry teeth of the ocean 31 years earlier, after a Japanese torpedo ripped the guts of HMAS *Perth* open in World War II. He knew what it felt like when a ship reached such an angle in the water that there was no way of recovering it.

Suddenly, without warning, the *Blythe Star* was going down. The unimaginable was happening.

Now battling to walk given the angle of the deck, Cliff was thinking of the men from the previous watch, Mick and Mal McCarroll, slumbering below. Someone had to rouse them and get them out of their cabins before the slippery fingers of the ocean made their way to them and trapped them.

Minutes before, when the ship had rolled sharply to starboard a second time, the sleeping Mick had been hurled from his bunk. Landing with a bruising crash on the cabin floor he was awake instantly. Horror overtook him as he looked at the porthole and saw it was entirely submerged under the water. Spinning, he saw water pouring into his cabin from the doorway, its icy touch already grasping at his legs. As Mick's brain struggled to comprehend what his eyes were seeing, he remembered watching movies about ships sinking. What he always feared was water pouring into his alleyway and cabin. *Shit, this thing's sinking*, he thought. *This water is going to come in here and drown me.*

Now his body was pumping adrenaline, numbing the cold from the water that was already at his knees and rising rapidly. Mick now had one thought: survival. In nothing but the jocks he'd been sleeping in he took off, splashing out the cabin door and up the alleyway. He pushed against the water that was pouring in as if it was trying to force him back into his cabin.

In moments everything had changed. Time could no longer be trusted. It seemed like a thousand things were happening simultaneously in an instant but also in warped slow motion. It was like, in this moment, when his whole life boiled down to the blood pumping in his veins, his muscles forcing him into action, time wasn't following the usual rules.

Mick clawed his way forward, half-walking, half-crawling on the walls, the ship so far over that the floor was no longer beneath him. When he reached the laundry doorway, Mick looked in and saw Mal McCarroll wrestling with the porthole. It had been left open, and now water was cascading in and drenching Mal, who was trying single-handedly to hold back the weight of the sea.

Mal turned as he heard Mick, his eyes wild, the terror written plainly in the whites. They looked at each other for what felt like forever but was only a few seconds, seeing in each other's chalk-white faces their own shock and fear reflected. At the same moment, they shook their heads at one another.

'Upstairs. Let's get out of here, it's gone,' Mick said.

Needing no further prompting, Mal abandoned his fruitless effort to seal the porthole. He let go and the porthole was flung from his hands as water coursed in, now completely unfettered.

Mick led the way up the companionway, water pouring everywhere. The ship was now floundering at 90 degrees on its starboard side. Pulling themselves onto the poop deck, Mick and Mal saw Alf Simpson and Cliff Langford joining Tas Leary there. Relieved to see Mick and Mal, Cliff abandoned his attempt to get back to the accommodation.

'What the hell's going on?' Alf asked.

'I don't know, but I'm going to get this raft over the side,' Tas replied, making his way as fast as the ship's angle would allow to where the life raft was packed tight and stowed away.

Mick and Mal managed the gruelling 30-metre clamber across the sharply listing deck to join the others. Reaching them, Mick came alongside Alf. 'I think she's going over,' Mick said, disbelief pairing with horror at the scene unfolding around him. Mal kept moving past Mick, up to the boat deck that sat above the poop deck at the rear of the ship.

On the bridge of the doomed ship, Mick Power was still holding fast to the wheel, doing what he could to try to keep the ship sailing and upright. There was no denying the all-out panic that hit him in waves now. The captain was still nowhere to be seen, but Power wasn't leaving the bridge while he thought there was still hope the ship might right itself. He still thought someone would appear any second and bark an order to change course, or try to ground, or do *something* that would put things right.

But the captain wasn't coming. When the ship had first lurched to the side, Captain Cruikshank had been walking across the deck. He'd been caught unawares and thrown sidewards, just like Cliff Langford and Alf. Losing his feet beneath him, George Cruikshank had slid under the starboard lifeboat. It was then he had the realisation that they might be in trouble and that the list he had dismissed just minutes before might have been a first warning that everything was not okay. Spying the open galley skylight set in the deck a short distance away, the captain had slowly pulled himself up. Scrabbling with his hands and arms, he managed to manoeuvre himself over to it, where he could stand. Gingerly he'd then made his way in the direction of the bridge. When he reached the wheelhouse bulkhead, the ship was slowly but surely lumbering ever further sideways into the water. As the ship slipped from 75 degrees to 90 degrees, the captain watched, frozen.

While Mal had been desperately trying to batten down the laundry porthole to keep water out and while Cliff was thinking desperately about rousing the sleeping watch, Captain Cruikshank stood, rooted to the spot, watching with dread as the starboard rail disappeared under the relentless ocean swell. Finally bringing himself back into the moment, his mind turned to the bridge and chartroom beyond, where the radio and portable emergency radio were situated. If he could reach them, he could radio a message to the world, sound the alarm to alert the crew and collect the emergency radio to take on the lifeboat. But, only metres away, the bridge and chartroom might as well have been on another ship. Deciding there was no way he could make it to the bridge, he gave up any idea of trying to retrieve any of it, and the captain instead grabbed whatever handhold he could and pulled himself around to the poop deck.

Down in the bowels of the ship, the chief engineer, John Eagles, was struggling to get above decks. He had headed back to the engine room after checking in with the captain on the bridge. Then he had headed around to check the ballast in tank number 3. Before he could make it, the ship had lurched violently, throwing him onto the burning engine.

A burn more than two centimetres wide was seared from knee to ankle on his right leg. The only bit of luck – if you could call it that – was that the wound cauterised. Still, John didn't lose his mind. Noting the steadily increasing list and realising the ship was lost, he put aside any thought of the state his leg might be in and gingerly made his way around the scorching engine to switch it off. The engine's growling roar shuddered to a stop. The shriek of an alarm – tripped by the dying engine – tore the air, but it couldn't drown out the terrifying sound of rushing water. John knew he had to get out. When a ship goes down, you don't want to be below decks.

Up on the bridge, Mick Power gritted his teeth and held his ground, waiting for any direction to come his way. Suddenly, the engine shut off and the wheel beneath his hand seized. Where usually a finger could spin it, now it wouldn't budge. The wheel had lost power and he could no longer steer. Power realised there was nothing more he could do. The ship was lost. It was sinking. There was no point in him waiting any longer for directions. It seemed they weren't coming. Certain there was nothing more he could do to save the ship, he said aloud: 'Fuck, she's going down. I'm not going to get off.'

He grabbed a life jacket from the rack above his head. Unable to stand, he crawled to the port side door. Reaching it, he kicked off his thongs to give his feet better purchase. Looking around wildly, he spotted a safety line hanging from the port lifeboat. He reached out and managed to grasp it and pull himself clear of the bridge, and swung himself around to the rail of the boat deck. As he did so, Mal McCarroll and cook Alf Simpson swung into view.

Heart pounding, free from the death trap of the bridge but by no means safe, Mick Power saw the fear and bewilderment in the faces of his shipmates. Their eyes were wide and panicked as they all tried to accept in this moment – with a million things happening – that their ship was lost.

CHAPTER 5

Sinking Realisation

Saturday, 13 October 1973 – *Blythe Star*

The grey ocean swell blended into the grey horizon of the clouds, and light rain swept across the scene. It was the sort of view that would feel cosy if you were sitting by a roaring fire with book and tea in hand, curled in the window seat of a seaside cottage. Clinging to the deck of the *Blythe Star* at 90 degrees, it was anything but. It was 8.25 am, less than half an hour since the freighter had first lurched sidewards.

Mick was dressed in nothing but his jocks, but thanks to the fear pumping through his veins he didn't feel the cold. It would come creeping in later. Since he'd been thrown from his bunk minutes earlier he had been in constant motion. Muscles taut as he held himself to the ship, Mick noticed the captain coming from around the starboard side of the bridge toward him. 'Did you get a mayday away?' he yelled across at Captain Cruikshank.

'No,' the captain yelled back simply.

The moment passed and Mick scrambled across toward the boat deck, where the crew were gathering one by one as they escaped from below deck. White and shivering, Mick made it across, and Mick Power handed him a bright, orange life buoy.

It only took a second for Mick to survey the scene and get the drift of what was happening. Mal McCarroll was casting around wildly for an axe to hack one of the wooden lifeboats free from its ropes. By now the starboard lifeboat was well and truly out of reach under the inky ocean. But if they could get the port lifeboat afloat, they just might have a chance.

It would be a desperate move. With the ship leaning so heavily, cutting the lifeboat free was a dangerous proposition. The falling boat might well collect them all on its way down. But desperate was exactly what they were as they watched the ship sink inexorably lower in the water with every passing moment.

Seeing Alf Simpson, Mick passed the life buoy to him. Then he moved further aft and turned his attention to joining the search for an axe. The other men grabbed at whatever they could to lower themselves down to the poop deck. Each moment brought new and more visceral panic flooding through them. 'Where's the axe?' Mal yelled in desperation, seeing it nowhere.

The crew looked around at Mal. The axe was meant to live in the lifeboat. What did he mean where was it?

Then Mick Power called a reply. 'It's in the bridge.'

SINKING REALISATION

Not much fucking use there.

Mal and Mick realised that, without the axe, which was nestled safely on the bridge along with their radios, there was no hope of getting the lifeboat away. They abandoned their efforts to free it and turned their attention to reaching the poop deck. There, a rectangular-shaped white box about a metre long was now their only hope. Tucked inside the box was an emergency life raft. It didn't have the sturdy wooden sides of a lifeboat, nor the oars or manoeuvrability, but it was all they had.

Tas Leary was wedged awkwardly into the cramped space where the raft was stowed in its box. He ripped off the strap holding the box down and tried to loosen the pins locking it in place. There was no room for anyone else to join Tas and help, so Mick stood back alongside the rest of the crew. As he waited, heart pounding, all the action of a moment before drained away in the wash of the rain. Completely powerless, he watched as Tas wrestled with the raft box. Thoughts started to creep into the void left in the wake of action.

What a miserable way to go, Mick thought. As he watched his world disappear from under him, he was convinced that his race was run and time was up. He was certain that this was how it was going to end, standing on a ship as it took on more and more water, freezing cold in nothing but his jocks and waiting for the water to claim him.

Movement and action had kept the cold at bay. Now it crept in. Mick's toes were numb against the deck. As he contemplated his last moments, he never turned to a higher being to plead for his life. Standing there, he was ready to do anything asked of him to help get himself and his shipmates to safety. But he wouldn't demean himself by trying to strike up a deal at the 11th hour with a god he didn't believe in.

Tas's hands grappled with the wingnuts on the back of the two pins that held the raft fast. It was a fiddly job on a good day, but with the pressure of time and his crewmates' lives hanging on his every move, undoing the nuts was excruciating. After what felt like an age, the nuts finally fell away, tinkling as they bounced down the deck and into the freezing water below.

Tas wiggled the raft box and managed to yank the first pin free. He turned his attention to the second, but, try as he might, he couldn't move it. Cursing, he kept trying to free it from the swollen wood jamming it in place, as though willpower alone might convince the pin to move. But nothing ever came unstuck just because you swore at it.

'Has anyone got a spike? The bloody thing's stuck and I need something to hit it free,' a wretched-sounding Tas yelled, looking for the pointed metal tool used to work with ropes, or anything, that might help him free the jammed life raft. His desperation was infectious, and the crew immediately searched for something that might help.

Mal McCarroll pulled a wooden wedge from somewhere. 'Here,' he said. He tossed it to Tas, who jammed it under the life raft, using the wedge as a lever to force the life raft free. But the wedge was clearly not up to the task and the life raft remained immovable. Tas looked around for something else

SINKING REALISATION

that might help. He spotted a lump of timber a metre or so long and dived at it, grabbing it like it was a gift from the Big Man himself and thrust one end under the box holding the precious raft.

He threw his whole weight onto it. With everything he had he used the wedge and wood to try to free the raft. The rest of the crew watched on in despair. Nothing. Tas eased off for a moment to gather every buzzing morsel of energy in his body. Then he tried again. For a moment, nothing happened. Suddenly, unwillingly, the raft shifted and began to lever over the side.

Smelling victory, Tas started belting at it with the timber. As it neared the top of the rail, he threw the lump of wood to the side and kicked at the raft, forcing it over the rail. The raft plunged into the water below, just a metre or so from the now still propellers. If John Eagles had not had the foresight to head deeper into the engine room to turn off the propellers, they would have shredded the raft as it sailed downward.

Tas kept his hand on the end of the 26-metre-long rope, called the painter, which snaked out and disappeared into the box bobbing in the swell. He began hauling the painter in, hand over hand, until he neared the end.

As the raft box drew closer and the painter tautened, Mick's breathing became shallower. Tas had one chance to get this right. The painter was attached to a gas canister packed up in the life raft. When pulled with enough force, the painter would trigger the canister to explode and the raft would leap into existence. But the device was notoriously unreliable. Not every canister exploded, and if this one didn't, the crew of the *Blythe Star* were out of cards.

Barely pausing to consider, Tas gave an almighty tug on the painter. It seemed to Mick like the world stopped turning for a beat or two. His heart pounded as if in slow motion.

Boom.

Boom.

Boom.

Then, the canister exploded, unfurling rubber and hope. Inflating fully, the orange dome-shaped life raft – about the size of a three-man tent – seemed miraculous to Mick. Not even the feeling of Collingwood winning a grand final could compare to the elation he felt seeing it come to life before his eyes.

Tas leapt into the raft, keeping a firm grip on the painter. With his other hand, he tried to keep the raft free of the edge of the ship so it wouldn't be damaged in the final mad dash to relative safety. 'Get in! Everyone get in!' he yelled.

Mick Power was closest and needed no prompting. He leapt into the raft and quickly moved under cover of the canopy to make room for the next man. Mick turned to Captain Cruikshank again. 'Did you get a mayday away?'

Before he could hear the answer, Tas yelled again. 'Bucko, move it! Get in the raft!'

Mick's turn was up and he dived into the raft, followed by John Eagles. Looking back, he saw that the ship was now wallowing entirely on its side.

Still on board the ship, John Sloan was reluctant to get into the raft. He was saying something and gesticulating

SINKING REALISATION

wildly. But it wasn't the time for hesitation. The *Blythe Star* could sink at any moment and suck the raft and crew down in her wake. They needed to get clear.

In the end, the prospect of staying behind on a sinking ship forced John Sloan onto the raft, followed by Captain Cruikshank. As the other crew scrambled to get inside, Cliff Langford looked across at John and saw that he was white as a sheet. Alf Simpson was the last to clamber aboard.

Someone thrust a knife at Mick, yelling at him to cut the raft free of the painter. They needed to get the hell out of there. Mick grabbed the knife and started hacking at the taut line connecting the raft to the sinking ship. Now it was his turn to feel the weight of eight men's eyes on him, their survival in his hands.

'Hurry up, get it off,' the crew cajoled.

But the more they harried him the harder it bloody got. Mick's hands were shaky and slippery.

'Hey, where's Ken?' Tas Leary called out suddenly.

Shit. Mick realised they were a man down. But he still needed to cut the raft free of the painter or there'd be more than one man lost.

Minutes earlier when the *Blythe Star* had started her death roll and lurched to starboard, Ken Jones had been asleep in his cabin. Waking to see water over his porthole, he'd rushed to the door and tried to push it open, but it didn't move. Ken had realised immediately the pressure of the water building up on the outside of the door had pinned it closed.

He'd put his shoulder into it and threw himself at the door in an attempt to budge it. Nothing.

Darkness enveloped him as his cabin sank further. The water was now snaking its way in, spurting and gushing around the door and through any crevice it could find. Ken knew there was no way he was getting that door open until the pressure equalised. So he stood and watched with forced patience as his cabin slowly filled with water. Each litre that poured in brought him closer to being able to open the door – but also closer to drowning. It was going to be a tight-run thing.

Ken had kept trying the door, checking to see if he could move it. While he watched his world turn aquatic, he grabbed a life jacket and a cardigan and threw them both about his shoulders. Finally the pressure equalised and Ken could coerce the door open. He took a deep breath, thought of Francis and Susan, and swam for it.

Lungs feeling fit to burst, Ken swam along under the deck, making his way toward the companionway, where he'd be able to surface and get clear of the ship.

In the raft, Mick cast his eyes about desperately with the others, the dread of losing the first mate coursing through him. Time slowed again for Mick. Then he saw splashing. 'Here he comes through the water,' someone behind Mick yelled.

'Over here, Kenny,' Mick called out. Ken didn't respond – he hadn't heard. Mick called again, and this time Ken heard him and struck out toward the raft.

SINKING REALISATION

As Ken came closer, Mick saw blood streaming down the first mate's face. A great chunk had been taken out of his nose. The crew aboard the life raft called to Ken, willing him to make it over. As he reached the side of the raft many hands reached down in welcome, grabbing him and hauling him into the raft. Mick could see that Ken's legs were lacerated, with chunks of skin missing here and there, torn off in his desperate swim for survival.

It only took a moment longer for Mick to get the painter free. The little raft started to float away from the ship, its gentle, bobbing progress, like a rubber duck on bathwater, at odds with the desperation of the moment. The crew watched, awed and silent. Their ship was now entirely lying on its starboard side, her dripping and exposed hull in the air. It's a perspective no seafarer ever wants to experience.

In less than ten minutes, with the raft still barely 30 metres away, the ship's bow rose out of the water. The stern, which until just minutes ago they had all been standing on, sank beneath the surface. Then, without fanfare, the rest of the ship slipped away, devoured by a careless ocean.

Mick couldn't believe his eyes. He couldn't believe that a ship could just disappear like that. He felt like there should have been more noise, or destruction or ... anything. Something to mark the momentous nature of losing a ship. To show that his entire world had just disappeared from under him. But there was nothing. Not so much as a gurgling bubble. It was simply there, and then gone, leaving ten crew shocked and disoriented, trying to grapple with their new circumstances.

The crew were now adrift in a life raft 10 kilometres west of Tasmania's South West Cape in the hostile Southern Ocean. They were about to find out just what they were made of.

CHAPTER 6

In the Shit

Saturday, 13 October 1973 – Life raft, Day 1

The dawning realisation that they were totally alone and at the mercy of their wits came slowly to the ten-man crew. Following their escape from the clutches of the *Blythe Star* and still shaking from shock, fear and adrenaline, they were flooded with elation. They had stared into the watery face of death and escaped by the skin on their knuckles – some of them quite literally. Relief brought a kind of hysteria over them, and they began talking loudly across each other.

'Did you see that—'

'What was that you saw—'

'Did you see when—'

No one was able to finish a sentence and no one could hear what the others were saying. Realising someone needed to take charge of the situation and bring them back to their immediate problems, first mate Ken Jones tried to silence the babble bouncing around the little, orange-domed life raft. After a few tries the conversation died off.

For the third time that morning, Mick turned to Captain Cruikshank. 'Did you get a mayday away?' he asked.

'No, I didn't have time to warm up the transmitter,' came the reply.

'What about the emergency wireless?' pressed Mick. 'Did you get the portable radio?'

'No, I didn't have time,' the captain said again. He added with a note of defensiveness, 'It was too dangerous to go into the chartroom to get it. I would have got trapped in there.'

This silenced the crew far more effectively than anything else. Reality started creeping in. Mick realised they might have escaped the sinking ship, but they were still in a bit of shit. Their only means of telling the world what had happened was trapped in the chartroom and plummeting down to the ocean floor.

Mick couldn't believe what he was hearing. Surely the captain was having a laugh – albeit in poor taste. How could he not have got to the chartroom? It comes right off the bridge.

Clearly other minds were running on a similar track. Someone asked the captain how he couldn't have had time to take the few steps from the bridge to the chartroom.

Then came the admission that he wasn't on the bridge when the ship went down. He insisted to the shocked men around him that it would have made no difference to firing up the radio. 'It's a cold set,' he said. 'It takes a couple of minutes to warm up. I wouldn't have fancied being in there waiting for it to warm up.'

Mick didn't buy it and felt a rising tide of anger toward the captain.

The bedraggled and battered men were sitting hunched, shoulder to shoulder. Mick's skin was raised in goosebumps as the cold October air of the Southern Ocean flayed his exposed flesh. He had nothing to cover it except his watch and a pair of jocks.

Mal McCarroll, in undies and a T-shirt, wasn't much better equipped. At least those men who had been up and about on shift when the ship went down were a bit better set up. The captain's shirt and tie (along with jumper, pants, socks, slippers and windcheater) were glaringly incongruous with the shambolic scene around him. Alf Simpson was still in his white cook's uniform, while the chief engineer was in his boiler suit, which now sported a gash down the leg where the engine had burned through to his skin.

The rest of the crew were wearing pants and shirts which, while better than Mick's get-up, were hardly the perfect choice for the situation they now found themselves in. Realising the uneven distribution of attire, someone piped up, 'Skipper, give your windcheater to Doleman. Poor lad's bloody freezing.'

Between the ten of them were only two life jackets – the one Ken Jones had the foresight to grab hold of when he made his desperate swim for the surface, and the one Mick Power snatched as he abandoned the bridge after it was clear no man would be able to save the ship.

By now the adrenaline that had kept them fuelled and moving as they escaped the sinking freighter was wearing off. Pale faces looked around at their new vessel disconsolately. With the captain's words hitting home, Power lurched to the opening of the raft and Mick heard retching and splashing as Power brought up the contents of his stomach.

A few minutes later, the captain followed suit before falling back into his place, pale and shaken. 'That's the ship gone. The next thing's the inquiry,' he said. 'It's all right for you blokes, but if we get out of this there'll be an inquiry and they'll want to know why I wasn't on the bridge.'

George Cruikshank had always dreaded being hauled before an inquiry and being asked to justify a decision or action – something that had had disastrous consequences.

'Where were you?' someone asked.

'In my cabin. I'd gone down for a glass of water.'

Conversation started murmuring between the men again, although far more sedately than the burst of excited chatter that immediately followed their narrow escape.

'Why wasn't there a fucking axe in the lifeboat? There should have been one in there,' Mal McCarroll vented. He was thinking of how different their prospects might be looking just now if they were in the far sturdier wooden lifeboat, with oars and some capacity to be directed and navigated. Captain Cruikshank responded in the general hum that he had taken it out when they were on shore and put it on the bridge.

'Fat lot of good it does there,' came a tart reply.

Cruikshank turned to Cliff Langford beside him. He spoke in a low tone to him, emphasising how quickly everything had happened, that, whatever he had done, the *Blythe Star* was doomed.

Dazed and trying to take in everything that had happened, Cliff was only half-listening.

'Cliffy, you'll agree, won't you, that nothing could be done to save the ship?' Cruikshank implored.

Cliff didn't bother answering.

Slowly, Captain Cruikshank fell into silence and almost into himself. Looking across at him, it looked like he had checked out. His mind had either shut down or gone somewhere the others couldn't see or reach.

As the minutes ticked by, the men again felt the shifting nature of time as it warped and twisted without any activity to mark its passage. They rose and fell gently on the swell of the ocean, the occasional shower passing over and adding a gentle whisper to the constant sound of water moving against the black rubber of the raft's base.

Mick wasn't the only crew member looking for someone to step into the void and give them direction. Ken Jones, square shouldered, moustache perched above a humorous mouth that was now set grim, stepped in and took charge. 'Alfie, you better take charge of the rations,' he said. 'Take a look in the box and see if there are any flares in there.'

Alf manoeuvred himself over to the cardboard box that held all the raft's emergency supplies. Already the salt water was soaking into the edges, the cardboard turning pulpy.

'It's cray season, isn't it?' Mal McCarroll asked. 'One of them might see a flare.'

'Nah, I don't think so. The season closed a while back,' chipped in Tas Leary, who had recently been shooting the breeze with the resident fishermen at Grassy on King Island.

But the rest of the crew were certain there'd be an itinerant cray fisherman around who might spot a flare and raise the alarm. They might yet be having a warm shower and tucking into a big feed before slipping into a cosy bed that night.

While this conversation was going on, Alf unpacked and assessed what was in the ration box. He passed a rocket flare across to Ken Jones who clambered his way across to the raft opening. He rolled the flap up and tied it in place.

Wedging his leg against the edge of the raft he leaned out as far as he could and extended his arm toward the grey sky. Hand grasped firmly around the tube of the flare, he took hold of the red-ridged cap at the base and unscrewed it. A small string fell down that Ken grasped and pulled hard.

The smell of burning gun powder and a sizzling hiss filled the air as the flare fired off. The luminescent bright red scorched the eyes at close distance, and even the men under the raft's canopy could see the red projectile fly 300 metres into the sky, where it seemed to hang before slowly descending. The 40 seconds it burned were 40 seconds of dreaming of warm tea, a cigarette, of wives and girlfriends and children just a few hours away. As the flare faded, those dreams faded too.

Then, they waited.

How long would it take for someone to reach them after seeing the flare? A rocket flare like that could be sighted up to 15 kilometres away, so it might take a while. The seconds and minutes ticked by. It was hard to know when the waiting became the giving up, each moment bleeding into the next. Each second brought the promise of the next, that the next minute would bring their salvation. And yet each minute also brought the crushing emptiness of the waves around them.

Ken Jones realised the danger of the empty minutes to the men's minds so he got them into gear. 'Right, lads, we need shifts,' he said – all business. 'Twenty minutes apiece, one rowing and keeping lookout, then swap to the next man.' He turned to the cook. 'Alf, what have we got in there?'

Alf had been picking through the meagre supplies he had unpacked from the emergency rations box – a collection of food, water and other emergency kit. 'We've got another rocket flare, and six handheld flares,' Alf replied.

'We better save those for when we see someone,' Ken said. Always it was *when*, not *if*.

Taking inventory, Alf had also noted some cans of water – although some were well out of date – as well as protein biscuits, glucose powder, one three-cell torch with three spare batteries, some fishing hooks and a can opener. What he hadn't found in the box were matches or space blankets to help keep the cold at bay.

Ken turned to Mick, who was shivering. 'Mick, get hold of one of those paddles and make a start toward land.'

Mick picked up the short leaf-shaped paddle and leaned out over the water to dip it in. A life raft is hardly the most aerodynamic creature, but it's better than nothing. Surely a few hours on the paddle would get them closer to land?

As each 20-minute block was up, the men would shuffle around in some bizarre, cramped game of musical chairs to let the next person taking up the paddle move forward to the opening. But as the day wore on, Mick, Power and Mal McCarroll became the main paddlers.

When it came time for the captain to take a turn, however, he couldn't be roused. He refused to take the paddle and was barely responsive to their cajoling. It seemed to Mick that he was almost in a state of semi-coma. The shock of the sinking had caused George Cruikshank's body to shut down. His brain couldn't process what had happened and what was unfolding around him, so it protected him by switching off.

After only a few hours, the cramped conditions started to make themselves felt in aching muscles, caused by the awkward sitting position and lack of movement. Conversation ebbed and flowed throughout the day. No one said anything of the thoughts that hid at the edge of their minds. They still expected someone would be along to get them soon. They might not have got a mayday off, but a ship couldn't just sink without anyone noticing, without someone coming along soon enough to get them. Could it?

Mick was hardly in the most comfortable place in his life, but looking over at John Sloan he noticed that the other man seemed to be far more unsettled. John was no stranger to doing it tough. An adoptee in a loving but poor family, life in those early years was hard, as it was for many of the crew. Like Mick, John grew up knowing what it felt like to go to bed with a growling stomach.

John Sloan might have spent the past two decades at sea, but his heart was on the land. He loved farming and riding horses and as a young man all his spare time had been spent working on farms. Unlike many in the maritime industry, he didn't drink or smoke. He'd joined the decks of a ship after training as a marine engineer with dreams of seeing the world. It was on a voyage to Japan as second engineer on the SS *Taiping* in 1957 that he met a young 24-year-old called Joan, who along with her mother, Thelma, had booked a three-month cruise on the ship.

Joan was a country girl, and she and John soon hit it off. They bonded easily over their shared love of farming and horses. The seeds of a great love story were sown in the romance of the high seas. Later that year, the two were married and tried their fortunes on the land together. But making a life out of what the land and rain provides is tough, so John had gone back to work at sea part-time to keep the cash flowing.

Originally, John wasn't even meant to be on the *Blythe Star*, but another ship's delay had left the Tasmanian freighter in need of a second engineer and John stepped in to fill the gap.

Sitting in the slick of water that swilled in the bottom of the raft, John was deeply agitated. Someone asked him if he was okay. Then he dropped a bombshell on the rest of the crew.

They had all lost precious things – Alf his cherished chef's knives, Mick his cassette player loaded with AC/DC and some spare Slade cassettes to get him through the long days at sea. But John had lost something far more important – the medication he needed for a thyroid condition, now trapped in the steel hull of the *Blythe Star* fathoms below the surface.

The crew suddenly understood why John had been so reluctant to get aboard, even as the *Blythe Star* was slipping away from under him.

'If we don't get picked up in two or three days, I'll be in trouble,' John informed his shipmates. 'I didn't have time to get them. Everything happened so fast.'

Their certainty that they would be rescued in a day or two was about to be tested. Because if they weren't right, then John Sloan would be in all sorts of strife. But, by and large, they still thought that someone would come to get them before then.

Ken Jones reassured the men, telling them it wasn't a matter of if, it was when. 'Chin up, lads, we'll be right,' he said, his confidence giving them confidence that somehow everything would iron out.

Late in the day, Alf Simpson, without anything to cook but still in charge of dishing out sustenance, cracked open a can of water.

It was like a pass the parcel game, where each player got just a sip before handing it along to the next. As the water touched Mick's mouth it felt heavenly. Already, his lips were dry and chapped from the wind and salt, and the water seemed like a miracle to his dry tongue. Even though the water had a brackish tang, Mick took his sip with relish. Brackish water is still water, and he was glad to have it.

Alf then gave each of them a biscuit from the emergency rations. Mick looked at his unappealing rectangular biscuit, brown like chocolate, and took a bite tentatively. With the taste of cardboard and texture of chaff Mick thought wishfully of meat pies at the footy. God what he wouldn't give for one of them now.

Beside him, Mick Power was having a harder time of it. Not even through his meagre ration of one biscuit and he was retching, his stomach refusing to accept it. Tas Leary was the same, his body refusing to take in the protein biscuit that was meant to keep them alive until they were rescued.

Alf opened up some glucose powder and told Power and Tas to put out their hands. He poured the brown-coloured powder into their palms. They lifted their hands to their faces and licked them clean, tongue scouring the cracks in their palms to pick up every crystal of the sweet powder.

Once their meal of one biscuit each – for those who could stomach them – was polished off they were back to sitting cramped together. Ten burly men in a far too small space trying not to think about just how uncomfortable they were.

As evening approached with curling fingers of darkness, the wind picked up and the thin rubber of the raft's canopy fluttered and snapped. The water around them began to heave, as though a creature was waking ready to hunt the night. The little speck of the raft was being blown further south and east, away from Tasmania and civilisation.

Gloom settled into the raft, so John Eagles pulled out the matches he'd had in his pocket and lit up the last cigarette the men had been able to scrounge between them. The match hissed to life as John struck it. He held the little dancing flame to the end of the smoke, which blazed electric orange as he drew the tobacco-stained air into his lungs.

They passed the cigarette between them. Each man took a drag before sending it across to the man next to him, careful to catch the falling ash so it didn't burn the rubber raft. Each smoker relished the taste of tobacco on their tongue and the rush in their lungs, unsure how long it would be until their next cigarette. John carefully wrapped up the little package of matches in some plastic, secured it closed with tape stripped from the emergency ration box and tucked them fastidiously into the breast pocket of his overalls. This little packet was all they had to start a fire should they ever need one.

Suddenly, the call came down from the man keeping lookout and maintaining a steady rhythm on the paddle. 'I can see a light!'

Elation flooded the raft like a wave. This was what they'd been waiting for! This godawful day would be over and they would all get out of this okay. It would be a story they could tell over beers at the pub.

Ken took charge of the moment again, as he had since he was pulled bleeding and soaked from the water into the raft.

Quickly shuffling over to the opening, he poked his head out. After a quick discussion, the men decided the light must be coming from Maatsuyker lighthouse. It couldn't be more than three miles away. And there must be a keeper on watch up there. Someone with eyes seaward who would surely spot them.

'Quick, get me that other rocket,' Ken said.

Someone thrust their second and last rocket flare into Ken's hand. Again, he unscrewed the bottom, took hold of the firing wire and pulled hard. But this time, instead of a light arcing into the sky, a disappointing fizzing sound could be heard then silence and darkness.

'It's a dud,' Ken said, cursing and pitching the rocket casing overboard.

'Fucking oath,' a frustrated voice responded. Someone handed Ken one of the six handheld flares. This one ignited in a spitting blaze of red, the molten sparks falling onto Ken's exposed hand. Gritting his teeth against the searing of his burning flesh, Ken tried to protect his hand from the falling fire. All the while he held the flare aloft for the watching eyes of the Maatsuyker lighthouse.

The flare, blindingly bright at close range, blazed for a minute. Then it burned out, but Ken wasn't ready to give up. 'Pass me the torch instead.'

The torch was passed around the circle to Ken's waiting hand. He flashed it on and off.

Short-short-short.

Long-long-long.

Short-short-short.

SOS, the international signal of distress. Ken's eyes stayed trained on the light burning out of the Maatsuyker lighthouse. Little did he know that, just twelve hours earlier, lighthouse keeper Tony Parsey had been watching the labouring progress of his ship.

As dusk turned to night, Ken kept signalling, even though it appeared there were no eyes looking their way. Now the floor of the raft was transformed into a clinging dampness. Scantily clad as he was, Mick had felt the cold all day but with the setting of the sun he came to understand what it was to be cold on a whole new level.

Darkness on the open ocean isn't like anywhere else. Lit only by the cartwheeling expanse of the Milky Way above, the inky black remains untouched by any man-made light. As the raft kept time with its rolling gait, up, down, up, down, all perspective was lost. The ebony of the ocean bled into the black sky. No horizon was visible to get their bearings, the mesmerising shush of water against the raft relentless white noise.

It couldn't have been more than an hour since Ken gave up signalling Maatsuyker, conserving their few batteries, when into this disorienting landscape floated a set of lights. Sitting low, the lookout recognised the shape of another ship. He called down excitedly to the others.

The crew knew the shipping routes well, and based on the time and their rough location, they deduced that the ship was the MV *Mary Holyman*. Ken got hold of another flare. This time he wedged it into the emptied water can, wrapping a bandage around it and down his arms. Even with this protection, once he ripped it open and it sputtered into life the white-hot burning of falling flare still seared his arm. Ken waved the flare overhead, as high as he dared without falling into the drink. As soon as it died, he picked up the torch and began signalling SOS again.

Wretched frustration wedged in his chest as the *Mary Holyman* appeared oblivious, sailing on her set route unperturbed by the human tragedy playing out just six miles away. Up in the Maatsuyker lighthouse the head keeper had lit the kerosene lantern, sending its beam into the night. He spotted the *Mary Holyman* and recorded its passing in the logbook. But he didn't notice the blinking and flashing coming from the little bobbing raft.

As the *Mary Holyman*'s lights dimmed with distance, the spirits of the men on the raft sank. Eventually, the ship disappeared over the horizon and her lights winked out.

The wind hadn't dropped and continued to drive them in front of it. With no way of steering the raft they were at its mercy. It was barely past nine o'clock and the cold had made its way into their bones. Mick's body shuddered involuntarily and he crept closer to the man beside him, who gave off a faint warmth. By now they had been pushed south past Maatsuyker.

As the raft passed out of sight of the island Mal McCarroll started to feel uneasy. He knew the ocean had more terrors to throw at them than just dark and cold. To the south of Maatsuyker there was a hulking mass of muscovite granite rock, a top fishing spot that would make mincemeat of their raft in the dark. Leaning out of the canopy, he took over paddling as he cast his eyes around. Then he saw something unmoving and dark in the near distance. Mewstone.

Mal watched apprehensively as the raft continued its course south-east toward the island, which is around 12 kilometres south-east of Maatsuyker. Its sheer cliffs rose proud and brutal from the ocean, as though the only way land could survive the savagery of the weather was with menacing indifference. The highest part of the island loomed above them.

Although weary, Mal felt a surge of fear at the sight of the island. His heartbeat rose as he imagined them being dashed against the rocks. But the wind had other plans for them that night. As though playing with them, it drove them on a close skirting path past the rocky island. Mal breathed a sigh of relief, wondering just how far the wind was going to blow them. If they thought it was cold now, they would stand no chance if they headed further south, where the biting Antarctic chill would be waiting.

It seemed Ken Jones was thinking similar thoughts. 'If it keeps up like this, tomorrow we'll be down with the penguins,' he joked.

Earlier in the day the men had set the drogue in the water in an effort to slow their drift. A conical-shaped tube, the drogue was attached to the raft by a rope and dragged behind. The resistance of the water being funnelled through supposedly slowed them. They all hoped it would be enough to keep them from being pushed too far south overnight. But they realised that there was little they could do now to change their course. Already cold, exhausted, with thirst and hunger starting to lick their insides, they huddled together and tried to sleep.

While the close proximity of the men had been uncomfortable in the day, it now proved a blessing. Mick might only have met these blokes two nights ago, but now he cuddled up to them to share their body heat. It wasn't much, but it was all the heating they had. In his jocks with the bare skin of his legs pressed against the cold rubber beneath him, Mick was desperate for any warmth he could snatch from the bodies of his crewmates around him.

Cliff Langford shifted uncomfortably. It wasn't just his body that was giving him grief. In Cliff's mind this ordeal started to merge with another from 31 years earlier. As a young 22-year-old, Cliff had done what so many other young men had done and signed up to serve king and country in World War II. Aboard HMAS *Perth* on 1 March 1942, 25 minutes after midnight, Cliff had heard the rumbling crunch of a torpedo explosion blowing out her side. It had been followed by another, then another, as three torpedoes found their mark, putting paid to the 141-metre-long navy ship. In the darkness HMAS *Perth* hadn't sunk right away. It had lurched and listed to starboard in an eerie precursor of another sinking, three decades later. Then, it had rolled to port and slowly gone down, leaving the debris of man and metal scattered across the ocean surface.

Cliff and the sailors around him had swum as fast as they could to get clear of the ship. Then the Japanese convoy following behind the torpedoes steamed right through them. A man is no match for thousands of tonnes of metal. The captain of one of the Japanese destroyers called to the survivors of HMAS *Perth*, asking in impeccable English if they wanted to come aboard. Treading water, soaked through and freezing, the Australians said no. Instead, they just kept on swimming, trying to escape the disaster that was unfolding around them.

Cliff would spend eleven hours in the waters of the Sunda Strait, which connects the Java Sea and Indian Ocean between the Indonesian islands of Sumatra and Java. For a while he clung to a life raft alongside a cluster of other men. Eventually they were picked up by the Japanese and sent, along with thousands of other men, to work on the Burma Railway, known as the Death Railway due to the tens of thousands of POWs and forced labourers who died among the horror of the work camps. Cliff had endured terrible conditions for three and a half years, years he said he would rather forget. The suffering he'd experienced was etched in the lines of his face.

Now, at 53, Cliff was shipwrecked again, this time in the freezing Southern Ocean. Cliff was one of the older men in the raft and was feeling his age. Earlier that night, as the light was stolen from the sky, he'd looked out to the horizon and seen the ghosts of his long-dead shipmates. Now, in the darkness, he heard their desperate calls for help echoing across time. The sea was a graveyard that held the bodies of his old comrades, and he knew it would claim who it could.

That long and cold first night was not the last time during the days to come that Cliff would wonder if all the world had forgotten them.

CHAPTER 7

We've Lost a Ship

Sunday, 14 October 1973 – Doveton

As Doveton slowly came to life on a sleepy Sunday morning, Joanie opened her eyes in her warm bed. She lay for a moment, holding the business of the day at bay for a few seconds longer. Today was her birthday, and she was meant to be looking forward to a restaurant cruise with Mick. Instead she'd be spending the hours trying not to notice he was gone and the hole he left behind. She sighed and rolled the covers back.

Okay, enough, let's do it, she told herself. *Mick's not here, but it'll be okay. Let's be happy and you can celebrate the next birthday with him.*

Joanie's mum, Carmen, realised that, with Mick away, the day would bring a pang of sadness for Joanie. So, when Joanie was up and about, Carmen made a suggestion. 'Why don't we have some friends around and we'll have a bit of a party.'

'That sounds great,' Joanie said. In a household of eight there would be enough busyness and laughter to keep her mind off things. Add in some friends and she might just have a lovely day.

* * *

Sunday, 14 October 1973 – King Island

Early that morning about 250 kilometres away on King Island off Tasmania's north-west coast, Jim McKenzie was up and at 'em. McKenzie was the Tasmanian Transport Commission's man on the island. It was up to him to make sure the freighters bringing their essential supplies could berth and depart on time with minimum fuss. It was an important job. God forbid the beer delivery should go awry.

Following a well-worn routine, McKenzie checked for a telephone cable that was due to have come in from the *Blythe Star* at 5.30 that morning. It would have all the details about when the ship would come sailing into view. He was expecting it somewhere about 10 am, but the cable would confirm that. When, at quarter past seven, still no cable had arrived from Captain Cruikshank, he headed over to let the labourers who'd be unloading know that they wouldn't be needed until 11.30 am. That done, he continued on to the wharf. Once there, he fired up the radio and tuned in to VHF channel 16 in an attempt to raise the *Blythe Star*.

Captain Cruikshank had something of a reputation for being elusive on the radio, and so it seemed he was today. Nothing but crackling silence came back.

Little did McKenzie know that the radio he was trying to reach was under 150 metres of water, far beyond the reach of George Cruikshank.

* * *

Sunday, 14 October 1973 – Life raft, Day 2

It would be a stretch to say Mick woke with the dawn seeping into the raft on Sunday, given he'd hardly slept. Through the night, exhausted, he would doze off, but his body, frozen and in shock, wouldn't let itself rest completely, and he would soon be awake again with nothing but his thoughts to occupy him through the long and desperate hours.

Morning shed light on their grim, bedraggled reality, where waking was far worse than nightmare. It hit them like a lump of rock slamming into their guts and settling in their stomachs, heavy and nauseating. The optimism that had filled the raft immediately following their miraculous escape from the *Blythe Star* had long since evaporated. Mick met the day feeling grim and couldn't help but think that they weren't getting out of this.

'Morning, Bucko,' Ken Jones muttered in his Liverpudlian accent. 'Slept like a baby, I bet?' Sensing the fear curling around Mick's stomach, Ken cracked a joke. He knew that

Mick needed bolstering. 'Today's the day, lad! They're coming for us today! Nothing surer.'

It wasn't just Mick drinking in Ken's words. With Captain Cruikshank still huddled off to the side, vacant and shut down, the remaining crew were looking for a beacon to pin their hopes to and Ken provided it. Ken was a man who, like all great leaders, could intuit what people needed. When everything had quite literally been ripped away from under their feet, this crew needed structure and routine. First up, he re-instigated the paddling shifts, 20 minutes apiece before swapping out. Each time the raft flap opened it let in the cold sting of unfettered wind. Speaking with a natural grace and authority, Ken made it clear that, as the raft was their vessel for the moment, it needed to be kept orderly. There was to be no slovenliness. Each morning, they would tidy and do what they could to keep the small dome of rubber as habitable as possible. If nothing else, the movement of 'keeping house' would be good for their bodies.

In the daylight, it was clear that the raft seemed entirely inadequate to carry the weight of ten men. Its arches were soft and sagging, and the rubber canopy hung flaccid and heavy over their heads. However, while the emergency pack in the raft may have been wanting in many regards, it did have a small hand-pump. Shaped like bellows, the pump was about 40 centimetres long with wooden handles. The men attached the pump to the raft's air valve then took turns pumping the bellows, their muscles feeling the lack of any real food since they'd leapt to safety the day before. Pumping more air into the raft would become a daily ritual for the crew, as they tried to eek a few more hours of life out of the raft.

After the bitter night they'd endured, they decided to inflate the raft bottom while they were at it. As the air was forced into the floor it gave them some cushioning from the watery world below. But it presented another problem. Now the floor bulged, rising in lumps around them, causing the slosh of seawater that was a constant in the raft to pool in the depression made by each man. Suddenly, bailing was all the harder as they tried to navigate their new undulating floor with a small jug.

Mick turned to anything that needed doing. He wanted to do whatever he could for himself and the crew. Men who, until a few days ago, were complete strangers to him. He would never get the chance to know them as shipmates. He was getting to know them as survivors. And from the outset he could see how some stepped up and grew into the chasm of uncertainty before them, while others shrank away.

When the ship was sinking, the crew's bodies flooded with adrenaline and cortisol. Their higher-order brain function narrowed in on surviving moment to moment. Their bodies were in fight or flight mode. But stuck immobile in a raft when there was nothing to fight and nowhere to run, this survival response can trip into freeze and denial. Shutdown. The brain and body are no longer able to process and respond to what's happening. For the second day, Captain Cruikshank remained inert and silent, a shell of a man who seemed to have broken under the weight of the situation and responsibility.

Within each of them, a battle was being fought that would determine their odds of survival: hope they could keep going against the daunting likelihood that they wouldn't be saved.

Already their bodies were feeling the effects of exposure. The human body is not designed for continuous cold. It felt like the numbingly cold water was settling into their bones. Their hands and feet were pale white, their peripheral circulation shutting down as their bodies pumped blood to the vital organs in the torso to keep their lungs breathing and hearts beating. This influx of blood to the torso could overload the kidneys, which would then offload all this extra fluid as urine. Already shocked and suffering, having drunk only an eggcup of water each during the past 24 hours, that fluid wasn't going back in.

Dehydration was setting in, an additional pressure on brains that were already suffering from extreme cold and stress. It also caused the blood in their veins to thicken and the risk of heart attack or stroke from blood clots was real. At the very least their cognitive function was tanking as the viscous blood tried to make its way through their brains.

The thirst would become like a beast at Mick's throat, always there. But John Sloan, deteriorating without his medication, felt the thirst far more. Alf Simpson decided they needed more formal rationing than simply passing the water can around for a sip each. He carefully measured off two ounces (around three tablespoons) for each man each day. John Sloan, however, was furnished with a can of water entirely to himself. But even that didn't seem enough to feed his desperate body's insatiable need for fluid. It was clear that he was already in far worse shape than the day before. Still, he would stoically take up the paddle and have his turn trying to move the raft toward the mirage of land on the horizon. There was a quiet courage in his silence as he attempted to spare his shipmates the agony of his existence while his body fast-tracked into shutdown.

As the first light of dawn touched the raft, it revealed a problem. The cardboard box that had neatly held their rations was disintegrating after 24 hours in constant water. And out flowed their supplies – fishing hooks, knives and the jagged ends of cans, their sharp points threatening to puncture their precious raft. To a man they decided the sharp objects needed to go. Their fingers carefully scrabbled around the raft gathering everything up. The fishing hooks and all the other sharps, besides one knife and a can opener, were collected and pitched over the side. Mick breathed a sigh of relief watching them go. Alf took careful custody of the knife and can opener, wrapping them as best he could in the remaining scraps of cardboard and carefully stowing them into his clothes. They might have needed fishing hooks if they were going to be out here for long, but they needed an intact raft more. They might have jettisoned the most dangerous, sharp objects but there was little they could do about all the water cans now loose in the raft, slipping and sliding around their bodies.

As they continued the monotonous routine of paddling, the sun rose in the sky. It quickly became clear the raft wasn't well designed for paddling. Kneeling, they'd lean their torsos entirely out of the raft so the paddle could reach the water. The only way to move the raft forward was to strike the paddle out in front and pull it back underneath you, forcing the water under the craft – hardly hydrodynamic.

It wasn't long before the pain set in. When it was Mick's turn, his hamstrings cramped. It was agonising, and he had to hand the paddle to someone else while he recovered.

Suddenly, there was a holler. The lookout could see something on the horizon. It was Pedra Branca. Bleak, sheer and savage, the rock islet is about as wide as a football field and a bit over twice as long. Eighty-one kilometres from South West Cape, it rose sheer out of the ocean. Dark dolerite at the bottom, the peaks along its length were dusted white as if by snow with the deposits of gulls and gannets. And those same rocks would happily shred the *Blythe Star*'s life raft. Which was a problem, as the wind resolutely blew them toward it.

Eight months earlier, Pedra Branca had proven just how vicious it could be. A Japanese fishing vessel struck the island and was ripped open and sank swiftly. Twenty-one crew died, only one surviving by clinging to the inhospitable rocks. Pedra Branca is not the sort of place you'd pull up for a picnic.

The men inside the raft were blind to just how close they were to the rocks. But soon the sound of the waves throwing themselves ceaselessly against the rocks grew louder. Then they all realised they needed to paddle hard.

As each man took his turn there was renewed vigour in their movements, but the paddles were hopelessly short and the handles far too small to hold easily. Someone suggested they try to get to the other side of the island, where the mass of rock would give them a break from the wind. So they tried to manoeuvre the raft away from the vicious rocks and around the island. Having paddled for 24 hours straight, they hoped they might be able to rest their bodies without fear of being blown to Antarctica.

Around Pedra Branca was the only shallow water for miles – the rest was deep ocean. As they drew closer, the raft, surrounded by broken water, bobbed and swirled, and the sound of the waves breaking on the rocks became a roar.

For hour after hour, they took turns paddling, desperate to keep themselves free of the rocks. Each time a new crew member took the paddle, he would have to scramble past the inert figure of the captain. Far from having the wherewithal to help paddle, he seemed barely there at all.

The day wore on and Mick, Mick Power and Mal McCarroll, being the youngest of the crew, took on the lion's share of the paddling as the others tired. As Mal looked across the whitewash, paddle in hand, beating out a slow rhythm in the water, he thought it was the bleakest scene he had ever laid eyes on. Every time his paddle dipped in the water, he said the name of his wife, Joan, or one of his four kids, only for the wind to snatch it from his mouth and carry it away. It was a nice thought that perhaps the wind would carry those words all the way across the waves and they might land in the ears of his loved ones and they might feel the whisper of him in the air. It was the closest any of them could get right now. Maybe the closest they would ever get again.

As they tired, spirits began to flag, but Ken Jones encouraged them to keep going. It might be odd to think of being inspired in such a horrific situation, but Mick was endlessly inspired by Ken. He chivvied and cajoled and encouraged them. Just one more. Our lucky break is coming next. We're going to get out of this.

But Lady Luck wasn't going to be handing out good fortune so easily. Before the morning was done the rope of the drogue, which had gone some way to slowing their path southwards, snapped. Suddenly the raft was entirely unfettered in the water, with nothing to slow its path. *Shit*, thought Mick. How the hell were they going to stop themselves from floating even further south, and ending up freezing in the Antarctic water around Macquarie Island?

'Get one of those water cans open, Alf,' Ken said.

Alf cracked the water can open and shared it around. Then he passed the now empty can to Ken. After punching some holes into the can's upper rim, Ken managed to loop the remainder of the torn rope onto the can. Then he shuffled over to the raft opening, threw the can into the water and watched as it caught. It might not be much but it was the best they could do with the materials they had to hand and might go some way to slowing down the raft.

Mick's turn paddling was up. The crew all shuffled around, and Mick handed the paddle to John Sloan. Fatigue was becoming like a physical weight and he fell back against the side of the raft. He zoned out and thought of home.

It was Joanie's birthday today. He wondered what she was doing. The vision of the cruise he had planned for her floated in his mind, taunting. He wondered if she had any idea yet that his ship had gone down. Would she ever? Or would he just disappear, no explanation or trace? His mind played over memories of home, of family dinners at Joanie's, of good company and safety. Thoughts of home were both a comfort and a curse.

Leaning out of the raft opening, John Sloan didn't speak. He was putting all his energy into the painful task of drawing that wooden paddle through the water. His skin had taken on a poor pallor, his movements becoming ever more sluggish. But still, without complaint, he did what he could, taking the paddle and his turn. As he paddled his body's final protests began. His stomach retched and he vomited between paddle strokes. Stomach empty, stinging watery bile would heave out.

When the others caught on that John was pushing through as his body broke down, they took the paddle from him and sat him back in the raft. 'That's enough, you rest,' someone said.

John leaned back, his eyes closing and breath shallow.

As the raft careened closer to Pedra Branca, the paddling became more fevered. Each man who took the paddle hurled himself into the job. No one needed to spell out what would happen if they didn't, if the raft hit the rocks. The hours dragged on, and still they weren't clear of Pedra Branca. It was as if the rocks were magnets drawing them close no matter how hard they paddled to get away. They needed to make land, but not here. They wanted to come ashore some place where they would have a fighting chance of getting out of the raft before it was pulverised and they were pounded on rocks.

Finally, by afternoon, their paddling and the infernal wind sent them scooting around and past Pedra Branca. They breathed a sigh of relief. But as the islet faded from sight, their south-easterly drift continued, taking them ever further from land and safety.

Back on the paddle, Mick looked up and saw a grey sky completely devoid of life. No dark shadow of birds circling or screech of wheeling gulls. He began searching for birds, but no matter how he scoured the ocean and sky around him there wasn't one to be seen. He realised just how far they must be from land. And still they were headed south. A terrifying loneliness swept over him. He didn't know where he was or where he was going or where they'd end up. And never had that been more terrifying.

The men kept paddling, pushing their sluggish and vapid bodies, hour after hour, with nothing to mark the passage of time except the rise and fall of each swell. Finally, the ceaseless hours of paddling seemed to have paid off. There, on the horizon, was a smoky smudge of land. Bruny Island. Civilisation. Safety. It was the injection they needed, the fuel to keep them paddling. Trying to keep it in sight as the raft rose and plunged between the waves, the view of the island gave them hope. Excruciatingly slowly, they got closer and were able to see the Tasmanian coast. Mick dared to dream that maybe this ordeal would soon be over. Perhaps he would make it through. Dangerous thoughts.

Finally, the seemingly endless day drew to a close. It seemed unbelievable that they'd spent one night adrift on the open ocean in a life raft and now, as dusk fell, Mick realised they were about to endure another. And the wind was turning on the crew of the *Blythe Star* yet again. As darkness came, the night-time hours saw them blown south again. The glimpse of land became nothing but a glimmer of something they'd hardly dared hope for before it was snatched away again. The optimism of the afternoon faded and Mick realised that they might be spending many more nights out. What had seemed unthinkable now looked possible, even probable.

* * *

Sunday evening, 14 October 1973 – Doveton

In Doveton, Joanie's impromptu birthday party had begun. Already the McGrath house was full of people, as it often was. About 25 people crowded into the living room, hugging Joanie and wishing her happy birthday. She stopped on her way to get a drink to say hello to Mick's mum. The hum of laughter and chat and music created a warm and happy ambience. Surrounded by people only too willing to help her forget that Mick wasn't there, Joanie found that the hours slipped by.

By 11 o'clock everyone was sitting around talking over the music. A family friend, Marree Henwood, her brown hair up in a big bun, was chatting to Mick's mum and Mick's best mate, Steve Henwood. Out of the corner of her eye, Joanie suddenly saw something go flying. She realised pretty quickly that a cream bun had flown past and had landed in Marree's perfect bun, courtesy of her brother, Buffy.

For a moment the chatter died away as everyone held a collective breath. Marree's face was a picture of shock as white cream dripped from her hair. Then she burst out laughing and fired something back.

'Okay guys, that's enough. No more cake fight,' Joanie's mum, Carmen, called out. As you would if you were the one who'd be cleaning up.

But Buffy was known to be a bit of a character, and the smell of fun was in the air. The next bun to go flying was aimed straight at Carmen. A moment's pause again. Then it got the better of her. Bursting out laughing, Carmen threw one back at him, giving as good as she'd got.

It was on, no holds barred. Birthday cake and cream was flying all around the living room. With cream in hair, on faces, dripping down clothes, everyone was cackling uproariously. Joanie's cheeks ached from laughing.

It was the last laugh she would have for a while. She wasn't to know that while her birthday was unfolding in wild style with a cake fight of epic proportions, a shivering Mick was wondering whether he'd make it through another night.

But that dawning was about to come crashing into Joanie's orbit.

* * *

Sunday afternoon, 14 October 1973 – King Island

On King Island, Jim McKenzie had spent the day trying hourly to raise a response from the *Blythe Star*, receiving nothing but deafening silence. By mid-afternoon he'd given up on seeing it coming ploughing up to the wharf that day and had dismissed the men hired to help unload. With a growing sense of unease, he continued trying to get through to the ship that had pulled a disappearing act. He made his final call over VHF 16 at five that afternoon. Still nothing.

McKenzie picked up the phone and called Captain David Bond, who had sat with Captain Cruikshank in his office just two days prior and convinced the other man to head up the west coast which, although more treacherous, was faster. Captain Bond listened to McKenzie's report and responded with annoyance, convinced that Cruikshank had holed up to wait out some weather and had turned his radio set off.

Captain Bond was irritated. Why couldn't the bloody man follow simple cable instructions? 'I'm sure he'll get there overnight,' he said to McKenzie.

Another hour passed and McKenzie sent a final message to the *Blythe Star*, with instructions for berthing the next morning. The news that the *Blythe Star* was incommunicado had started to make its way through the gossip mill.

* * *

Sunday evening, 14 October 1973 – Hobart

A young and hungry political journalist, 27-year-old Trevor Sutton, was at home enjoying a relaxing Sunday night when the phone rang. 'Hello?' he answered.

The voice at the end of the line had a tip-off for him. 'There's a ship missing. We've got a ship missing off the coast of Tasmania somewhere.'

A journalist is never really off duty and Trevor immediately began asking questions. He usually covered politics for TVT6 – the big story that was gripping the small island state was about the Hydro Electric Commission's decision to flood a pristine little glacial lake called Lake Pedder to shore up their power reserves. A missing ship? Well, it was something different at least.

Trevor hung up. He'd make a follow-up call the next morning. But, thinking it over, it sounded like the ship was just delayed. It would probably turn up tomorrow, so there was no point losing sleep over it now. He'd deal with it when he was in the office.

CHAPTER 8

The Search that Wasn't

Monday, 15 October 1973 – King Island

Monday dawned wet and heavy. Jim McKenzie was up early and found a cable waiting for him. But it wasn't from the *Blythe Star*. It was from another of the Tasmanian Transport Commission's ships, the *Straitsman*, which was due to berth at six that morning. The captain of the *Straitsman* said he had heard the shipping authorities in Melbourne trying to get through to the *Blythe Star* all night, without success.

The nagging worry that had tickled at McKenzie yesterday now blossomed into serious concern. Where the hell was the ship? And why wasn't the captain answering? Because he didn't want to? Or because he couldn't?

He picked up the telephone receiver and dialled the number of the exchange. He needed to reach Captain Maddock, Shipping Manager of the Transport Commission.

He waited while the operator tried to connect the call.

'Sorry, sir. That number is disconnected.'

McKenzie wasn't about to give up. So, he gave the operator the number for Captain Bond. This time he heard the click as the line went through.

'Still no sign of the *Blythe Star*,' he said. 'Nothing all night, not a peep this morning and Melbourne hasn't been able to get anything out of her.'

A short conversation later and McKenzie rang off. He had to go and start preparing for the *Straitsman*. This ship at least was accounted for and scheduled to unload. Dragging himself to wakefulness, Captain Bond showered and dressed before having a quick breakfast. Two hours after speaking to Jim McKenzie on the phone, Bond was on his way to Captain Maddock's home to brief him on the missing *Blythe Star*.

* * *

Monday, 15 October 1973 – Hobart

Slowly, Hobart was cranking into gear. It might have been the capital of Tasmania, but it was no Sydney or Melbourne. It still retained the air of a glorified country town, the morning rush hour still decades away from genuine gridlock. Journalist Trevor Sutton slid into the driver's seat of his brown Morris Marina, turned the keys in the ignition and drove out into the traffic.

It was only a short drive to the red-brick TVT6 newsroom. Once there, he quickly made his way up to the second floor.

Passing the edit suites, he nodded hello to his colleagues and stopped to have a quick chat.

'Heard about this missing ship?' he asked.

'Yeah, anyone know anything?' a colleague replied. 'Do we know what ship it is?'

It didn't take long to realise no one was any more enlightened than he was. Trevor headed into his office, and settled in for the day. Then he made the first of many calls to the Tasmanian Transport Commission that morning.

A young woman answered. Trevor outlined what he'd been told, and asked to speak to someone who could tell him what was going on. Could they confirm a ship was missing? What ship was it? How many crew were aboard?

He was stonewalled. 'This is a matter for the Minister for Transport,' came the reply. 'We can't confirm anything.'

As he rang off, Trevor wondered how the hell the Transport Commission couldn't confirm whether or not a ship was missing. Surely it either was or it wasn't – how could you not know?

Trevor picked up the phone again, ready to call every contact he had to try to get to the bottom of what was going on.

* * *

Meanwhile, at around a quarter past nine in Captain Maddock's home, Maddock and Bond made a call of their own.

Associate Commissioner of Shipping Captain Thomas Morehead picked up, and Maddock and Bond ran him through the situation.

'Well, he might have holed up on the west coast, but the weather's been clear,' Morehead said. 'Doesn't make much sense.'

There was still a feeling between the three – though no one need mention it – that Captain Cruikshank was known for going incommunicado. It was probably just the usual flakiness that he couldn't be bothered or hadn't remembered to make his regular shipping calls. All the same, they decided to make one more call.

This time Maddock rang the Regional Controller for the Department of Transport, Captain Maurice Brahan. Eighteen months earlier, Brahan would have been the go-to man for a missing ship. But then the Marine Operations Centre in Canberra had been created, a centralised point of operations for all search and rescue missions – under federal control.

Unfortunately, that's not how Tasmania worked, especially in the 1970s. It was a place that was about working with people you knew. Deals were still sealed with a handshake and the old maxim 'it's not what you know, it's who you know' was almost a point of pride.

Maddock spoke to Captain Brahan, himself on board a ship, about this infernal ship that wasn't showing up. Maddock informed Brahan that the *Blythe Star* hadn't made port that morning, Monday, as planned and was incommunicado. The problem was, Maddock was a day behind. The *Blythe Star* was meant to have shown up 24 hours *earlier* than that.

'You should ring Marine Operations,' Captain Brahan said. 'I'm not much use. I can only make local calls out of here.'

'Look, it's only a few hours. I think it's too early to go hitting the panic button,' Maddock said. 'Tell you what – I'll get back in touch at four this afternoon if there's still no sign of her.' He didn't say it, but presumably he didn't want to be the red-faced fool who called in a major search operation for a ship that then came sailing gaily into harbour a few hours later. That sort of embarrassment wouldn't do the commission, or him, any good. Best just to wait it out. No doubt the ship would turn up. After all, it was only a few months ago that Captain Cruikshank had turned off his radio while he waited out some weather for three days.

On that occasion, Cruikshank had downright refused to stay in touch with the commission, only staying in radio contact with McKenzie on King Island. Maddock had read him the riot act, and was readying himself to kick it up a notch when the bastard finally did show up.

Repeating that disappearing act was the sort of thing Cruikshank would do, Maddock thought. Hell, he was so unreliable he might have just as easily gone as far as Maatsuyker Island before turning around and heading up the east coast after all.

Maddock's Monday morning was not shaping up to be a good one. Playing a guessing game about when the bloody ship would turn up, he was behind already and the day had barely started. 'I'll take a flight up the west coast this afternoon if we haven't heard anything, and see if I can see her. I'll call you back again after that,' Maddock told Brahan.

* * *

Over in Parliament House, the Minister for Transport, Neil Batt, was taking a call from someone at the Transport Commission, who was filling him in. 'Where is it?' he asked.

Bluster came through the line to the disbelieving transport minister.

'Well, which way did it go?'

'We don't know.'

As the minister tried to wrap his head around what, exactly, he was being told, the person on the line tried to reassure him. 'Don't worry, we'll find it.'

As Batt hung up the phone, he wasn't worried. After all, Tasmania is just not that big a place. It couldn't be *that* hard to find a whole ship out there.

By now, Trevor Sutton, having hit a brick wall on the Transport Commission switchboard, was calling the Minister for Transport's office, trying to get some sliver of information. But the silence from the ship was only amplified by the silence from the authorities. No one could tell Trevor what was happening because they didn't know. And, honestly, they still weren't that concerned.

Despite the urgings of Captain Brahan to call the Marine Operations Centre in Canberra, the Transport Commission officials were holding off making that call. Instead, at one o'clock that afternoon, Captain Maddock and Minister for Transport Neil Batt walked out onto the tarmac at Cambridge airport, 15 minutes east of Hobart. The *Blythe Star* was missing, not a peep, but instead of calling in the official search and rescue authority, they'd decided to go looking themselves. Literally go looking. In a light aircraft. It didn't seem like a super strategic approach.

The south-west of Tasmania is a wild part of an already rugged island, the savagery of the landscape surpassed only by its beauty. The bush is dense and runs right down to the white sands of the beaches. The weather can turn in an instant and throw the ocean at the land as though it's trying to tear chunks out of it.

High above in a light plane, Neil Batt started to feel a little green. To say he wasn't a fan of flying would be an understatement. Flying left him terrified and paranoid and this trip had him white knuckled. Nevertheless, he and Maddock looked out the aircraft's small windows, trying to spot any kind of slick on the water below, some debris, any sign that a ship once existed out here on the inky expanse.

The pilot was directed to fly directly at the cliff face, the sheer rock looming ahead, before dropping away suddenly and sharply to give the passengers a view of the side of the cliffs to see if there were any marks. Pass after pass they came up blank and circled around again.

Finally, much to the relief of the now queasy and shaking Neil Batt, they turned away for the last time and headed back

Neil Batt was left to answer questions about the missing *Blythe Star* once it failed to show up in port. The authorities didn't know which route the ship had sailed. *(Courtesy of the Tasmanian Archives: PH30/1/8326)*

toward civilisation and safety. They had seen nothing. Not a glimmer, absolutely zippo to show for the ship that had supposedly sailed this way a couple of days earlier.

Back at Cambridge airport, as the plane tyres skidded on the tarmac, the two officials realised they had no other option. They would have to make the call to Marine Operations and tell them a ship was missing. Which, in itself, wasn't the worst bit, because they'd also have to explain that they didn't really know which way the ship had sailed around Tasmania – east or west. There also appeared to be some confusion about when it was meant to have showed up at port on King Island. Even the most laid-back paper pusher would struggle not to get red cheeked.

As the afternoon neared five o'clock, Maddock and Batt made the call. A short time later, Hobart Police headquarters were furnished with a list of names and addresses of the next of kin of those men aboard and tasked with the unenviable job of telling them that the *Blythe Star* and her crew were missing.

Meanwhile, Neil Batt called a press conference in his office at Parliament House. Trevor Sutton, who had been nervously watching his deadline marching closer, raced down to attend. As he waited outside Batt's office on the first floor of the stately Georgian sandstone building, he exchanged notes with the other journalists and camera operators. Eventually, the door opened and they were invited into the large office for the briefing.

After the minister made a statement, he opened to questions. At last, Trevor had his chance to ask the questions he'd been trying to get answers to all afternoon. But the minister's easy tone and his assurance that the ship was just running late and was sure to turn up soon took the sting out of the story. Not overly concerned, Trevor did at least find out that the ship was the *Blythe Star*, it was captained by George Cruikshank and carried a crew of ten.

Trevor raced back to the news office, tearing in to get the film processed in time to get his report to air. He made the local 6 pm bulletin – a ship was missing, suspected to be running late and due to turn up any moment now. Which wouldn't have been the most reassuring news for the *Blythe Star* crew as they battled on. Just as well they didn't know what was being made of their absence on land.

* * *

THE SEARCH THAT WASN'T

Monday, 15 October 1973 – Life raft, Day 3

As light dawned for their third day on the raft, Mick poked his head through the flap. He could see nothing but heaving, grey ocean and roiling sky. There was no land in sight. There was no sight more lonely or frightening.

A small mercy was the fresh rainwater beating its rhythm on the raft's canopy. It meant water, as much as they wanted to drink. Intake valves on the side of the raft captured the rain and they could drink their fill. Little rivulets of fresh, clean water trickled down the orange rubber of their raft and they took turns to drink greedily. Never had rain seemed so miraculous. However, hard on the heels of the rain was the wind, driving weather and waves before it. But for now, they'd take the water.

Looking around the raft, had it not been so serious the scene might have been comical. All the silver paper from biscuit packets and flattened aluminium water cans were strung up around inside. They hoped the metal would help them show up on the radar of any of the planes searching for them.

It was another of Ken's ideas, as much to give the men a purpose and hope for the rescue as to actually achieve much. Like some bizarre craft group, the men would sit in a circle and carefully use their can opener to cut around the seam of each can to flatten it, being painfully careful not to let any sharp edges catch their precious raft. When they'd finished, they would vigilantly wrap up the can opener. Then they'd hang up the shiny silver reflectors. The inside of the raft was starting to look like an outlandish Christmas tree, but the task gave them purpose. And hope. In those moments where they were gainfully employed their spirits rose. It gave them agency in the chaos, a sense of control in an entirely uncontrollable situation.

While they worked, they would talk and share stories. No one can spin a yarn like a sailor, and here they had ten sailors with nothing to do but weave stories for each other to take their minds to a place that wasn't that damned cold and wet raft. Ken Jones continued to bolster them, encouraging talk of home. Mick Power would later say that if it wasn't for Ken, everyone would have gone to pieces and just laid down and died. But there was no way Ken was letting that happen on his watch.

Their shifts on the paddle continued, although the captain remained largely unresponsive and John Sloan was no longer able to help. As the third day in the raft progressed, John became quieter. He lay crumpled across the raft, mumbling occasionally. Delirious, he was no longer making sense. Perhaps he was finding relief in the sanctuary of his mind, speaking with his beloved Joan and their son, Peter. The other crew could only hope so, because God only knew the present was no place to let your mind linger.

No one spoke about his condition. No one wanted to be the man to say the unthinkable – maybe he wasn't going to make it. Out of respect for John, they held their thoughts to themselves and tried not to dwell on how far behind him each of them might be.

THE SEARCH THAT WASN'T

John Sloan wasn't the only one starting to show the effects of the situation. It was hard not to notice the long cauterised burn on the chief engineer John Eagles' lower leg. He was also looking a bit sluggish when he was paddling, his movements slow and uncoordinated. But there was nothing they could do about it. The medical help they all needed was a long way off.

They hadn't seen land all day, and the wind that had got them within sight of the Tasmanian coast the afternoon before was impishly fickle. Swinging around, it was now pushing them south again. As the day wore on, the weather deteriorated. The wind whipped up into a frenzy, flaying the waves until they heaved 12 metres high. The howl of the wind carried the whispers of fear the men refused to voice outright. The little raft bobbed and spun wildly, entirely at the behest of Mother Nature. Mick gritted his teeth. *I'm not going to let this beat me*, he thought to himself. He tried to focus on Joanie's face in his mind, and to think of his brothers and sister, his mum and dad.

The weather worked the ocean up into such a fury that a wave crashed over the top of the raft, forcing water inside the opening and drenching them. Without pausing to contemplate what could happen next, the men jumped to it. Someone picked up the small plastic jug and started bailing. Now their thoughts were not so much of rescue, but of the far more immediate task of keeping their raft free enough of water to stay afloat. If they ended up in the water they'd suffer hypothermic shock in a matter of minutes.

As the raft plunged into the trough of each wave its rubber sides would rise up to meet each other in some bizarre embrace. The men inside were thrown bodily into each other, arms and legs flailing. It felt like they were being beaten to a pulp. Still they desperately tried to keep bailing.

As the Tasmanian Transport Commission was finally calling through to the Marine Operations Centre in Canberra to let them know they didn't have comms on one of their ships, the crew of the *Blythe Star* stared down the barrel of another night at sea. Never before had they realised how torturous the human body can be when it is cold, unfed and thirsty. This vessel of flesh and blood that held each being, suddenly became like an enemy of the mind. Unable to shut off the cold that pierced their skin, or the soaking chill from sitting in 20 centimetres of water, their bodies would take over their brains.

Like a demon it would hijack their thoughts until they could think of nothing else but the cold. And the despair would creep in that morning would never come. That maybe they might never again feel the warming bask of sun on dry skin. Night holds terrible things, but none so terrible as the things hidden in the mind, just waiting for circumstance to unleash them.

CHAPTER 9

Headless Chickens

Tuesday, 16 October 1973 – Doveton

It was a fair morning in Doveton when Joanie McGrath started work for the day, not at the bridal shop where her whirlwind romance with Mick had started just a couple of months ago, but at the Doveton chemist. Easing herself into her workday, she was tidying the makeup section when Mick's mum, Irene (whom Joanie called Clara), came through the door.

'Oh, hi, Clara. How are you?' Joanie chirped.

'Not good, Joanie,' Clara replied. It took a moment for Clara's grave expression to sink in, then something congealed in Joanie's stomach.

'I wanted to come and tell you,' Clara said. 'We've just got news. Mick's ship is … it's missing at sea.'

'What do you mean?' Joanie was struggling to make sense of the words. This wasn't something that happened. It wasn't *meant* to happen.

'We got a call. The *Blythe Star* is missing. They can't reach her and don't know where she is.'

'Is this serious? How bad is it, his ship being missing at sea?'

'Well, it's bad, Joanie, it's bad. They've got a search out for it.'

'What happens now?' Joanie asked, still trying to come to grips with Clara's news and what it meant. 'It's a big ship, and with search and rescue out there looking for it … they'll definitely find it, right?'

'Well, let's hope so,' Clara said. 'Look, I've got to go and get back home. We've got a lot of people there, people from the union and all sorts, but I wanted to tell you myself.'

Shell-shocked, radiating distress, Joanie thanked Clara and turned to her boss, Basil. 'Can I go with Mick's mum? We've just been told his ship is missing at sea. Everyone's at his house,' she said.

'No, you'll need to finish your shift,' Basil replied. 'You can go down there after work.' Basil was a blow-in. Not a Doveton local, he was new to managing the chemist and didn't understand that, in this town, everyone had each other's back. He had no idea of the shockwaves that were about to ripple through the tight-knit Housing Commission community. Mick was well known and loved, and Doveton was the kind of place where losing one of your own could tear the fabric of the town.

'I'll see you after I finish work,' Joanie told Clara. Her mind racing and with a million questions, she turned back to the neatly packed shelves of makeup.

Basil might have stopped Joanie from heading up to Mick's, but he couldn't stop people coming into the chemist. And come they did. Few of them had ailments or prescriptions to collect. They came to see Joanie.

'Joanie, have you heard?'

'Did you hear the news?'

'Mick's ship is missing, do you know?'

'Are you all right, love?'

Joanie asked everyone who came in for any information they might have. Did anyone know anything more? Had the authorities been back in touch? But just like Trevor Sutton the day before, there were no answers to her questions. Except Joanie had a hell of a lot more skin in the game.

Time dragged as Joanie counted down the minutes until her shift was over. Finally, as the tills were tallied and cashed up, the sign brought in and things put away for the night, Joanie's sisters came in. As soon as the doors clicked closed behind them, they all ran, flying up the street to Mick's place.

As they rushed through the front door into the living room, words spilled out of Joanie. 'Have they found it yet?'

Mick's place was packed. During the day it had become a headquarters for people looking for answers and comfort. Clara was there, and Mick's dad, Tommy. Then there were union men, seafarers on leave, friends and relatives. Joanie looked around. The pool table that had pride of place in the centre of the living room was covered in maps and charts, and groups of people sat around the centrepiece with cups of tea in hand. Tommy was surrounded by union men and seafarers, ash dropping from lit cigarettes as they discussed where the ship might be. The smell of anxious cigarette after cigarette clung to the wallpaper.

No one had good news, unless you counted no news as good news. There was still no sign of the *Blythe Star*.

Finally, it hit Joanie. This was bad. Very bad. She sank down into a chair, her sisters either side of her, and tuned in to the muted chatter going on around her. She gleaned every last detail she could, although, God knows, it wasn't much. The discussion continued for hours. Cups of tea were put away and beers came out, casseroles were loaded into the oven.

As midnight approached, someone offered to drive Joanie home. She climbed into their car at the end of a day that had seismically shifted since morning. She had walked out her front door happy and carefree and walked back in tired and frightened.

* * *

Saturday, 13 October to Tuesday, 16 October – Crib Point, Mornington Peninsula

Three days earlier, not too far away in Crib Point on the Mornington Peninsula, a 15-year-old girl, Robyn Simpson, had an uneasy feeling. Her mum, Kit, a shift worker, wasn't on that day, and was pacing restlessly across the brown flowery carpet in the lounge. It seemed Robyn wasn't the only one on edge.

'What's wrong, Mum?' Robyn asked.

'I've just got a feeling something's not right.'

Neither of them could put their finger on what was wrong, but there it was – something in the air.

Days earlier Robyn's dad had said goodbye to her, the youngest of three. Her brother was at work and her sister was away, boarding at navy school.

'See you later, pet. Look after Mum,' he'd said as he gave her one of his bone-crushing hugs that left you gasping for air but totally convinced of his love.

Then he picked up his Gladstone bag, packed with some spare clothes and his precious knife roll, and headed out the door. His solid frame filled the doorway for a moment, then he was out in the sunshine, bending down to get into a taxi and then gone, off to work.

Alf Simpson was a cordon bleu chef, but he wasn't heading off to a high-end restaurant. He was off to cook for hungry sailors.

Alf had trained as a chef in Melbourne but then, in 1952, perhaps with dreams of adventure in the air, he'd joined the Royal Australian Navy. Already fully qualified, he was promised that he would climb the ranks quickly. As it turned out, 15 years later he was still a chief petty officer.

But he served his country with distinction and commitment. When 1962 brought Australia into the Vietnam war, Alf was decorated for his service.

When he came home he never did recognise those medals, even if his daughter Robyn would treasure them. 'You don't get medals for doing your job,' was his view. He was that kind of man.

He did make it back into a restaurant after he was discharged. But cheffing isn't a family-friendly career and the lure of a sailor's week-on, week-off work schedule, which would allow him to spend more time with his children, convinced him that he should head back to sea.

Which he did, signing up to the merchant navy. His first call-up was on a 44-metre steel freighter carrying cargo from Hobart to King Island on Tasmania's north-west coast. So he packed his bags and headed to Hobart to join the *Blythe Star*, with a hug for Robyn on his way out the door.

Alf being away at sea wasn't new for Robyn or her mum, Kit. He'd worked for more than a decade in the navy and they were long accustomed to him being at sea. Nevertheless, that Saturday they both felt something wasn't right. They told themselves it was nothing. They weren't to know that Alf was soaked, frozen and shaken in a raft being pushed ever further south in the Southern Ocean hours after his ship had disappeared without a trace.

That night Robyn could hear Kit moving about the house, still restless. On Tuesday morning, Robyn was getting ready for school and her mum for work when the phone rang. Her mum picked up the receiver. There was a pause.

Robyn looked at her mum.

The phone was in Kit's hand and she was shaking her head. 'I can't believe it,' she said. 'We haven't been told.'

Then shaking took over her whole body and tears gathered in her eyes and spilled down her cheeks.

Robyn rushed over as Kit hung up the phone. 'What's wrong, Mum? It's okay, calm down.'

Robyn put her arm around her mum and tried to quell her tears while also trying to make sense of what could have possibly been said to leave her mother in this state. She put the kettle on for a cup of tea. Her mum looked like she could do with something a lot stronger but given she didn't drink alcohol, tea would have to do.

Then it came out. Robyn's dad was missing at sea.

Dad, who gave the best hugs. Dad, who would roll his eyes as they played another game of Spotto or I Spy on the long road trip to visit his sister in Adelaide, Robyn squeezed onto the shelf behind the back seat. Dad, who always cooked Christmas dinner for the family.

Robyn's Aunty Stella had just heard on the news that a Tasmanian Transport Commission ship called the *Blythe Star* was missing and uncontactable. She was on the phone right away to Kit. Did she know? What was going on?

Once she'd regained her composure, Kit got back on the phone and called the authorities. She must have been hoping to hear, 'Oh, sorry, madam, all a mix-up. No your husband is fine.' Instead she heard the words she dreaded, the news that made sense of the foreboding she'd felt a few days earlier.

It wasn't long before the phone was running hot as the news got out and Kit let people know, and Robyn's brother arrived back from work.

In the spirit of tight-knit communities in the 1970s, casseroles, scones and sausage rolls started appearing at their door. Robyn couldn't even think of school. Instead, she sat with her mum and brother at their blue Formica kitchen table as cup of tea after cup of tea was made. Robyn's sister, a cadet at navy recruit school, was unable to get permission to leave the academy to join the family as they stared into the abyss of the unknown.

Robyn's eyes were soon tired from crying, her mind tired from imagining. *The ship's missing. It could have sunk. Maybe it could have blown up ...* Anything could have happened and all she had was her imagination to fill in the gaps.

The family wasn't alone, with a steady stream of people dropping in and out, checking to see if there was anything they could do. But there was only one thing Robyn and her family needed, and no one could give it to them – the call saying, 'The ship's been found! Alf's okay!' That call didn't come.

During the interminable wait for news, time became amorphous, an hour disappearing in the blink of an eye and then minutes feeling like hours.

At one point, Kit answered the shrilling phone to hear the voice of her sister, who she hadn't seen for years. Some things transcend distance and time. 'Is there anything I can do?' Aunty Pattie asked.

It was arranged for Robyn to go to her aunty's for a few days. It would give her mum a breather as she tried to hold herself together and it would get Robyn out of the maelstrom until they had more information about what had happened.

By four o'clock that afternoon, they'd drunk more cups of tea than they'd care to mention. Robyn's mum took herself out to collect the mail. It was something that resembled normalcy, and gave her a few moments in the fresh air to blow away the clinging cobwebs of fear that she was trying to hold at bay for her children.

When she returned, she held out a white envelope. 'Here's a card from your father,' she said to Robyn.

It was something Alf had done for every birthday he had missed at sea. He would always remember to head into whatever local shop or post office he could find in whichever port he was in to pore over the meagre offerings and select something for his little girl's birthday.

Then he'd stand there in the post office for half an hour trying to get the words right. It was the only way he could let Robyn know how much he loved her and that he was thinking of her on the day she'd come into his world.

Taking the envelope in her hand Robyn shivered. She turned it over and opened it carefully.

The card had kittens and bunny rabbits and little flowers on it. *Dad, I'm not a baby! I'm 16!* The thought sprang unbidden into her mind. It was immediately chased out again when she read the words on the front of the card. 'Sending you love with this greeting. To my beautiful daughter on her birthday.'

Her breath hitched as Robyn opened the card and read the carefully penned words inside. 'Missing you, love Dad.'

'I'm missing you too,' Robyn whispered as she showed the card to her mum and brother, tears taking over her.

With this card in her hand, that had last been held by her dad just days before, Robyn couldn't imagine he could be gone. After years in the navy, he was supposed to be finally spending more time at home. *I don't want to lose my dad*, Robyn thought. The moment was somehow both surreal and razor sharp at the same time.

Robyn still couldn't comprehend how they could just lose a ship. Much like Joanie, she thought, *Well, it's a big ship. Surely it'll turn up soon?*

But that night in bed, sleep wouldn't come. Her mind played out all the scenarios she could imagine to explain her dad's absence. It was like some horror movie but she couldn't leave the theatre because it was her mind. She could hear her mum walking around the house all night. Clearly, the still and silent darkness held things she didn't want to contemplate.

* * *

Tuesday, 16 October 1973 – Hobart

On Tuesday in the TVT6 newsroom, the missing ship was the talk of the office. 'How can you just lose a ship?' was the common refrain. The bemused journalists watched on, disbelieving at how bamboozled the Tasmanian Transport

Commission appeared to be. At least there appeared to be a search now, Marine Operations in Canberra having finally been called in late the previous evening. But Trevor Sutton was somewhat cynical about that too.

Trevor got the impression that the search was conducted to appease seafarers and the public that the authorities were taking action. He thought that it was what in more recent times might be called an 'arse-covering exercise'.

Trevor's cynicism was perhaps understandable given everyone he talked to continued to dismiss any real possibility that the ship had sunk, instead saying that it was probably just late or holed up somewhere. Where? It was a good question, and one they seemed unable to answer.

Despite Captain Cruikshank's conversation with Captain David Bond the day they sailed, when they'd decided the ship would sail up Tasmania's west coast, the Transport Commission somehow didn't seem sure the ship had in fact gone that way or whether, instead, it had gone the longer but safer east-coast route. Trevor was gobsmacked that they didn't know which way the ship had sailed.

When he'd questioned the transport minister about it, Batt had responded, 'Look, the skipper, Captain Cruikshank, that's his decision. He makes the decision which way he goes.'

Tasmania operated a rapid-fire bush telegraph and already news of the missing ship was spreading through the community. Wherever Trevor went, whoever he talked to, the first question to pop up would be, 'Does anyone know where the ship is?' Once unheard of, the *Blythe Star* was now being discussed over beers, dinner tables and in offices.

At least the Marine Operations Centre in Canberra had swung into gear. The problem was, as searches went, theirs was ... patchy. Try as they might to get a clear point on where the ship was last known to be or where it could have gone, they couldn't pin down a possible location because the Transport Commission didn't know.

Instead, they had to search an area that comprised the entire coast of Tasmania. All 2200 kilometres of it.

The breadth of the search area and the finite nature of their resources meant they simply couldn't cover it all. So, the question was, should they do a thorough search of a smaller area – which might not even be the way the ship sailed? Or, should they broaden the search? They went with the latter, even though the search pattern would only have a 30–40 per cent detection rate. Ten men's lives hanging on a search with less than 50 per cent chance of success.

* * *

3 am Tuesday, 16 October 1973 – Maatsuyker Island

There was one person who could have ended speculation about the ship's route – young lighthouse keeper Tony Parsey on Maatsuyker Island. While the raft was being pushed about the untamed ocean around Maatsuyker, Tony was still blissfully ignorant that he was the last person to lay eyes on the *Blythe Star*. He had the missing piece of information that could entirely change the picture.

Tony was on the night shift again, keeping vigil over the burning kerosene light. Those winds that had lashed the tiny raft, screaming across the ocean and that had last touched land in Africa, had been buffeting the lighthouse and tearing over the roof of number-2 quarters.

The light lanced through the black, glinting off the rolling swell. In the weather room below the lantern, Tony noted down his observations at regular intervals. At around 3 am, he heard the radio come to life with a call from Cape Bruny. He answered and heard the crackling and tinny voice of Harry, the Cape Bruny lighthouse keeper.

'We have a fellow from Marine Operations in Canberra on a call. He wants to know if you saw the *Blythe Star* go past yesterday?' he asked.

It was a crucial moment, one where fate dances a line. A slightly different choice of words and things might have been different. But when Tony heard 'yesterday' he assumed he was being asked about Monday. 'No, there were no ships that went past here yesterday,' he replied.

The thing is, the message from Marine Operations in Canberra had somehow been lost in translation. 'Yesterday' in the original message referred to *Sunday*. But it was now the early hours of Tuesday, so the correct meaning was lost, and with it a crucial opportunity to change the course of events that was barrelling ten men toward the unimaginable.

It was a simple mistake that could have been sorted out in short order by a visit to Maatsuyker. But it wasn't.

'Why, what's happened?' asked Tony.

'It's missing, they don't know where it is. It's a coastal freighter. Grey hull, with a white rear superstructure,' Harry said.

'I saw a ship matching that description, but it was a few days ago – three days ago,' Tony said, thinking back to the ship that appeared to be so low in the water it looked more like a submarine.

Tony waited for the radio to fire up again while Harry relayed his message to the chap on the phone from Marine Operations.

Finally, the radio sparked again. 'Oh, he said that wouldn't be the one,' Harry reported back.

Tony recalls an odd instruction following this – he wasn't to record the message about the missing ship. He remembers being told that since it wasn't an official message, he shouldn't bother writing anything down. Usually, Tony would note down any messages that came through by radio, so everything could be scrutinised by the head keeper.

Tony thought all this seemed strange. It was a hell of a coincidence; a ship matching the exact description of the missing vessel and making heavy labour of it just a few days prior. But as they signed off, he shrugged it off. Marine Ops must know what they were doing.

So, due to a simple misunderstanding, Tony's sighting was discounted. He wasn't instructed to keep watch for any signs of the ship or crew. Even though they weren't asked to keep an official lookout, Tony couldn't help but keep a keener eye on the expanse of ocean around them. He'd scan his eyes across the horizon regularly, looking for a ship adrift and being tossed by the waves. He supposed it was probably broken down without power and awaiting rescue somewhere.

If the radio message that the ship was missing had come through two days earlier, on the day the ship failed to turn up at King Island, Tony might just have spotted the men as they desperately fired flares from their raft at dusk near Maatsuyker.

But the Transport Commission's delay, their assuredness that the captain was probably just being a bit flaky, meant another opportunity to subvert the course of events was missed.

Even now, four days after the *Blythe Star* had sunk, the Tasmanian Transport Commission were still fuzzy regarding which day the ship was meant to make port. They'd told Marine Operations it was meant to be arriving at King Island on Monday, when Jim McKenzie on King Island had clearly raised his concerns about the ship failing to make port or contact a day earlier on Sunday.

As dawn broke on Tuesday, Tony headed back up to his quarters, his shift done. Later that day he chatted to the head keeper, John Cook, about the call that had come through in the wee hours and the ship he had seen a few days prior.

Tony said he was disappointed that his sighting had been discounted so readily. He thought it seemed significant, even if the dates didn't quite line up with what Marine Ops was saying. Cook asked a bit more about the ship Tony had seen, and Tony described it to him in detail. He even grabbed a pencil and a loose piece of paper and sketched it for him.

'Yeah, that's the *Blythe Star*,' John Cook said, deciding to follow up again with Marine Operations and throw the weight of his authority behind Tony's testimony.

So John fired up the radio, this time delivering an official message for Cape Bruny lighthouse to ring Marine Operations in Canberra to say that, based on sketches and a detailed description from his keeper, Tony, the *Blythe Star* had passed Maatsuyker. It was in the logbook as having passed on 13 October.

But he might as well have saved his breath. At this point Marine Operations had spoken to another lighthouse keeper off Tasmania's east coast who reckoned they'd seen the ship pass by that way. So, Marine Ops didn't bother following up on John's message. The dates didn't line up with the Transport Commission's dates, anyway, so it was probably a case of mistaken identity. Which it was, but it was the keeper on the east coast who was mistaken, not Tony.

So, the search area remained far larger than it need have been. The radio at Maatsuyker stayed silent. They didn't hear any more from the authorities for days. And the ocean remained empty, the raft by now having blown further east in the direction of Bruny and Tasman islands.

CHAPTER 10

Losing Time

Tuesday, 16 October 1973 – Life raft, Day 4

It was as though beasts were inside Mick's stomach, clawing at his guts. He was so hungry he could no longer tell if he felt hungry or sick or both. The darkness of the nights, the constant motion and the white noise of the sea washing against the raft were a form of sensory immersion that played tricks on his mind. And he wasn't the only one.

Daylight would bring relief, with the mercury creeping up a few degrees and light at least giving shape to their experience. A strong wind continued to push the raft, this time north toward mainland Tasmania's south-east coast. They were entirely at the mercy of the wind and currents, a plaything of whatever gods oversaw this savage part of the world. The rain had stopped and with it the swell ceased its relentless efforts to get inside the raft's canopy.

Tuesday dawned clearer. It was their fourth day adrift, but already they were losing sense of time passing. Monday blended into Tuesday as the men's sleep-deprived and dehydrated brains struggled to distinguish one day from another.

Bosun Tas Leary had a stub of pencil and a scrap of carefully guarded, soggy paper on which he noted down their estimated position each night. It was some small effort to track the passing days and drift, proof that they were still alive and existed and moved in a real world beyond the raft.

Conversation swelled and lulled with their moods. Most often they would talk of their lives and loved ones. Memories and musings.

As Tuesday dragged on Ken Jones was clearly thinking of home. 'My girl Susan's turning four on Saturday,' he told Mick. 'We'll have to be picked up by then. I'm not missing my little girl's party.' Ken was a vivacious and humorous man, not to mention something of a charmer. He played the ukelele and could often be heard booming out a song in his strong Liverpudlian accent. Susan was the daughter from his second family in Victoria. He'd left his first family in New Zealand when he sailed across the ditch to Australia to pursue a blossoming romance with Susan's mum, Francis. Articulate, charmingly open and honest in the love letters he penned, it's easy to see why women fell for him.

In letters to Francis, Ken wrote of their hopes and dreams. Of the yacht he would buy and take her sailing on. Of the empty feeling of missing her, and how it would be an awful feeling were it not for the fact that it spoke of the depth of his love for her. A gift giver, Jones would often turn up at home with some token of his affection. This trip had seen the kitchen mixer he had bought as a present for Francis plunge to the bottom of the ocean.

He was generous with everything: gifts, his love, jokes, words and hope here on this raft.

Somehow Jones's certainty that their rescue was simply a matter of when, not if, fed Mick's own hope. He shared stories of his family. Of Joanie. He thought of her often.

'Here I am stuck in a raft with ugly blokes, and I've just met the most beautiful woman in the world,' he joked wryly. 'What on earth did I do to deserve this?'

Over time, discussion turned to what had happened to their doomed ship. Why had it gone over? Inevitably they turned to the loading of the cargo. Throwing it around, they decided that some of the cargo must have shifted below decks, throwing the ship off balance, and then the heavy loading of deck cargo had further compromised stability.

After four days, Captain Cruikshank was at last stirring back to life. Finally, he could be roused enough to join the paddling and lookout. He joined the discussion, surmising that perhaps if he had turned a bit when the ship first took on a list they might have fared better. But it was all hypothetical. The early list was dismissed, and the captain absent from the bridge when the *Blythe Star* began its death roll.

In the long minutes and hours that ticked by, Mick's mind would linger on what would happen if they did get out of there. There'd be an inquiry for sure. He didn't think the captain was in a fit state when the ship sailed. He suspected Cruikshank's senses had been dulled by the influence of liquor. Should the world know? The question bounced around in his mind, with nothing else to distract him.

Meanwhile, Ken Jones turned the discussion once again to the shipping schedules to and from Hobart. What ships would be passing by when? Maybe one of those held the key to their rescue. Once more stepping in to give hope to his crew, this discussion kept the men's spirits buoyant. He continued to instil a sense of purpose and routine in the days that stretched undisturbed by any event of significance.

Ken insisted on the 'housekeeping'. They would scoop water from the hollows around each man, although truth be told they could never clear it entirely and their skin was showing the wear. It was wet from constant submersion, not to mention pale from the reduced blood flow as their cold bodies tried to preserve the warmth in their core. Their skin was disintegrating. But there were only so many times they could clean a small tent-sized raft. Once it was done, with nothing looming on the horizon to break the monotony, the boredom set in.

Mick realised that boredom meant nothing good, and that if he was to see his way out of this hellhole then he'd have to block out where he was and what was happening. In an effort to hold the boredom at bay, they would try to get some games going, but they never really took off. You can play only so much I Spy in a raft. Mick joined in all the conversations and threw himself into the cleaning tasks, such as they were, to keep his mind occupied. He didn't like what lurked there when it wasn't.

John Sloan was deteriorating by the day. He grew more and more still, his mumbling less and less coherent. Desperately trying to do what they could for him, but knowing they couldn't give him what he needed, they gave him more water in an effort to keep him holding on. While the other nine men would share a can of water, John would have one to himself. But their best efforts were clearly no substitute for the medication he needed, which was fathoms deep and far out of reach.

Mick's body was feeling weak and at times his head danced with lightness from lack of food. The snatches of sleep he could claim were a respite for both his mind and his wrecked body, a body that was trying to hold on to whatever energy it could, while getting precious little from one protein biscuit and a palmful of glucose powder a day.

Tuesday afternoon brought an exclamation from the lookout.

Land!

Their makeshift drogue was only just slowing their ripping pace, with the wind chivvying them along. They'd been pushed northward and were now east of Bruny Island and still heading north. The direction favoured them. If the wind kept up and they stayed on the paddles they would make it into Storm Bay – into which the Derwent River emptied from Hobart. Their adrenal systems spent, it still gave them a burst of energy.

They each took up the paddle to row with renewed vigour, keeping the sight of land in their eyes to keep them going. Mick was flooded with hope. In a strange way he found the sight of land comforting. He knew that it was out there, and they weren't completely lost to the world. The sight beat back the crushing loneliness of the vast expanse of ocean, without even a bird overhead. They just needed someone to find them.

Having had their fair run of shit luck, surely they were due a break? Surely there'd be a passing fisherman or another freighter going past who would spot them? Now, when Mick's turn came, he wielded the paddle fervently, willing the land closer with every stroke, daring to dream …

Mal McCarroll didn't find the land dancing off on the horizon quite so comforting. After a while seeing it but being unable to reach it started to eat away at him. It felt like someone was messing with them, showing them a glimpse of warmth and food and water, but always at arm's length. He'd have given anything for something warm inside him, to burn out the chill that had set in his bones.

The wind that was snapping at the raft's canopy might have been pushing them closer to land, but it also exacerbated the cold, which was inescapable. It never left them. There was only cold, and colder. It had started to consume Mick's waking hours, eating away at him until he thought he might go mad. As he took the paddle for his shift each time, he'd fumble and grip it tightly, having long lost feeling in the tips of his fingers. He didn't like to ponder what the grey tinge they'd taken on meant.

The day passed in a repetitive haze of paddle, lookout, rest, paddle, lookout, rest. As dusk fell, the clouds closed in, bringing dark early.

The men's spirits were buoyed by their last glimpse of land before night swallowed it up. They were sure that tomorrow's dawn would bring them the blissful sight of land within spitting distance, sure that there was only one more night to hang on, muscles aching from the shivering and cold.

There was no glimpse of moon or stars through the heavy set of the clouds, and the darkness that enveloped them was once again complete. Unable to see a hand in front of their faces, they talked to each other in the dark until they lapsed into silence and sleep – or as close to sleep as they could manage.

The constant motion of the swell beneath them increased as the night wore on. Mick found himself clutching what he could to hold himself still in the raft. He was holding on grimly for dawn – at least light would give them some perspective in the roiling water. Before dawn gifted them daylight, however, the weather turned vindictive.

Heavy raindrops hammered on the raft, as though affronted by their presence out here on the ocean, and the waves grew taller until they were as high as power poles. As they crashed down and over the raft, water gushed in the door flap and once again the men would desperately take turns bailing before they were doused again. They would perform a frantic dance, scooping up the water in their plastic jug before trying to fling aside the opening wide enough to empty the jug without letting in more water before they managed to drag it shut.

As the raft shot up the crest of each wave, Mick's body tensed in anticipation of the crunch to follow as the raft sandwiched in half, throwing them all inwards. They'd be smashed into each other's space, headbutting someone they couldn't see. It was as physical as the worst punch-up he'd ever been in, but there was no one to fight back against. He felt powerless, at the mercy of the weather and the endless motion and ferocity of the sea.

White caps foamed along each wave's crest, a furious spray of wind and water flying off with the shrieking gale. What Mick had thought a shipwrecking might be like paled in comparison to this present moment. He could never have imagined the pure unadulterated savagery of the ocean in all its awe and terror. He was acutely aware of nature's indifference.

Mick's fear was a living thing. He was consumed by the idea that the bottom of the raft would tear apart and they would fall through it to their deaths. For hour after hour, the ten men endured. Wave after wave. Taking turns bailing, exhausted, soaking and aching, they were desperate to keep their little raft afloat. It was horrific.

* * *

Wednesday, 17 October 1973 – Life raft, Day 5

Eventually the grey hue of Wednesday stole over them. It seemed miraculous, as though such a normal thing as the sun rising was impossible in this heaving hell of water and wind and spray.

But the day brought them no relief. It just meant they could see their flailing limbs as they were pitched together again and again. Someone, as they emptied the bailing jug, braved a peek outside and had grim news to report. The weather that had punished them all night had blown them back off the coast. Their glimpse of land had disappeared. The hours of paddling to get closer, the hope of watching it ever so slowly grow on the horizon, had been for nothing. The wind had swung around and pushed them mercilessly back out to sea.

The news was crushing. The men did their best to protect John Sloan, who had already been in bad shape before the hours of bodily assault. But there was a limit to what they could do, each just trying to hold their own space in the raft and hold their own thoughts together.

Cold, dehydrated and now suffering from the physicality of fighting the weather, their bodies were continuing to shut down. The battle in their minds was just as ravaging. Mick didn't know how he'd find the strength to endure another wave or endure the next moment. And yet the next moment would come and then he would be looking at the next, wondering how he could make it through that one.

Time shrank and expanded, with every second felt in the beating of their hearts.

It seemed as if everything was in Mick's mind at once. It was constantly ticking over trying to work out the consequences of every action he could take. He was desperate for control over any small part of his existence. He was mindful of nature, and its ability to kill him. He desperately hoped that wouldn't happen. *I'm not gonna lie down and let it happen. No way,* thought Mick as he gritted his teeth through another bone-crunching rollercoaster down a wave. He was going to do everything he could to save his and his fellow seafarers' lives. Right now, that meant enduring the unendurable.

Even though fear lurked in each man's mind they tried to keep smiling for one another. None of them wanted to say out loud what they feared inside. If they hadn't had each other to keep smiling for, maybe they would have curled up in the raft and accepted the inevitable. But they found strength for their shipmates, and in doing so found it for themselves.

Ken encouraged Mick, telling him that they would get through this. They would be okay. 'What's a bit of weather, eh, lad?' he'd joke.

Ken was a voice of encouragement in a raft full of pessimism. 'We're not done yet,' he'd tell Mick. 'We've just got to keep going.'

Alf told the others that they'd bloody better make it out – it was his daughter Robyn's birthday today. He wondered if she knew he was missing. He told the others about her. Every memory. The road trips to visit family, Robyn squashed onto the shelf behind the back seat. He told them proudly about her swimming and netball. As if by sharing his memories of her, of all his children and his wife, Kit, he could somehow make them more real to him.

It was a way to get through.

* * *

Wednesday, 17 October 1973 – Maatsuyker Island

Tony Parsey sat by the heater in the kitchen and looked out the window. The bad weather had set in. It swirled around the low house and battered the windows. The swell was eight metres high, pounding and breaking over the sharp trail of rocks called the Needles, which were 45 metres high. He thought of the missing ship and hoped it wasn't out there. He knew they wouldn't be seeing any boats today. All the fishing vessels and small freighters would have pulled up stumps. Everyone knew better than to be out on the ocean when it was in this mood.

* * *

Wednesday, 17 October 1973 – Doveton

Joanie woke to the crushing memory of the news from the day before. Mick was missing. She was tired from the late night, but rushed to get up to see if any news had come through. She flicked the radio on, but there was nothing. Somehow, she got herself ready for work at the chemist and walked down.

Her whole world had undergone a cataclysmic shift and it felt as though everything else should have changed too, that the birds in the trees, the people making their way to work, the school children running late should all have stood still, just as her world had. It would be that way until she knew what had happened to Mick.

At work she went through the motions. 'Morning,' she said to her boss, Basil. 'Mick's ship is still missing. Can I please have the radio on?'

Basil shook his head. 'No, it's too disruptive.'

'Well can we just put it on in the background? I need to know what's going on.'

'I'll think about it.'

Thinking was all Basil was going to do and, sure enough, the radio stayed silent.

During the morning family and friends of Joanie came and went, all bringing the latest news and rumours. It wasn't a great deal, but at least she wasn't completely in the dark.

She looked up as each person entered, hopeful they might have more information. When her lunch break came, she ran out of the shop and back home. Racing inside, she flicked on the television and listened for any news.

Back at work, she watched the clock, counting down the minutes. Just like the day before, as soon as the doors closed behind her at the end of her shift, she headed to Mick's family home. There, the living room was still full of people, the seafarers still discussing what might have happened while poring over maps and charts. A heaviness hung over the house. A shiver crept down Joanie's spine. It was an eerie feeling.

Everyone had an opinion about what could have happened, but their speculation shed no light and gave no joy. For Joanie, the seriousness of Mick's situation had sunk in, but she drew comfort from the fact that all these people were gathered there for the same reason – because they loved Mick.

CHAPTER 11

Bickering and Delay

Thursday, 18 October 1973 – Hobart

It was Jennifer Lee's fourth day at her new job at the Tasmanian Transport Commission. Just 17 years old, she was, by her own admission, 'well-proportioned' and had already caught lingering glances at her chest.

The new job was a big step up for Jennifer. So was the pay – she'd be going from 24 dollars a week to 45 dollars. But it was also a step up in responsibility, as she moved from being the office girl doing the banking and other lowly tasks, to the telephonist and receptionist of a major government organisation. She had her own desk, sitting by herself downstairs at the front.

On Jennifer's very first day at the new job, news had broken that a ship was missing. Not realising the baptism of fire she was about to experience, she greeted her new workmates. There were the married ladies with kids, the one whose hands were

BICKERING AND DELAY

so dry they crackled when she put on hand cream, and Crystal, who was secretary to Captain Alistair Maddock. Crystal sat upstairs outside Captain Maddock's office and seemed always to be trying to get someone onto a diet.

Jennifer would catch sight of Captain Maddock in passing. He was a big man, broad shouldered with greying hair. She didn't speak to him – he was the boss, after all – but she clocked him and memorised his name.

That first day had passed in a blur as Jennifer tried to get her head around the expectations of her position. She was the only telephonist and the media was calling on repeat throughout the day to try to get answers about the *Blythe Star*.

Jennifer watched from her desk as people came and went as they tried to figure out where this ship had gone. She overheard snippets of conversations and observed the building maelstrom of confusion that unfolded around her over those first few days. She got the impression there were concerns about who might be held accountable at the end of all this. As the days passed, the Transport Commission higher-ups contemplated ever more outlandish ideas about what might have happened. They even pondered whether it might have been hijacked, before, eventually, commonsense prevailed. Pirates would probably have little interest in fertiliser and a pallet of beer. Somehow this option was on the table, but no one seriously entertained the idea that the ship might have sunk.

There were the usual seafarers coming and going from the office, with the commission's everyday operations still running. It didn't take Jennifer long to get the measure of the place. Not unlike many workplaces in the 1970s, it was somewhat misogynistic. Everyone had their place, and a woman's place was sitting at a receptionist's desk listening but not speaking. There were wolf whistles and suggestive comments that Jennifer took to be part of the job. It was also apparent early on that alcohol was a big part of the Transport Commission's culture. When crews would make land it would be straight off to the pub. They were big drinkers.

Speculation about what might have happened to the *Blythe Star* swirled around as Jennifer took it all in, bemused, and answered the ongoing calls from journalists such as Trevor Sutton, who were all sniffing around for the latest update. On Wednesday afternoon, the journalists got an update from the Federal Minister for Transport, in which he repeated the wrong information he'd received from the Tasmanian Transport Commission, that the ship had been expected on Monday – a day later than it had been expected in reality. The statement also outlined that all resources were being thrown at the search, and no expense would be spared.

Certainly, by then, the RAAF had been called in to help with the search. The trouble was, they'd been given an impossible task, having been asked by the Marine Operations Centre to search an unreasonably large area. The RAAF had rejected this request in no short order – it would have taken 46 Orion patrol aircraft to pull that off. They didn't have 46 Orion aircraft. They only had ten.

To be fair, the Marine Operations man heading up the search from Canberra knew it was a ridiculous ask but, given the paucity of useful or reliable information from the Transport Commission about where the hell this ship might be, he didn't have much choice. It was like throwing a dart at a map on the wall. In turn, the RAAF commanders were frustrated by the lack of information from the Marine Operations Centre.

While the RAAF and Marine Operations debated the search approach, the ten men in the life raft were hanging on to hope that someone out there was looking for them. If they'd known the state of the search, the loss of hope might have done them in. In their ignorance, they assumed the best was being done, and perhaps it was better that way.

Finally, after ministerial intervention, a new search area was agreed. But those lost hours couldn't be brought back. In the end, only one Orion along with three other aircraft took part in the air search. The Transport Commission was also holding to the view that the ship was probably fine, so the searchers were instructed to look for the ship – not a lifeboat or life raft.

Each day the thought bubble about where the ship might be was different, and the searchers were asked to focus on a different area – from a sweep of the entire Tasmanian coast to Schouten Island on the east coast, to down past Maatsuyker Island in the south. A few more aircraft joined in the search, but even though it grew into the largest sea search in Australia's history to date, the chaotic and patchy approach didn't help their chances of success.

The search for the *Blythe Star* was the largest sea and air search at the time, with RAAF planes scouring the ocean around Tasmania. *(Reproduced by permission of the Australian Broadcasting Corporation – Library Sales © 1973 ABC)*

The grim news didn't end there. When the RAAF had been called in to help, they'd brought sobering information. The rations provided on the life raft were only sufficient to keep the crew alive for 72 hours. While the Transport Commission appeared only now to be contemplating the prospect that something may indeed have happened to the *Blythe Star*, the ten crew were well outside that 72-hour survival window. The clock had been ticking and, according to the experts, time had run out.

Luckily no one told the crew that.

* * *

Thursday, 18 October 1973 – Life raft, Day 6

Thursday dawned over the *Blythe Star* crew calm and clear, with just a thin covering of misty cloud stretched above, a blessed relief after the punishing hours of weather the day before. Mick was bruised and stiff from the pummelling. But as the youngest of the crew, he was faring better than many of the others.

Cliff Langford, one of the three crew over 50, was feeling the effects of the exposure and the total physical and mental fatigue. Over the days he became more ill, and there was a slackness in his face and a dullness in his eyes. Delirium started to creep in as his grip on their terrifying reality loosened.

But it was John Sloan who was their greatest concern. He was clearly not doing well and they weren't sure how much longer he could hang on. For hours he would lie still, just mumbling occasionally. The other men would massage him and hold him tight in an effort to share some warmth with him, as if by keeping the cold at bay they could somehow stop the hands of death creeping around him too.

Mick had never sat next to a dying man before. But the men still refused to voice their fears in the face of death, which was now curled in the corner of the raft, biding its time. Their spirits weren't helped by the realisation that again they had lost a chance of making landfall. The previous night had once more seen them pushed within sight of the land, only for Mother Nature to steal them back out to sea under the cover of darkness.

Having their hope snatched repeatedly from their desperate grip inflicted a mental injury that was devastating. Survival out there was as much a mental game, a game not for the faint-hearted.

In a life or death situation, there's much that needs to go right for you to survive. The luck of getting off the ship cleanly and without injury, the strength of a body to keep going long after it should have shut down, and the battle in the mind to keep going when logic would tell you to lie down and accept your fate. By now their feet were showing signs of frostbite. The salt from the ocean crusted wherever it dried, and their lips were hard and cracked from lack of water.

That Thursday morning, they were huddled in the shade of their raft's canopy, when they suddenly heard a noise that sent a current through their bodies.

'Did you hear that?'

It set off a hum of chatter in the raft.

A plane.

The distant drone of a plane was the first sign that there might be a search, that anyone out in the world had noticed they were missing and was looking for them.

Finally, after six days in the raft, could this be their search party? They discussed the sound of the plane, debating what sort it might be. Chief engineer John Eagles identified it as a bomber. He'd heard that buzz before when he served in the war.

Full of excited energy as the plane approached, they looked at their metal-festooned raft, the crushed water cans, the metal biscuit wrappings. Would it be enough to show up on the plane's radar?

Ken whipped them into gear. If this was their moment for salvation, like hell were they going to miss it. They were going to bloody well pull out all stops. The torch was pulled out again and he flashed an SOS signal in the direction of the plane. The heliograph, an emergency signalling mirror that had been in the emergency rations box, was also passed quickly to the raft opening and flashed in desperation.

Ken seized one of their precious remaining flares and wrapped his hands to protect them as best he could from the molten spray of the flare. Then he ripped the top off. The iridescent light blasted – a tangible beacon of hope burning into the sky.

They waited with bated breath, listening. The distant roar of the plane grew louder then slowly faded off into the distance again.

The same question was in everyone's mind. 'Do you think it saw us?'

Nerves stretched to breaking, they sat in silence and tried to listen for the sound of the engine over the incessant hush of water around them. Time stretched on, moment bleeding into moment with nothing but the wind and the waves.

They couldn't help but be buoyed by the sign of life and the evidence of a search. Looking over at John Sloan, it was clear that their deliverance from the raft couldn't come soon enough. If they were found that day they would all get out of this okay. They would have a hell of a story to whip out at the pub, but they'd be okay.

A few hours passed before they heard another unmistakable mechanical drone of a machine drawing closer. They got back into action with the heliograph and waited for it. The roar got louder as the plane approached. When it sounded like it was right above them, they took turns poking their heads out of the raft opening. Then they saw it. On the white canvas of the high, misty grey cloud, the shadow of a plane.

'It's seen us!' came the jubilant cry.

It was like fire injected into their veins. There it was above them! They waited and listened and watched as it seemed to fly in search patterns around them. Up, across, down, across. The square flight path couldn't be a coincidence. It must be their search! They flashed the heliograph and hoped the jangling cans would fire off the radar. If only they still had a rocket flare, they might have fired that off and caught the eye of the plane. But with one fired and the other a dud they would have to make do with the heliograph and torch.

The plane continued its deliberate pattern, slowly getting further and further away. The fire that brought them all to life and animated them faded. Why was it still searching? If it had seen them, what else could it be looking for?

With no choice but to sit and listen to the excruciating sound of the plane fading into the distance, Ken Jones had a task to stop the men sinking into despair.

'They're searching for us,' he reminded them. 'It's only a matter of time until they come back and find us.'

Mick barely dared to look across at John Sloan. The rest of them might have time to wait for the searchers to come back, but it didn't seem like John did.

The men did the only thing they could. They kept up their rotation of paddling shifts, trying to bring themselves closer to rescue. They plugged away at it, ill-equipped as they were with a too-small paddle and a round bobbing raft.

The afternoon brought news from the lookout at the raft opening that they could see land again. Like a fresh breath of wind, it brought some life back into the raft.

Ken seemed to realise the importance of the men seizing this moment of action. He knew that the crew could only take so many disappointments. Looking at them curled around the raft – those cuddling close to John Sloan and massaging him to keep him warm, Cliff Langford becoming less lucid – he knew they needed to either make land or find another soul to raise the alarm.

He pressed them to paddle hard, and kept them at it continuously for 36 hours. The land smudging the horizon was Tasman Island. If they could only get close enough to catch sight of the lighthouse, they might signal the keeper.

Thursday had gifted them calm and quiet seas. At this point they would happily take any luck they could and used it to their advantage, pushing themselves to make progress while they weren't waylaid by rolling swells and winds pushing them offshore.

As Alf handed around the rations that evening, John Sloan seemed to have an inexhaustible thirst. He took as much water as Alf could give him, and still needed more. It didn't improve his condition. It was a cruel form of torture to not have more water for him. They made him as comfortable as they could.

The evening dusk descended and still those men who were able to paddle kept up a relentless rhythm in the water.

Sometime between 10 pm and midnight by their best reckoning, the men were sitting around soaking up the cold and the dark, trying to keep their thoughts at bay, the sound of the long-distant plane echoing in their heads. The silence it had left behind was deafening.

Ken was at the opening looking out when he saw something. Coming from the direction of the Tasman Peninsula, about half a dozen lights materialised on the inky line that marked the horizon. He called down into the pitch of the raft.

'Oh my gosh, I can see a ship,' he said as he dropped back into the raft. 'When it gets a bit closer I'll hit it with the SOS.'

Ken was chafing at the bit. He wanted to make sure it was close when he fired up the torch. He was sure the lights were from a Japanese fishing vessel and had heard that they'd scarper if they saw lights. They weren't keen to risk getting caught fishing in waters they shouldn't. Which was one thing when they were just fleeing from a passing freighter, but an entirely different thing in the current situation.

Ken marked the ship's progress with a commentary to the men inside. When he thought the ship was about half a mile to a mile off, he started flashing SOS on the torch. The ship appeared to come toward them. It was working!

The men inside the raft watched the glow flashing on and off through the small opening in the raft canopy.

Mick sat there, desperate to get up and have a look. For a young man who was used to action and taking his destiny into his hands, having to remain prostrate in a raft while waiting and unable to even see what was going on was agonising.

Ken popped back down again to give them an update. On his way back out through the opening he grabbed one of their last few remaining hand flares.

Mick heard Ken tear the flare open. Its hiss sputtered into the frigid southern night air, the acrid smell of burning settling in the raft. The flare lit up the night.

'Are they coming?' asked a voice from the raft.

'Yeah, I think she's coming,' said the delighted and almost disbelieving Ken.

The flare burned down, burning Ken's arm. But he held it high and steady. Once it burned out, Ken took up the torch again. He resumed his flashing of the SOS signal across the waves. But a light was dancing in front of his eyes, lingering from the brightness of the flare. He squinted and tried to see through the darkness.

Mick shuffled over and relieved him at the opening. He took the torch and took over the signalling. On and off, he didn't break as he sent the light bouncing across the waves toward the ship. Once Ken's eyes recovered from the flare's piercing light, he took over again and Mick sat back in the raft.

The minutes passed. Ken followed the course of the ship with rising dread. As it became clear what was happening, he watched in disbelief. 'No, she's turned away. She turned away from us,' he said, then cursed.

Ken could hardly believe it was possible that seafarers would turn and leave other seafarers to the mercy of the ocean when they were clearly in distress. He kept watching to see if the ship would turn again. But no, it had veered to port and seemed to be skirting around them. It had turned away.

Ken sat back down in the raft. Not yet ready to give up, the crew each stood up in turn and turned the torch on, watching the ship. The SOS continually flashed into the night, unanswered by the steady deck lights of the ship. The mysterious ship stayed within sight for almost an hour, moving away all the time. Finally, the ephemeral lights were swallowed up by the night, leaving them once again in darkness.

Mick felt a heaviness in his chest at yet another lost chance. He felt like crying. He wasn't the only one. As the men tried to comprehend what had just happened, they talked it through. They were convinced that the ship was a Japanese fishing vessel poaching in Australian waters. Even so, they were in disbelief it would leave them in clear distress.

To be prepared to sacrifice lives to avoid prosecution was unimaginable for those ten men of the *Blythe Star*. It was a body blow. The hopeful air that had filled and buoyed the raft deflated again, leaving Mick and his crewmates mired in depression.

In utter powerlessness, they could do nothing with their anger, desperation and despair other than curl up close to one another again and try to cling to whatever wisps of warmth they could find. Periodically they picked up the jug and bailed, trying to keep the raft as dry as they could, and shook each other awake for the lookout and paddle shift.

Up until that night, the men had managed to keep the demons from their minds in the dark. But after losing both plane and ship to the void it was hard not to let those thoughts loose. The past 24 hours had seen them built up and knocked down repeatedly, and it had taken much of their limited mental reserves to ride the waves of hope and despair.

Whatever's going to be done, we're just going to have to bloody do it ourselves, Mal McCarroll thought to himself as he sat in the dark. He knew it was almost a week since the ship had sunk. The search couldn't be going on all that much longer before they were given up for dead. It was a terrifying thought. He knew it was all on them now.

Also realising there was no one coming for them, Mick was thinking along similar lines. They would either save themselves, or wouldn't be saved. He hoped the rest of the crew was in the same frame of mind as him.

If the strength of his wish to escape that bloody raft was enough it would have willed them to safety. Instead, he just cursed the cold and the dark and the absent searchers and the ship that had left them behind.

John Sloan was still and quiet. He seemed to have fallen into a deep sleep that evaded the others. Alf slept fitfully, but at some point in the night he realised that John was slipping away. Time was up for his crewmate while, for the rest, deliverance from this nightmare was seemingly as far away as ever.

CHAPTER 12

Goodbye

Friday, 19 October 1973 – Life raft, Day 7

Day seven on the raft dawned clear and cool. Alf Simpson's first thoughts were for John Sloan. Alf looked across at his crewmate. John was deathly still.

Cramped and huddled, Mick stirred and also looked across at John's prone figure. 'He's pretty quiet,' he said softly. 'Is he dead or alive?'

Ken Jones clambered over the tangle of bodies to John and searched for a pulse. The moments while he waited, trying to feel a faint throb through his cold and numbed fingers, seemed to drag on. Finally, Ken said, 'He's dead.'

It wasn't a surprise. The grey tinge of John's skin and the slackness in his face told their own story. Still, hearing it spoken aloud was like a molten rock falling through Mick's insides. He'd never seen a dead body before, and now he was sitting feet away from one. As the other crew came to, the realisation that they'd lost one of their band of ten settled across the raft like a sickness, poisoning the well of hope they were holding.

For a long time no one spoke. No one wanted to say the things that would have to be said in this awful reality.

'What do we do with him?' came the inevitable question eventually.

There was a quiet discussion as the remaining survivors tried to make an impossible decision – what to do with their dead shipmate's body when they were still fighting for their lives themselves? In their minds were the close calls of yesterday. The planes were a sure sign that a search was underway.

The decision was made by consensus. 'We'll hang on to his body so we can take it home to his wife,' Ken said. It was the least they could do for John Sloan's family, who had no idea where he was or if he was okay.

The heaviness of John's death brought Mick's thoughts of his family and Joanie closer. He was tinged with fear and despair that maybe, just like the second engineer, his loved ones might just get his lifeless body back. If they were found at all.

With the decision made, Ken and Alf sat with John resting between them, supported against the side of the raft. There was not enough room to lay him out.

Mick might only have met John Sloan a week before, but getting to know a man in those circumstances created a bond. It stripped people back to their core, and Mick thought John was a decent bloke. Despite the anguish of his final days, he had tried to spare his shipmates from the agony. Mick couldn't stop thinking about the wife and child John had spoken of those first couple of days in the raft when he was still able.

Mick had not yet had death touch his life. Now he was staring it in the face. He was trapped in a tiny raft where death had taken a seat in John's place. Mick was just 18, barely older than a lad, when he'd walked up the gangway onto the *Blythe Star*. But sitting in the raft that day he was no longer that boy. He was a man, with no choice but to try to harden himself to the circumstances he found himself in. To have done less would have seen him sink under the weight of exhaustion and fear and despair.

A glance out of the raft opening brought another letdown. Despite their continual paddling throughout the darkness, the night wind and tide had taken their raft back out to sea again. With the tenacity of desperate men, they struck out yet again in the direction of the land. What else could they do?

'Keep paddling, or we'll get nowhere,' Ken encouraged. 'We've got to get a break soon, today might be the day.'

In a raft of despair, with nothing else to latch on to, Mick grabbed hold of Ken's beacon of hope and positivity. He used it as fire to fuel him when it was his turn to paddle, to strike the water continually to try to draw the land closer.

Slowly, excruciatingly, hour by hour, land came back into view.

The Tasman Peninsula lurked once again like a distant memory or dream on the horizon. The sunshine mocked them, making a joke of their pitiful existence. In a desperate bid to make more headway, they raised the drogue and opened the raft's door flap, hoping to catch the wind with their raft. As the raft filled with the gusting wind, they held the paddle in the water like a rudder to try to keep some control over the course of the raft as it scudded across the waves. The wind was finally blowing the right direction and they managed to make more headway.

Eventually, they decided they were within 15 or so miles of the Tasman Island lighthouse. They could see the sun glinting off the lighthouse, a small finger visible on the land ahead. They figured it was close enough that they should be visible if they could catch the keeper's attention.

The heliograph was taken to the opening again. A rectangular-shaped mirror with a small eye through the middle, they could sight their target and know they were flashing directly at it. Lining it up, they began signalling the lighthouse, and it seemed as though their little mirror was flashing on the very light at the top of the tower.

Sitting cramped in that raft, John Sloan cold and still beside them, they barely dared dream that their signal might be picked up. But as the hours crept by, depression sinking deeper into their sodden skin, they gave up the idea as another false dream.

The deadly repetition of the last few days, paddling incessantly toward land only for it to be snatched away after dusk, was eating away at them. It was like a horrific dream they couldn't escape, as if they were destined to an eternity of cold and hunger and thirst with no end.

Somewhere in the mire of time that stretched out across the day, Mick Power, stationed at the opening with paddle in hand, called back down to the others. He'd seen a fin breaking the water, cutting a white streak. Then another and another. 'There's bloody killer whales out here!'

Fucking hell! Could we ask for anything more? Mick wondered. Fear permeated him.

Just when they thought their existence couldn't get more fraught! At the sound of the massive orcas sliding in and out of the water, expelling great sprays of air from their blowholes, their eyes grew wide with fear. Not daring to move, the crew stayed totally silent. They didn't even dare whisper. They all had the same thought. Would the killer whales realise they were there? And if they did, what would they do?

Barely daring to breathe, Mick strained his ears to try to track the animals' movements. Blinded by the raft's canopy, every sense was tingling. At any moment, he expected the flimsy canvas to tear open in front of him, the first he would know that the creatures had taken a fancy to them for lunch.

It was hard to put the brakes on his imagination as it played out the scene in his mind. Confusion. Chaos. The feel of sharpened teeth tearing at his flesh, rendering it open to the salty water. A cold sweat washed over his body, his heart pounding through his shrunken frame and seeming to land somewhere near his Adam's apple.

But after what seemed an eternity, Mick Power spoke again quietly. 'It's like they're curious, just checking us out,' he said.

Thank Christ, Mick thought. *I'd be pretty bloody dirty if they're curious to find out what's in the raft.*

A nervous laugh rippled through the men when someone joked that it was lucky Power was on the paddle, not a better-looking bloke, as his mug must have given the creatures a fright to send them on their way.

'It's not every day they get a nine-course meal floating past. Thank goodness they're not taking up the opportunity!'

As the sound of the orcas faded, the men dared to move, shuffling over to the opening to tentatively peek out past Mick.

'They're gone,' Mick Power reported, relieved.

So, their endless routine began again.

Mick would paddle until his body gave out, then call up the next man – usually Mick Power or Mal McCarroll – to take over. They would clamber over each other and their shipmates, shuffling around so each person could reach the opening. All of this happened around the prone figure of John Sloan.

As the hours wore on, with no sign of another plane, they began to wonder how long they could keep John aboard. But no one wanted to be the one to start that discussion. Finally, as the day drew to a close, there was no escaping it anymore. 'I don't know if anyone's coming for us today,' Ken said.

After a short discussion, the crew agreed they would have to give John a sea burial. They'd sat sentinel over his body for the entire day in the hope they could bring his body home for his family, but now they had to let that go.

GOODBYE

The logistics of burying a man at sea from the cramped confines of a tiny life raft filled with ten grown men weren't straightforward. As the men prepared to move John's body to the opening, Mick spotted warm socks on feet that could no longer feel their protective comfort. Still in his jocks with bare, blue and goose-fleshed legs, the thought of socks seemed like an impossible luxury.

Unsure, he asked Ken if he could take the socks. 'I'm sure he wouldn't begrudge me?' Mick said.

The rest of the crew agreed.

'It's fine lad, take them,' Ken said, a grim compassion in his voice.

Mick peeled the socks off John's still feet and rolled them onto his own. It was one of the hardest things Mick has ever had to do in his life. Then the men lifted John's body and shuffled him across the slick rubber floor of the raft. They paused for a moment, dreading what had to be done next.

Then they found purchase on his clothes and lifted him as gently as they could to the opening.

Captain Cruikshank cleared his throat. 'John Sloan, you haven't been with us very long,' he said, the gravity of the situation like gravel in his throat. 'You've done your job well and been a good shipmate to all of us. We're sorry it has to be done this way but wherever you go we hope you'll be happy. God bless you.'

There was nothing more to be said. Slowly, they slipped John Sloan over the side.

There was gentleness, dignity, horror and respect in that moment. The strain was written on the crew's faces, and as John disappeared, a silence so complete it seemed to dull the white noise of the ocean temporarily descended on them.

They all knew that, the way things were going, the chances were they too would die in the next few days.

There was no holding back the wave of despair that took over Mick. No one spoke. They had lost their first casualty, and a rescue seemed more distant than ever. In each man's mind was the question of whether they would be next. Above it all, Mick mourned the man he'd just met. He mourned for John's family. For the sheer waste of his life. John hadn't deserved to die like that. There was no justice or reason to a death out in a place like this. It brought the realisation that Mick could be next.

As Mick sat there, he began to think about life and legacy. Rolling back through his memories, he saw them through a new lens. It ignited a spark in his soul to get out of this, so that he would have the chance to become a better man.

If I can get out of this unscathed, I can do anything, he thought. *I can be anything I want, but I've got to make sure I'm the man that can do it.*

Mick thought about the anger he'd struggled to temper at times, the talking he'd let his fists do, and he made a promise to himself. *If I get outta this, I'll be a better person.*

That there was a reason to live. A reason to keep enduring. A way to move forward when everything in Mick's body and mind was screaming at him to lie down and give up.

The day's empty sky and sea had proven to Mick that there was no one coming for them. If they were going to get out of here, they would have to save themselves. *I'll be buggered if I lie down and give up*, Mick said to himself. *I'll do everything I can to get myself and my shipmates out of this alive.*

As Mick was waging his own inner battle, Ken could see the state of the men around him. The death of John Sloan had been a body blow to them all. They'd begun to feel there was a curse on them. He knew they needed something else to focus on. So, with a supreme power of will, he put aside his own doubts and fear and depression and encouraged them not to give up.

He instructed them to pick up the paddles again. 'Come on, we were close to land today, we've got to keep going,' he said. He said anything he could to rouse them, knowing that unless they had something to channel their despair into, something to focus on, they would all give up. Once the mind has resigned itself to death, it isn't long before the body follows. Through his character and willpower alone, Ken somehow brought the eight men around him back from the brink.

Mick picked up a paddle and made his way yet again to the opening and slowly started the gruelling process of paddling to exhaustion. When he collapsed, there was another man there to take over. And so, slowly, they pulled themselves through their darkest hours, trying to keep moving forward. They focused on anything they could to give them strength to keep going in the face of unimaginable odds.

That evening, they tried again to catch the golden sun with their heliograph. The flashes from their raft fired off in the direction of Tasman Island lighthouse. But no corresponding flashes came back. Neither was there the sound of any search party rushing out to meet them.

As night settled around them, their isolation seemed more acute than ever. There was a brutal savagery in being able to see land, but having had a man die all the same and knowing they might be headed the same way. It was just as well Mick had given up on God back when his footy team was getting trounced, otherwise he might have been having a reckoning.

As the currents and winds shifted, again they saw land recede into the distance. By now they knew the drill – the chances were that by morning they'd be blown out to sea, right back to where they'd started.

* * *

Friday, 19 October 1973 – Hobart

The remaining nine crew of the *Blythe Star* may have felt forsaken, but they were big news on land – or their continued absence was, at any rate.

Journalist Trevor Sutton had been filing stories every day about the mysterious disappearance. By now, the reporting had changed. The media no longer said the ship was expected to turn up late and in one piece, and was starting to question the laissez-faire attitude of the Tasmanian government and

Tasmanian Transport Commission. 'We can communicate with men on the moon, and yet we cannot communicate with the *Blythe Star*,' quipped one report.

Each day, Trevor took the short drive to the office and hit the phone to try to hunt down the latest on the missing ship. On Thursday, the day Mick and the crew had seen that tantalising shadow of a search plane overhead, Trevor got a call from pilot Vern Reid. When TVT6 needed aerial footage for a story, they'd call on Vern, a former policeman and sharp operator. Trevor had been up with Vern more than once, strapped in alongside the pilot. Vern would open the window and, with his seatbelt stretched taut, he would reach out of the window, both hands on the camera while his feet were on the plane's controls. Somehow, he'd hold the aircraft in a steady circle while he'd fire off his film.

Vern wasn't calling to shoot the breeze. He had a proposal for Trevor. 'Tomorrow's weather is going to be fantastic,' he said. 'It'll be the best weather we've had since the *Blythe Star* went missing. We can do a coastal search. We'll find anything that's on the shore.'

Trevor was interested. 'How would we do that?' he asked.

Vern outlined his flight plan, which was based on where he reckoned the ship would likely be washed up or adrift. They'd fly down to South West Cape, one of the most southern points of Tasmania, and along the coast back up to Hobart, refuel, and then keep going up the east coast right past the Tasman Peninsula and Eaglehawk Neck and all the way around to Maria Island.

'We've got a good chance,' he said, 'because the weather's on shore and very clear tomorrow.'

'It's a big ask isn't it, to travel all that way?'

'No, no problem. I'll put up a drum of fuel. Would your station give a drum of fuel to the search?'

Trevor was excited. 'Yeah, I think so,'

It was a chance to do something when it seemed like nothing was happening. Not to mention, a chance to break the biggest story of the week.

'Then we'll have it covered. Go get the okay and call me back.'

Trevor was buzzing as he strode around to the news editor, Bill Walkley. But when he put the idea on the table, Bill wasn't picking up the vibe. 'Well, that's a bit of an off-the-top-of-the-head idea, isn't it? We don't know whether it's gone east about or west about to King Island and you want to go flying down south?'

'Vern Reid reckons that's the place to search,' Trevor argued. 'He's a pilot, knows the area very well. I've been with him down on the southern coast a few times.'

The excitement was draining out of Trevor, replaced with frustration. He could feel that Vern's idea was a good one. He trusted Vern and if Vern said this was the place to fly over then Trevor believed him. But he could read the writing on his editor's face.

'I don't think I could support that idea,' Walkley said. 'It's really out of the ballpark. What gives Vern Reid the idea that he might find something when everyone else has just drawn a blank?'

Trevor was surprised. Surely it was worth a go? Vern was even going to stump up half the fuel. For just the cost of one 44-gallon drum they'd be able to search the entire coastline from Maria Island right around to South West Cape.

Trevor walked out of the news editor's office disappointed. He felt in his gut that Vern's idea was a goer. It was low risk for a potential high reward, both for the story and for the missing crew of the *Blythe Star*. As Trevor beat a retreat back to his office he contemplated going over the editor's head to the general manager. But he was only a young journalist, and on balance he thought that wasn't a prudent idea.

Trevor picked up the phone to call Vern back. The news went down about as well with Vern as it had with Trevor. They both knew they were missing a golden opportunity to have a proper look. They knew the shemozzle that had unfolded over the official search, and here was a chance to know that at least someone had methodically worked their way along the coast. Not just anyone either – Vern was a seasoned pilot with intimate knowledge of the coastline.

But the decision had been made and it was above their heads. They had to let the idea go.

Despite the authorities' public reassurances that every resource available was being thrown at the search, many of the crew's families, much like Trevor and Vern, had reservations.

Cliff Langford's father, Roy, was disgusted that there weren't more planes in the sky and boats scouring the seas.

'I'm quite sure that if some VIP were lost the whole air force, and possibly the navy would be out looking for them,' he remarked to reporters. 'Here we have ten men who are missing, men who are doing a useful job of work, and we find that it's considered not important at all.'

Fed up, Roy hired his own plane to scour the south-west coast, where he thought it was most likely to find his son.

He set off hopeful and determined. Had he gone just a few days earlier he may well have spotted the orange bobbing dot of the life raft being tossed by the waves. But as he took to the skies, his son Cliff and the other eight devastated men had been pushed east and continued to drift in and then heartbreakingly out from Tasman Island.

As the light plane touched down, Roy's optimism was replaced by a grim heartache. Maybe he was wrong. Maybe his son Cliff, survivor of the Burma Railway, seafarer, mischievous practical joker, just wasn't there to be found. 'I'm not without hope, but as you must realise my hopes are getting rather low now,' he said.

* * *

Friday night, 19 October 1973 – Life raft, Day 7

In the raft, the hopes of the crew had dwindled, along with their supplies. Hardly plentiful to start with, their emergency rations were diminishing rapidly. They had given as much water as they could spare to try to keep John Sloan alive, and they were now counting down their last clutch of water tins. Sometimes, when they cracked open a can, it would have a murky tinge to it and a brackish taste but they were long past caring. Water was water, and they couldn't afford to be fussy.

Mick Power and Tas Leary still hadn't managed to keep down any of the protein biscuits and were surviving on their meagre ration of water and their dusting of glucose powder alone.

The darkness of Friday night failed to bring the blessed relief of sleep, the cold all-pervasive, their shattered bodies in a permanent state of tension. After the days of cold and hunger, followed by the death of a shipmate, something snapped. Their grip on reality, getting ever more tenuous, gave way. Mick wasn't sure how it started, but he looked around and realised a couple of the other men appeared to be chatting and laughing. One of their precious cans of water was cracked and a head was tipped back, the precious liquid cascading into the open mouth beneath. There was a laugh and a joke and someone threw Mick a can and the can opener.

'Mate, crack a cold one and welcome these blokes in proper style,' someone called.

Mick opened the can and drank, his body aching for the liquid that tasted better than any beer he'd ever had. By now water cans were being cracked around the raft and the sombre weight of the afternoon lifted as the crew joked and laughed, passing around cans and drinking their fill.

To a man, the crew were convinced that some Norwegian sailors had joined them. The Norwegians were welcomed with much hilarity and were passed some water. Or was it beer? Hard to tell. Mick and the others were having the time of their life, joking with their new sailor friends and generally having a grand night out.

Only they weren't out. There were no Norwegian sailors. And that was their precious few remaining cans of water they were necking.

A group delirium had descended on them, and they imbibed and sang and talked. For once they didn't feel the cold, or the heavy weight of wondering if they would see their loved ones again. They lost themselves in the safety of delirium. It was sweet relief from the horror of the present, until, scattered across the floor of the raft, they fell into an exhausted sleep.

The whispering wind of the ocean stole away the Norwegian sailors their minds had conjured, just as surely as it stole them back out to sea.

As the sun rolled back the night, the crew stirred. Bleary eyes opened, and crushing realisations crashed down. They were still here. Sitting in a couple of inches of water, crouched under a claustrophobic plastic canopy that was the only thing stopping the Southern Ocean from ravaging them.

Mick looked around and saw the open and empty water cans strewn around. 'What the hell went on here?' he asked aloud.

The faces around him mirrored his shock. With mounting panic, he remembered the party of the night before. They quickly started scrabbling around to gather the empty cans and see how many they had that were still full. Can after can came up empty. For all their searching they found a single, lonely full can.

'Fuck,' someone said, pretty well summing up the sentiment in the raft.

Comparing notes, they all admitted with shame their fever dream of the night before. They realised they'd all shared the delirium. They'd all experienced the pub, the Norwegians, the good cheer.

None of the men could fathom what had happened and how they could have done it. Their precious water squandered, time was up for them. Shock set in as they comprehended that, however serious their situation had been the day before, it was worse today.

CHAPTER 13

A Last Push

Saturday, 20 October 1973 – Life raft, Day 8

Mick was distraught. With his head between his legs, his heart seemed to seize as he thought of his life, his family and friends. He was putting together a farewell in his mind.

'Don't worry, Mick, we'll get out of this,' came Ken's ever steady voice. 'We won't give up, this is it. We've got to keep pushing.'

Mick raised his head. Ken's words had pulled him out of his self-pity and ignited an ember of determination. He looked at Ken and drew a curtain on his despair. He reached again for the paddle. He wasn't going to be the one to let down his crew. If time was up, he wanted to go out knowing he bloody well did everything in his power to hold death at bay.

Mick was getting out of this, even if only to prove that he could be a better person who deserved to.

In the raft, the men's comfort level was closely attuned to what the weather threw at them each day. Saturday was a fair day, a small fortune when all other fortune appeared to have left them. Ken's insistence that it was when, and not if, they would get out of this roused the crew to continue and they struck out again for land.

As the mental hangover of their excess the night before dissipated, the men began to talk again of home. Perhaps the imminent void that had opened in front of them had brought the presence of those they loved onto the raft, but it felt to the crew as they talked that their wives, girlfriends, children and mates were there with them under the sun.

Just as it had on previous days, the Tasman Peninsula soon appeared and they could see the lighthouse once again, a beacon for an impossible dream of rescue. But today, they were closer than they'd ever been before. The land was no longer a mirage on the horizon but something real and solid, made of rocks and mud rather than indistinguishable smudges. They could even see a jetty. By Mick's reckoning they were about three-quarters of a mile from the lighthouse.

Mal McCarroll piped up. 'I reckon I could swim to that loading dock at the bottom of Tasman Island,' he said. 'I could get word out and come back for you and get you off.'

Mal thought this was the best chance they'd get, but Mick wasn't so sure. Nonetheless, he and Mick Power paddled hard for the jetty. Mal lay back in the raft resting before he attempted the swim, gathering any last reserves of energy from his depleted body.

As the raft bobbed slowly closer to the dock, Mick had to say something. 'Are you serious, Mal?'

'Yeah, I'm a reasonable swimmer,' Mal came back.

'Mate, that's a long way and you're not in a fit condition,' Mick argued. He was as desperate to get off the floating death trap as the next man, but he wasn't going to watch another person die in the attempt.

'You've been in this raft a while. It's really risky stuff.'

'No, I think I can do it,' Mal argued, suggesting a rope attached to him would link him to the raft and safety should anything go wrong.

'If you swim with a rope wrapped around you to that landing, what happens if a shark gets you?'

It's a fear all of them held, the previous day's encounter with orcas fresh in their minds. Mal's face looked uncertain. It wasn't something he wanted to contemplate.

Mick continued. 'He'll come back and find out there's more of us in the raft and you'll be the appetiser and we'll be the main course and dessert.'

Mal was silent, thinking it through. He could feel his body's drained and fatigued state. He looked out again at the landing, so tantalisingly close.

'You're probably right,' he conceded. 'We better not do that.'

Their window was snatched from them regardless, the wind swinging around and pushing them away from land. As he watched it recede, Mal could have cried.

But this time the land didn't disappear entirely, and as the hours marched on they moved northward up Tasmania's south-east corner. Even when, at the behest of the currents and wind, they drifted further away, they remained within sight of land.

Counting the nights that seemed to have blended into one long horror, Mick realised it had been a week since the slick decks of the *Blythe Star* had sunk. The continued silence in the sky told Mick that the search was either looking in the wrong place – or it was over. The pragmatist in him knew they wouldn't search forever. He'd known for a while that it was up to them now.

As the distant land slipped past, the idea dawned that the way they were going, it would be only a matter of time before they were washed ashore. But the towering spires of dolerite rock that formed cliffs up to 300 metres high filled Mick with trepidation. Just *where* were they going to end up? And would they be able to get out? Or would they be smashed against rocks they couldn't escape? By now, any faith in luck was long exhausted, and a nagging worry about their landing gnawed at Mick's stomach.

As they continued to drift, the sound of waves pounding at the feet of rocks grew louder. Shuffling to the raft opening to take his turn on the paddle, Mick looked out and saw a huge chunk of rock with sheer pillars 65 metres high looming ahead. Wasting no time, he picked up the paddle and thrust it into the water, in an effort to drag them past the rock before they came too close.

All the time, his muscles screaming at him, he kept half an eye on the rocks. They seemed to glow orange in the sun – the reflections dancing across the inky blue and velvety ripples of the ocean. Just another reminder of the many ways this ocean could kill them. But also a landmark.

Mal and Ken recognised the distinctive rock formation as Hippolyte Rocks and realised they must be east of the Tasman Peninsula.

Where the south-west of Tasmania is an endless wilderness of sharp rocks, bush and mud, where you could walk for days without seeing another living thing, the east coast opened up the possibility they might find help. Far more temperate, towns were scattered up the east coast. The weather was less formidable and there were stretches of white sandy beaches stolen from paradise and scattered between the cliffs. They were in a far better place to be rescued than they were when the ship sank.

A glance around the raft showed a sobering sight though. Cliff Langford was wasting away and clearly not well. John Eagles was sunken and silent. Each man held a heaviness that hadn't been there a week before, each man more gaunt with dull eyes. Mick was still one of the worst dressed. Although he now had John Sloan's socks, he was still bare but for his jocks. Even those more warmly dressed were barely better off. Their clothes were perpetually wet, clinging to their skin.

After a short conversation, the crew made the easy decision to try for Eaglehawk Neck, situated about an hour's drive south-east of Hobart. This was the best opportunity so far to make land and despite their shrunken and diminished state, they couldn't let it go. It was a daunting task. Even if they did make land, they would have their work cut out for them. Eaglehawk Neck is a small isthmus that links the Tasman Peninsula with mainland Tasmania. The Tasman Peninsula was one of the places in Tasmania to be settled by Europeans, looking for an Antipodean gaol, and was picked for its natural features, which was a far more efficient gaoler than any man. The sheer cliffs, the shark-filled ocean, the dense bush and remoteness suggested that the idea of convicts making a break for freedom was laughable.

Eaglehawk Neck itself was the only link to a less intimidating landscape, but in colonial times it was guarded by a line of nine dogs at its narrowest part, which was just 30 metres across. Even today, it is known as 'the Dog Line'. For the nine men in the raft, the landscape seemed as daunting as it must have to those beaten and enslaved convicts almost 150 years earlier.

Mists of rain swept over them as they drew closer to Eaglehawk. It was mid-afternoon when they finally found themselves offshore. The land looked so close and yet it might have been miles away in their depleted state.

Several of the men were very sick, the remainder fatigued and weak from lack of food and water. To complicate matters, not all the men knew how to swim. The best they could do was keep paddling, handing over to someone else when they were too physically destroyed to continue.

They waited and hoped for the tide and wind to change and bring them ashore. They thought they could see a strip of black winding beside the shore that may have been a road, and they could definitely see a flat shelf of rock on the water's edge, glistening under falling rain, that centuries of water had carved into a distinctive tessellated pattern.

'Can you see that?' someone asked.

'It's a car, isn't it?' came a reply.

Mick poked his head out. They could have sworn blue there was a car there, a brown Volkswagen. A woman was standing nearby. Behind her they could see the crisp lines of a building – maybe a hotel – something man-made in a world of movement and chaos.

The men hooted and hollered, trying to get the woman's attention. But by now no strangers to hallucination, they couldn't be sure whether she was real or a fantasy – and the memory of the fever dream of the night before was still fresh. The woman seemed to be looking out into the bay, but despite their best efforts she didn't respond. Mick supposed she might imagine they were just a group of lads enjoying a day's fishing and carrying on in good fun. All the same, their spirits were buoyed. They were the closest they'd been to land in eight endless, infernal days. The sight of the building – which was in fact the Lufra Hotel – had them joking through their exhaustion and planning what meal they'd order when they got ashore. Pie, chips and a beer. They reckoned they deserved one of those.

Then someone realised that Saturday was race day. The

Caulfield Cup was on in Melbourne – fancy frocks, dapper suits, frivolity and fun – hundreds of kilometres away.

The jokes continued about getting to the hotel to put a bet on. The idea tickled Mal McCarroll, who was a mad keen punter – it was in his family. As they bobbed off the coast, dreaming of the hotel just across the water, Mal told Mick about his brother, who was an SP bookie, an illegal bookmaker who takes bets on the horses. Well, he had been an SP bookie right up until he'd held up a handful of notes and said, 'Who wants some of this? Come on, get your money on the next race.' Then someone slapped a pair of cuffs on his wrists. That put an end to his bookie career, but not to Mal's love of the horses or a bet.

Mal had already put money on the Caulfield Cup before the ship sailed, and would have given anything to be warm and safe in the Lufra Hotel watching it unfold – feeling the thrill of seeing his horse bring it home.

'Well, I got a fair idea what the field is,' Mal said. 'You fellas each pick a horse and I'll commentate our own race.'

He listed the horses and they each selected a horse that took their fancy. Then, there in the raft within sight of the pub, wasted and desperate but still finding some good humour, Mal called the race that was only running in his head. The rest of the crew cheered and whooped, for all the world as though they were really barracking their horses down the last straight to win.

It helped pass the time as they waited for the tide to draw them in to shore. Except it didn't. The wind swung around again and started to blow them back out. None of the crew had much strength left to paddle at this point, and they could do nothing as they watched their great hope, their dreams of pies and chips, once again snatched from their grasp.

Still, Mick Power had the paddle in hand, trying to maintain some semblance of control over their course. Through the raft opening, Mick could see Power laboriously keeping the paddle in motion.

'Mick, look!' Power called through the opening. 'You better have a look at this. We're getting too close to these rocks.'

'Nah, it's a beautiful day,' Mick said.

Somewhere between consciousness and oblivion, his mind wasting from lack of fuel, Mick was lying back and enjoying the warmth the sun cast over their little shelter. He thought it was almost like a sailing day, just on a very different sort of yacht.

Power insisted that Mick take a look at what he was seeing, so Mick slowly roused himself and slid past the prone figures of the other men to the opening. As he did, he noticed that Cliff Langford was looking even worse today.

When Mick poked his head out, what he saw sharpened his focus, breaking through the cobwebs of his mind. In horror he looked up at towering pinnacles. 'Shit,' he said. Even their starved minds knew that to come much closer to these needle-like spires would be the end of them. With nowhere to cling onto and waves pounding at them relentlessly, they wouldn't last long, even if they were in good condition. And they were far from that.

'How the fuck did we end up here?' Mick was buzzing again with urgency. He took over the paddle, hoping that, having rested, he'd have the strength needed to skirt the fearsome rocks. He started paddling like mad, putting everything he had into the water. In just a couple of minutes his muscles were screaming, his hamstrings and calves cramping up. Power took over again.

Mick and Power took turns for around three minutes a stretch, about all they could manage before their bodies gave out and they needed to pass the paddle back to the other. They used every ounce of remaining energy to push them forward but they were still being drawn closer to the rocks, as though by a magnet.

'Do you think we can fit through the gap between the rocks?' Mick asked hopefully. He didn't know if they could make it around, but maybe heading through might give them another option.

'No way,' Power replied. 'We've just got to paddle hard.'

They both knew what that meant. The nine lives on that raft were in their hands. As they thrashed their bodies to keep going, time once more seemed to slow, and their world shrank down to those fingers of solid, immovable and indifferent rock, their valiant efforts to move themselves on, and the heaving inky water between.

There was no time to think of family, parents, siblings, partners. There was only one question. Could they make it? A whitewash of water swirled around the raft, whispering menacingly of the welcome the rocks had ready for them.

Mick couldn't quite believe it, but slowly they moved around the rocks. Body on fire, the entirety of his legs cramping, he started to think that maybe they might make it. Then they did. Mick breathed. They had another chance. But how many more?

With the terror of the rock pinnacles behind them, they could see a bay ahead. Could this have been their last hurdle? Could there be on the other side a place they could finally make land. Could they put this godforsaken experience behind them?

Mick and Power fell back into the raft with exhaustion. Their muscles were limp, entirely spent. They turned to a couple of the others who hadn't touched the paddle in days, reckoning they must be the freshest.

'Can you have a paddle?'

But their words drew no response. Mick tried again, explaining the disaster they'd just escaped moments before, and the opportunity before them now. But he might as well have been speaking a different language. Their crewmates were slumped in the raft, sullen and unwilling or unable to pick up the paddle.

Ken Jones tried his best to get everyone to take a stint on the paddle. It's impossible to know why two of them refused to pick it up. One of those men, in another moment, had shown incredible bravery. Put his body on the line to save his shipmates. But in this moment, they left Mick and Power hanging, exhausted and unable to pick up the paddle after their exhaustion.

Maybe those two had given themselves up for dead already. Maybe they just didn't have the strength. Or maybe they were just human and could be many things in different moments. A hero in one, a disappointment in another. Everyone has a breaking point, maybe they had reached theirs.

Whatever the reason, the men missed the opportunity to make land. Tension crackled in the raft. After more than a week packed in like sardines, the comradeship of crew – thrown together entirely by circumstance – started to fracture.

Mick was dirty that, after his and Power's effort, which had cost them so much, their calls for help were ignored. There was a tangible frisson of energy buzzing between the sunken and sullen men. It felt like real mayhem could break out at any moment.

Fatigue, lack of water and food were taking their toll and Mick wasn't the only one at the end of his tether. He was angry, but he also understood that everyone was knackered. Whatever the reason, the drift continued. Looking out at one point, he saw what looked like a road along the foreshore in the distance and he and Mick Power paddled as close as they could manage toward it only for it to coalesce into another mirage. Not a road at all, but a formation of rocks.

Shadows crept into the sky and as the men faced another night the cheer of the day drained with the light. By now they were well and truly fed up with the routine of drawing toward and then away from land. Mick was ready to call it quits and get to shore anywhere. He didn't give a damn where, he just wanted to be out of this bloody raft. He'd take however bleak a landing as was offered so long as it meant he could get his feet on something solid and could get his frozen skin out of the frigid water that they could never completely clear from the bottom of the raft.

As night settled in, the men huddled together, shivering and desperate. Through the raft's opening they could see in the distance the shifting and bobbing lights of the Lufra Hotel again, tantalising with its lure of safety.

Then they saw something else, far closer, about 45 metres away. It was land – a place called Devil's Kitchen. But the hiss of the ocean as it sprayed up the sheer cliffs was a warning. The place wasn't called Devil's Kitchen for nothing – the churning, angry waves that crashed on the rocks had inspired the name.

The men had decided that tonight was the night they would finally get to shore, regardless of where. Now they looked up at the towering rock, stripped bare from the power of the waves that pounded it. It was a daunting sight. Once again, they were being pushed toward rocks that would smash them up and spit them back into the sea.

At the last moment they changed their minds. No one had the heart to throw themselves at the mercy of rocks called Devil's Kitchen. Instead, they decided to try their chances again, drawing the attention of someone on Eaglehawk Neck.

They'd been saving their final flare for when they made land. The emergency pack in the raft had contained no matches, and somewhere along the way the matches John

Eagles stowed so carefully in his overalls pocket after they smoked that precious, last cigarette had disappeared. They'd been keeping the flare to start a fire that could breathe life back into their frozen limbs.

But that was all theoretical unless they made it to land, and they had never had such an opportunity to do so as they did right now. They could see the lights of the hotel, sparkling a message out across the sea that there was life, people, a phone.

So they pulled out the last flare and Ken Jones again wrapped his hand and arm to try to protect it from the molten rain that fell from the burning light. Moving to the opening, he stuck his torso out and pulled himself as high as he could before cracking the flare. Once again, the smell of burning filled Mick's nostrils and the light burned onto his retinas.

The men languishing in the raft waited.

Mick's heart beat out the moments that stretched on long after the flare had burned out. Nothing. There was no response to this final desperate plea for help. It had gone unseen.

Mick knew they couldn't afford to be blown back out to sea that night. Each day found them more exhausted, less lucid and utterly depleted. They were running out of energy to paddle back to shore.

But now land, so close a moment ago, appeared to be sneaking away again. He desperately plunged his hand into the water. Thick, leathery kelp was swaying gently below the surface and Mick grasped it tightly and held on quite literally for dear life. Minutes ticked by, each one made longer by the tension in his arm, which was all that prevented the raft tugging them away.

Mick was determined to keep holding on until the wind changed again and pushed them back toward more hospitable, land where they might be able to attempt a landing. He quickly realised the kelp was also an anchor to stop them being thrown against the rocks, their softened skin shredded in the darkness.

When his muscles were screaming, Mick called someone else to take over. In a tight shuffling manoeuvre, he made room for Mick Power to take hold. The routine went on for hours. Every now and then the man on the kelp would feel it start to loosen and tear away, and would grab wildly for another waving tendril to tether them to safety.

The incessant sound of waves crawled into Mick's mind. It was both a reminder of safety and the danger still sitting between him and it. Sleep came in snatches and moments of half-consciousness. Their bodies never quite truly rested. Those waves crashing nearby were more foot soldiers in the war against sleep.

Midnight came and went. Sometime in the small hours of the morning, muscle fatigue and exhaustion overtook them. When the kelp they were clinging to broke away they couldn't catch another. Once again, they were untethered and adrift.

CHAPTER 14

The Best of Them

Saturday, 20 October 1973 – Maatsuyker Island

On Maatsuyker Island, Tony Parsey had only heard snippets on the radio about the ongoing search for the *Blythe Star*. Life as a lighthouse keeper was busy. There was keeping the light going, and then there was everything else – building and equipment maintenance, weather observations, gardening. There was always something to keep Tony busy, so he hadn't had a lot of time to ruminate on that strange ship sighting and subsequent phone calls.

But it still came into his mind from time to time. Especially a few days earlier when the weather had thrown rain at the windows and wind howled around the jolting and shuddering tower. In those moments he'd paused to think, *Hope those poor buggers aren't out there in this. I certainly wouldn't fancy it.*

The search for the *Blythe Star* might have been the biggest maritime search in the country's history, but Tony had yet to see any sign of it. He was still perplexed that his report of a struggling ship matching the description of the *Blythe Star* had been so readily discounted. The search clearly wasn't focused on the area that crucial information might have indicated. Instead, the odd snippet of news that came through the crackling and tinny radio speaker told him that the search was focused up the east coast. 'What are they searching up there for, when the ship went past here?' the keepers would muse.

Finally, during Saturday, Tony was doing his usual weekend jobs when he heard the hum of a plane crescendo to a roar. Looking up, Tony saw a grey military plane flying low toward them, so low, it drowned out any other sound.

The plane passed the houses on Maatsuyker then, circling, it did another low pass of the houses.

All three lighthouse keepers watched as it growled past. *Hello, they've finally taken notice of us*, Tony Parsey thought.

A short time later, the radio crackled to life. The lighthouse department in Hobart was reaching out to them. It had been eight days since the *Blythe Star* sank under the wash of the waves, at least six since the Transport Commission had put two and two together and realised something was amiss. Now, finally, Tony Parsey and the other keepers on Maatsuyker were being officially directed to keep a 24-hour watch out for the missing ship.

They fired a response back promptly that they already had taken it upon themselves to do that. All the same, they hadn't sighted anything and had nothing to report. Tony wasn't to know that by the time they'd got that first radio call about a missing ship – then assumed to be holed up against the weather somewhere – the crucial window when the men were drifting past the island with their signals and flares had already passed.

* * *

Thursday, 18 October to Sunday, 21 October 1973 – Doveton

In Mick's living room in Doveton, his dad, Tommy, was still poring over the maps laid out on the pool table. He kept going over them, thinking where the ship could be. Where it could have been going. Where, in his bones, he felt it was.

Mick's siblings, the brothers he'd grown up with cheek by jowl in the shared bedroom, and his sister, Marree, who'd been the catalyst for his burgeoning romance with Joanie – were beside themselves. As day rolled into day with no news, their faces were set and grim as they began to contemplate the unacceptable prospect that maybe no news would ever come their way.

The seafarers who kept constant vigil with Mick's family and Joanie still threw around their thoughts and opinions, by now well aired after days with no new information. They kept debating the same questions because it was all they could do, and it was better than sitting on their hands and giving up. At least this way their minds were occupied.

As the days wore on someone eventually ventured, 'Maybe the ship has sunk.'

'No. No, it hasn't sunk,' Tommy fired up at once. He was having none of that talk.

'Maybe it has, though. Nobody's heard anything, there's no sign of it ...'

Tommy wasn't having a bar of it. He steadfastly refused to accept the idea, and Mick's mum, Clara, backed him up. No, there would be some explanation but that wasn't it. Not that the ship was lost. Certainly not that Mick was lost.

Joanie was still spending all her time outside work at Mick's place, finding what solace she could in the shared experience. The edges of the absence of news slightly dulled in the collective. She took hope from Tommy and Clara's certainty that the ship was okay. Tommy had spent a life at sea; he knew about these things.

But still, it was hard to stop doubts creeping in.

* * *

Sunday, 21 October 1973 – Life raft, Day 9

Mick came around on Sunday morning to the sight of the ocean's wash around the raft. Exhaustion had finally claimed him after they'd broken free from the kelp and drifted again in the vast expanse of water.

Another close and grey day lay heavy over them, rain tapping out a dance on the canopy above. With the dawning light came the memory that they'd lost their kelp anchor. But when he heaved his lethargic body to the raft opening, the day revealed that land was still within their grasp.

The night had pushed them further north up the east coast, rather than back south and away from civilisation. The little raft, bedraggled after more than a week on the ocean, rose and fell gently with the swell about 100 yards from the cliffs. They could feel the tide tugging their raft, finally drawing them toward land.

Mick saw towering cliffs, with deep green foliage hanging over the top like a badly cut fringe. The rock was striped and folded like some giant hand had once kneaded it like bread. Each line represented an age, millennia, a depiction of time marching on impervious to the struggles of man. Those nine men barely hanging on in that life raft were but a blink of an eye to the rocks standing sentinel over the ocean.

In the raft, the scene wasn't pretty. All nine men were barely compos mentis, hovering somewhere between delirium, death and consciousness. Mick had long since become accustomed to the smell, but if he hadn't he reckoned it would smell like death in there.

Ken poked his head out to take a look at what was shaping up to be their landing spot. What he saw didn't inspire confidence. It was rocky, bleak and closed in.

'If that's where we end up, that's where we'll stay,' he said as he sat back down. 'We'll never get out of there. Shall we?'

Mick took the invitation to pick up the paddle again and gave another desperate burst to try to move them further along to a more hospitable section of coastline. Beyond fatigued, he was weak and trembling. He paddled until he dropped, only a couple of minutes. He had only a few minutes break before the next man also fell and he was back at it. But it worked. They got clear.

The raft crept around the corner, past the precipitous cliffs that crumbled into the ocean, great slabs of rock hiding the bay. As they slowly passed, their endless rocking rhythm eased as the waves' swell slackened in the lee of the rocks. To their left, a dark yawning chasm lurked into which the sea rushed in, hissing and spitting.

Inside the raft, the men barely had the energy left to register the safety and protection of the bay, the calmer water held in the embrace of the cliffs that wrapped around either side like arms.

Then, miraculously, Mick felt something brush against the bottom of the raft. Then something else. They had found the rocks on the floor of the bay. Mick, Power and Mal McCarroll pulled themselves up and splashed over the raft's side, into the frigid water. It was so cold the air seemed to freeze for a moment in Mick's chest, seizing, before the hands of cold loosened and his breath was released again.

They each grabbed a hold of the raft and stumbled and splashed over the uneven ground beneath them. They dragged the raft toward the shore, ignoring the scrapes and bumps and jaggedness of rocks beneath their softened, wasted feet.

Tasmania's east coast might be known for the picture-postcard white beaches seemingly stretching for eternity into the distance, but that wasn't what met them in this bay. The narrow beach was more a collection of rocks and boulders hemmed in on all sides.

But it was land. Blessed, solid, real, immovable land.

Mick, Mal and Power got the raft up to where the water kissed the rocks of the beach. Then they collapsed. They could hear the others tumbling out of the raft.

Pulling himself out of the water's grasping clutches, Mick tried to stand up and make his way further up the rock beach. But his legs, cramped and bent for so long, refused to cooperate. After more than a week of being tossed in the ocean, his body had completely lost its equilibrium, no longer sure what was solid and what was moving.

He tried to move forward, but his body was behaving as though he'd had a skinful of alcohol. Around him the others were equally debilitated, lurching and stumbling as they tried to regain their legs.

'Just crawl, don't stand up. Your legs will be like rubber,' came Ken's voice.

At these words Mick gave up and half-crawled, half-staggered up the beach. His legs kept collapsing under him. He realised just how much condition he had lost in the last eight days, and just how far gone his body was.

Finally, he managed to crawl back up behind the rocks to a small section of grass. Looking around to get his bearings, he heard a sound. Barely daring to believe, he was drawn to a trickling that promised water. He crawled over, hearing the others not far behind him. They delighted in the discovery of a small stream bubbling between some rocks like it was their first Christmas.

After a week of constant thirst, like a devil living in his throat, Mick Power went straight to the stream and drank it like a pig at a trough, barely able to get it down fast enough. Finally, stomach bloated and full, he moved away. He only had a few seconds before it all came back up again, too much for his shrunken stomach.

Mick took a long drink as well, the crystal water like silk in his mouth. Satiated for the first time in days, he looked around and realised that the little stream might well have been the only bit of luck they'd had landing there. As he surveyed the landscape, he thought that they might have jumped out of the fat and into the fire. All around were cliffs a hundred-plus metres high. The coastline was unforgiving and sheer, only the odd trailing grass able to cling to fissures in the cliff walls. Behind them, the land rose sharply, thickly forested and tumbled with rocks. Taking it all in, Mick thought that it looked near impossible to get out.

But at that moment, anything more than rest was beyond them. They all lay in the grass, inert. For the first time since they sailed from Hobart their world wasn't in constant motion. The ever-present fear of sharks had evaporated, and though they had a task ahead of them, at least they knew that they couldn't be stolen further into oblivion while they slept.

Cliff Langford lay spread on the grass, clearly in a bad way. George Cruikshank wasn't far behind him. Both men were wasted and shrunken, barely able to follow conversation and drifting regularly to a place within themselves the others couldn't reach. Mick wondered how much longer they had. Which clock would run faster – their rescue or their final reserves to hang in there?

Now out of the closed protection of the raft's canopy their varying stages of undress offered them little protection from the elements. The cold ocean breeze played a freezing dance across Mick's skin. He tried to ignore it.

A couple of hours later, the battered crew began to stir and once again contemplated the lay of the land. They discussed their next move. They were all daunted by the forbidding landscape.

'Maybe we should get back in the raft and try to find somewhere better to come ashore,' John Eagles suggested.

'You're kidding?' Mick fired. 'I'm not getting back into that raft for anything.' The very idea of it set a vice around Mick's guts. He grabbed the knife they had carefully guarded through the ordeal and went over to the raft. Without pausing he plunged it into the soft rubber and yanked it down. Acting as much on instinct as thought, Mick started cutting up the raft. He mightn't have known how they'd get out of this bay but he sure as hell knew he was never getting in that bloody raft ever again.

A moment later Mal McCarroll joined him, both of them slashing the raft as though they could somehow erase the torture of the last week by destroying the thing that had held all their misery.

The others watched on, either agreeing with the sentiment or too wrecked themselves to intervene. With the raft destroyed and any prospect of returning back to the hungry, clawing ocean, their choice was clear. Find a way out or die on this beach.

Mal dragged the two life jackets that had escaped the sinking ship and had sat beside them for days from the limp, deflated raft. Slinging them over his shoulder he clambered across the rocks, making his way painstakingly to the edge of the bay. Picking a large rock, he laid one of the bright orange life jackets across it facing out to sea. He then scampered across to the opposite side of the bay with the second life jacket and did the same. Maybe a passing ship would spot them and come into the bay to investigate.

On the grass near the trickling water, they took stock of what they had left. They were down to just two packs of rations and one can of water. Water at least wasn't a problem anymore, but the food was about to run out and that would be it.

With their matches long lost and their precious last flare used the night before in the hope of catching the gaze of some pub goer at the Lufra Hotel, they had no means of making a fire. Now they were stuck with no means of breathing warmth into their frozen bodies.

Ken Jones stepped in again. Just as he had them making radar reflectors from tin cans in the raft to keep their hands and minds busy, he suggested that they could use George Cruikshank's and Cliff Langford's glasses to focus the sun onto the grass to start a fire. The thought of flickering flames and radiating warmth was so tantalising as to be torture.

Cruikshank began fiddling around, trying to get a spark or smoulder. Somewhat revived by the fresh, clear spring water and the few hours' rest without the constant motion of the ocean underneath them, the rest of the crew looked around again. Looking up at the inhospitable surroundings, Mick was daunted by what lay ahead.

'Righto, we've made it to land. Now we've just got to get out,' the ever-encouraging Ken Jones said. They debated what the best approach would be. The bay was like the base of a steep-sided bowl. There was no clear incursion point on any of the surrounding hills.

Around midday, encouraged by Ken's continued optimism, Mick decided that, as the youngest and fittest, he had a better chance at making it out of this natural gaol. He headed back down to the raft, knife in hand, and again started hacking off pieces, yanking and tearing at the fabric while he sawed until he had some strips and a larger chunk.

Sitting down on a lichen-covered rock, Mick picked up one of the strips and carefully wound it around his foot. He tied the end off and tucked it in. It was rough, and sure wasn't a hiking boot, but it was better than nothing to protect his feet so he repeated the process with his other foot.

Then, standing up, he cut a slit in the middle of the larger section of raft canopy and pulled it over his head, poncho style. He hoped that would be enough to give his unclothed torso some protection from the bush. He headed back to the others clothed in his odd assortment of hand-crafted gear.

'Well, I'm gonna have a crack and go out. I'll come back when I find something,' he said.

Hearing this, Tas Leary roused himself again and pulled himself to sitting. He fished about in his pocket for a moment, then held something out to Mick. 'If you see a shop, will you get a carton of cigarettes for me?' he asked.

In his hand was a crumpled ten-dollar note.

Mick took the note, and looked at it for a moment. *Where the hell am I meant to put this?* he wondered, before shoving it down his jocks. That would have to do.

Mick set off, trying to pick his way through the rocks and trees and scrub. It didn't take long before he was lost to sight, entirely consumed by the landscape.

The uneven ground was covered with rocks, sharp sticks and a litany of unknown hazards, and his makeshift shoes barely kept his soft feet safe.

Down at the beach, George Cruikshank had abandoned his attempt to strike fire from focused sun rays. The men accepted that a fire was out of the question. Just another thing to dream about and wish for. The captain stood up and declared that he was going to find a way out too. He wandered off toward the gully leading up the steep incline behind them. The men could hear his laboured breathing and the snap and crunch of the protesting bush as he forced his way through.

The remainder of the crew stayed on the beach, trying to recover some energy. Then Cliff Langford, bowed and beaten by their time in the raft, gathered his last remaining strength and staggered to his feet. Delirium had long since taken him over. He muttered something about a cousin who was a taxi driver, who he thought had parked nearby, then tottered off to find the keys.

Realising that Cliff too had disappeared, Tas Leary heaved himself up and followed to bring him back to safety. As Tas led Cliff back to the beach, the sound of their grunts and curses as they pushed through the heavy bush drifted back to the men still on the beach.

The effort had sapped their remaining strength and, dejected and defeated, Tas and Cliff sank onto the small patch of grass and lay back. Both fit men before this, their ordeal had depleted every reserve they had. Tas's feet were shredded, streaked with blood from the rocks underfoot.

The minutes slipped past. With no sign of Mick or George Cruikshank, Mal McCarroll, Alf Simpson and Mick Power joined forces to try for an assault on the hill. They headed up the right-hand side of the gully, taking a route that was, if not likely looking, at least less intimidating than the rest. Immediately they were forced into single file as they pushed through thick scrub up a nearly 90-degree angle.

They blocked out any thoughts of discomfort. Their bodies might have been screaming at them, but they feigned deafness and kept trying to push through the seemingly impossible scrub. They hit dead end after dead end. A rockfall, a chasm, impenetrable bush – something would force them to turn back and try another way.

After hours of throwing themselves at the terrain Mal, Alf and Power realised that they weren't getting anywhere and one by one returned beaten to the beach.

'We can't find a way out,' they reported back, utterly spent.

They lay back again and let their bodies rest, trying to ignore the stinging lacerations on their arms and legs from where they'd tried to force their way through the bush. Tas wasn't the only one now with badly torn feet. Several of them hobbled as they moved around their small patch of safety on the grass.

Still labouring in the bush above the beach, Mick tried to carve a path forward, refusing to give up. He heard Ken Jones's voice in his head encouraging him to keep going. Mick didn't want to go back to Ken having failed. He didn't want to let Ken down, this man who had kept him going when he wasn't sure it was within him. So Mick tried again and again to penetrate the thick scrub. Surely eventually he could force the bush into submission with bodily effort?

But, after sticking with it for hours he was finally beaten. Dejected he emerged back into the open and saw the other men splayed around the grass. After days of continual immersion Mick had dried, his body crusty and uncomfortable. His feet were killing him, the jagged rocks having done a number on him too.

Noticing his return Ken Jones went over to Mick.

'Make another go, Bucko,' he said. 'Never give up until you're dead!'

Ken's words again stoked the fire in Mick's belly that he would get out of there alive. That he wouldn't be beaten.

Another rescue attempt was mounted. This time Mick, Alf, Mal, Power and Ken set out, trying another route climbing the north mountain of the cove. They didn't make it far before there was the sound of a curse, falling rocks and scrabbling hands. Mick hurriedly looked around. He saw that Ken Jones had taken a fall.

'I'm okay,' Ken called out.

But no one was taking chances and it was soon pretty clear that Ken's ankle wasn't in a good way. Sprained at least, maybe broken. Given they were only just above their makeshift camp the decision was made to send him back.

The rest of the rescue party sat tight and watched as he made his careful, halting way back down the cliff. His hands grasped at any small nook or piece of hardy shrubbery clinging to the rock. Once they had seen him safely arrive back at their camp they turned and refocused their attention on trying to find a way forward and up.

There was barely any talking, each man going to a place deep inside themselves where they could try to block out the all-consuming sickness, fatigue and pain. They just focused on each hand, each foot.

Looking over at Power, Mick saw that he was going downhill physically. It seemed he was going the same way as Cliff Langford. Mick thought about telling Power to turn around, but who was going to tell a man they couldn't try to save themselves? After all, wasn't that what Mick himself was doing?

Slowly they made tedious progress upwards. Not far from halfway to the top, Power was the next to fall. He landed with a sickening bone-crunching thud on a rock below.

'Shit, Mick, you all right, mate?'

They scrambled back down to him. Hearts pounding. Power was splayed across a rock. He stirred. The relief of seeing him move and the rise of his chest was short-lived, however. The groan that escaped told them it was serious.

Power slowly rolled himself over and gingerly manoeuvred himself into a sitting position. The others checked him over. It was pretty clear even to their untrained eyes that this infernal bay had gotten the best of this friendly, tough bruiser from Newcastle. They reckoned he had broken a rib.

Then, a hacking cough shook Power's body. He winced in pain. The cough brought up bright red blood that splattered onto the rocks at his feet. Shit, maybe it was worse than just a broken rib. A punctured lung? Whatever it was, it wasn't good.

After a short discussion, Mal McCarroll took Power's arm and helped him to his feet. With Power leaning his bulk on Mal, they too picked their way carefully back down, while Alf and Mick again turned back toward the cliff's edge, still so far above them.

They pushed on, but the further they went the worse the terrain became, steeper, with loose rocks and even thicker bush. Mick picked his hand and foot holds carefully. He didn't want to be the next one plunging back down. Maybe he wouldn't be so lucky. If a head rather than a torso smashed against the rocks it wouldn't be pretty.

Finally, the terrain beat them again.

'Let's head back,' Mick said. 'We'll take a break and rest for a day then try again.'

Alf and Mick turned back again, defeated.

After a careful downclimb they emerged from the scrub and eased themselves onto the coarse grass. As the men drew a collective breath, Alf noticed John Eagles. He was down near the water's edge, sitting in the rear of the life raft and staring out to sea.

Alf made his way over. 'You right, mate?'

A barely audible 'yes' came back.

Earlier that day, Mal McCarroll too had noticed John dragging himself uncomfortably back to the water and the remains of the raft. When he'd called out to him though he'd received a curt 'leave me alone'. So he'd left it at that.

Now, Alf turned around and made his slow way back to the grass with thoughts in mind of preparing their little patch for the night. It might only have been mid-afternoon, but he had nothing else to occupy himself. He felt as though he could have slept for a week solid, anyway. He started to gather up long grass and ferns, piling them together in an attempt to create some softness and warmth.

He gathered a rough nest of sorts from whatever foliage he could scrounge. Then he lay down and exhaustion overtook him again, and he fell into sleep. Every movement was an effort and needed recovery.

Mick sat down next to Ken Jones, who once again encouraged him to keep going, to never give up. Mick's arms and legs were crosshatched with scratches from bushes and rocks, and his feet were bruised and tender where they weren't skinned. The meagre protection of his self-styled raft 'shoes' was wholly inadequate for the hostile terrain.

'Bucko, have another go. See if you can't find anywhere we might be able to get out,' Jones encouraged him.

So, after a rest, Mick picked himself up again, turned his back on the ocean and looked at the landscape behind. He studied it, trying to see any weakness in it. Any small animal pad or break in the thick scrub. Any place that might be less formidable. But it was no use – it all looked as impenetrable as the rest. Still, he picked a new line and pulled his raft poncho tighter around him. He checked the knot on his rag-raft shoes and struck out again.

By now the day's exertions were catching up with him and Mick slipped and stumbled over hidden roots and rocks. His already low energy was drained and no amount of stumbling through the bush was going to open up a route out. It wasn't long before he turned back.

Desperate not to let Ken down, he felt the failure keenly. He knew many of the crew were in worse shape than him, knowledge that weighed heavily as he made the decision again to turn around. As he fought to retrace his footsteps, water dripped from branches and leaves. It landed on his bare face and arms, trickling down. His wet hair clung to his face and the ground underfoot was slick and sodden.

On his return, Mick reported another failed attempt and sat down. By now, it was around five o'clock. 'Let's batten down the hatches,' he said, exhausted.

Despite the late sun still glancing off the water in front of them, the rest of the crew were in agreement. After days at sea where real sleep was impossible, and their undernourished bodies sluggish and lethargic, sleep was now one of the few resources they had with which to restore themselves. They did what they could to make themselves comfortable.

As the others worked to establish whatever remnant of a bed they could, Mick picked his way slowly down to the water's edge to let John Eagles know they were all bunkering down. But John wasn't sitting in the remains of the raft, where he had been earlier. Moving closer, Mick's eyes caught sight of something moving in the water. The chief engineer was entirely still but for the movement of the waves.

Mick noticed John's overalls were set on a nearby rock. His body was stripped to underclothes. Mick wondered why, even as he took in the loss of another shipmate. A week ago, Mick had never seen death up close. Now he was staring it in the face for the second time in a matter of days. John Eagles had finally succumbed to the exhaustion and cold. The long, cauterised burn down his leg that he'd sustained in the death throes of the *Blythe Star* had only further drained his resources. Having finally made land, it had all caught up with him.

A World War II survivor, a man who loved opera and playing cards and tinkering with Land Rovers, was gone.

There was a family, a wife, kids, there were friends and shipmates he had sailed with who had no way of knowing that quietly, in a hidden corner of a small island, John Eagles had gone.

With no energy left for anything but practicality, and circumstances having hardened him to the brutalities of life, Mick walked closer.

I can't just leave him there, Mick thought.

Bending down, he put his hands under John's arms. Heaving, Mick pulled the man up onto the shoreline, pausing for breath and energy between each effort.

Further up the beach, Alf Simpson had woken up and was making his way down to check on the chief engineer also. His grim face registered the scene of young, 18-year-old Mick Doleman dressed in scraps of a raft, legs bare and blue-veined with cold, bodily dragging his dead crewmate to shore. He hurried over to help. Together, they managed to pull John Eagles' body behind one of the many large rocks on the shoreline in an attempt to protect it from the sea. It was all they could do.

Turning away, both men silently made their way back up the shore.

When they reached the others they told them what had happened. The weight of the news settled over the scene. Another man taken. Who would be next? As this question rattled around in their brains it felt as though the cliffs surrounding them were closing in, the austere immovable rock hemming them into this nightmare.

Already the air was chill, and the eight living crew members of the *Blythe Star* huddled together again for warmth. The cold was wrapped around them and penetrated their bones. The chill damp of the ground beneath crept up into them.

The cold seemed more acute tonight. The raft might have been a miserable prison, but at least the domed canopy had preserved some tiny modicum of their body heat and kept the wind off them. Without it, the sea wind danced across their freezing bare flesh and every wisp of body warmth evaporated into the night air.

After their ordeal at sea and the exertions of the day the men were practically comatose. They slipped into something that could have been sleep or delirium. But even when their eyes were closed and their minds drifting, somehow the cold was still there. Even sleep brought no relief.

As they drifted off Mick listened. He heard nothing. No sound besides the regular crashing of the waves over the life raft and the hiss as each wave retreated. The rest was absolute and complete silence. No distant hum of a car or plane, no voice carried to them on the breeze. It was deadly quiet.

Night crept over the men. From time to time the silence was shattered as one or other yelled out in their sleep. Dreams mixed with delirium and their nonsensical exclamations were the only noises aside from the ocean echoing around the bay.

The night dragged on. Each time Mick came to, the cold would hit him again and he would long for morning and the movement and relative warmth it would bring.

Sometime in the small hours, Mal McCarroll stirred. Huddled together as they were, each man's movement was felt by those around him. In the darkness, not entirely in the present, he thought he saw Ken Jones get up. Assuming he was just off for a wee or to get some water – a rare luxury they couldn't have imagined 48 hours earlier – Mal huddled closer to the man beside him and let the oblivion of sleep take him again.

CHAPTER 15

It's Over

Sunday, 21 October 1973 – Maatsuyker Island

It was another blustery grey day on Maatsuyker Island when Tony Parsey heard the distinctive thumping roar of a helicopter approaching. The keepers and their families dropped what they were doing and came out to watch as the aircraft descended and carefully settled its heavy belly on land.

A man jumped out and made his way over. Reaching them, he explained that he was from the Commonwealth Lighthouse Service. He had in his hand some pictures of the *Blythe Star* to show Tony, to check whether this ship really did match the one he'd seen.

Tony knew the moment the images were handed over. That was the ship, the one he'd seen making heavy weather of it more than a week earlier.

'That's it,' Tony said confidently. He saw panic wash over the man's face.

Shit. This information, information that had been largely ignored and set aside days ago, was actually critical information.

The man didn't stay long, realising there was nothing to be gained by staying for a cup of tea. With a whirl of wind, the helicopter rose and was gone.

Once again, Tony was gobsmacked that it had taken this long for someone to make their way out to visit with a photo. The misunderstanding that had sent them on a wild goose chase up the east coast could so easily have been avoided if they had taken the short flight to the island a week ago. It beggared belief, really.

But the rhythm of life on the island continued. The lantern still needed lighting, weather observations still needed to be taken, food prepared and maintenance done. So Tony went back to work. But the vision of that ship, almost submarine-like, stayed with him as crisp and clear as the day he saw it.

*　*　*

Sunday, 21 October 1973 – Doveton

It seemed impossible to Joanie that more than a week had passed since that carefree night of her birthday, when cake and cream were flying. It was a week of not knowing where Mick was or if he would be back.

The days had dragged by. Each morning Joanie would wake and refuse to let herself think that Mick was dead. Instead, she'd tell herself that today was the day he'd be found. How can a big ship like that just disappear? Today would be the day they'd find it. Mick was a fighter. Joanie was used to seeing him at a music concert in some scrap or other. The fighter in him would get him through.

But the gnawing emptiness in her stomach, the heaviness in her limbs and the tightness of her chest held the fear she refused to acknowledge. The fear that maybe he wasn't coming back. Maybe she would never know. Never say goodbye.

She'd speak to him, hoping that maybe, wherever he was, he might feel her thoughts flying through the wind to him. 'Where are you?' she would say. 'People are worried about you. We want you to come home.'

But no amount of pleading brought an answer. The simple act of getting through the day seemed hard, she felt like she was barely functioning. Her mind was foggy and drifting, random thoughts and memories of Mick floating through. The not knowing was like a weight that was always there. Inescapable.

Around her in Doveton, Joanie could see the hope fading from other people's eyes. She could see their expressions change as they tried to reconcile themselves to the thought that larger-than-life, friend-of-everybody Mick might not be coming home.

Where there had been long discussions about where they might find the ship, now there were declarations that the ship must have sunk.

But at the Doleman house, Mick's dad was as belligerent as ever that his son was not gone. Buoyed by Tommy's certainty, Joanie would think, *Okay, another day has gone by. It's not looking that good, but tomorrow is another day and there'll be some good news.*

At Mick's house, every time they heard the phone ring it set everyone's heart racing. Maybe this was the call that would bring news. Maybe it would be the call to tell them the ship was fine. Maybe Mick would be on the line.

Being at Mick's house Joanie felt closer to him, not to mention she didn't know where else to go. Sunday found Joanie again in Mick's living room. The usual fog of smoke hung low under the ceiling, the television on, tuned to the news, of course.

The newsreader started to introduce the item on the still-missing *Blythe Star*. Everyone hushed each other and the chatter died down. The crisp, clipped tones of a news reporter broadcast to the anxious crowd gathered in the Doleman living room.

Everyone took a moment to comprehend what the reporter was saying. Tomorrow would be the last day they would look for the *Blythe Star*. The search for the ship was being called off. The search for Mick was over. The best the authorities could do was announce a marine inquiry to try to get some answers about what had gone wrong.

The report ended and the newsreader moved on to the other stories of the day, oblivious to the bombshell going off in a lounge room in the tight-knit community of Doveton.

IT'S OVER

The silence was complete. You could have heard a pin drop. Everyone looked at each other, uncomprehending. Surely they must have it wrong? The authorities would have rung them, would have told them. Wouldn't they?

Waves of anger broke over the scene. Tommy stormed to the phone to find out if it were true. When he received official confirmation, everyone could feel the emotion radiating off him.

Many of those there that night may have suspected that the ship was gone, but to hear it announced on the news had a finality that hit them like a sucker punch. Mick was gone and wouldn't be coming back.

Joanie took the news like a physical hit to her body. Her body shook and tears flowed down her cheeks. Looking around, she could see her distress mirrored in the people gathered. They were bound together in their grief.

Joanie and Mick's family clung to each other, trying to seek solace from one another, knowing they couldn't escape the crushing truth that the phone call had brought careering into the house. The tear-streaked faces of the people who loved Mick showed the depth of their love and their loss.

After days of insisting that Mick would come home, his mum, Clara, finally accepted that he was gone. The knowledge that she had lost a child shredded her insides, the pain physical and debilitating. The world ceased to make sense in that moment.

Then, as people processed the news, anger started radiating out through the room.

'Why would they do that?'

'There were ten men on that ship. Why would they call it off so early?'

They were angry, unanswerable questions about a situation over which they had no control. In the end, whatever they thought, they had to accept it. Finally, that last glimmer of hope – the lingering 'what ifs' were dead. Mick was dead.

Through her tears, Joanie heard Mick's dad, Tommy. 'Mick's coming home. He's not gone.'

'Tommy, you've given us lots of hope through this, but I've got to tell you I'm starting to agree with everybody else. He's not coming back,' Joanie said to him gently.

'Well, I'm not giving up, Joanie,' Tommy said, refusing to back down. He was furious. That the search had been called off. That people would accept Mick was gone. That any of this could have happened in the first place. But he was certain that Mick was coming home.

Joanie left Tommy to it. She could sense the enormous well of anger in him.

As the news reverberated through the small community of Doveton, the town went into mourning. No one knew what to do with themselves, so they gathered at the Dolemans' place and shared their shock, trying to support the family as best they could.

* * *

IT'S OVER

Sunday, 21 October 1973 – Crib Point, Mornington Peninsula

In households across the country the people who loved those ten men who had sailed from Hobart on the *Blythe Star* were hearing the news that the search was being called off.

In Crib Point on the Mornington Peninsula, 16-year-old Robyn, who had returned home from her Aunty Pattie's, and had only opened her dad Alf's birthday card days earlier, listened as her mum answered the phone in the living room.

'No, no – why?'

Robyn heard her mother Kit's distressed voice. The sound was chilling. 'What's wrong, Mum? What's happening?' she asked.

'They've called off the search for your father. We have to presume he's dead,' her mother said, delivering to her child one of the hardest messages a mother can give.

Robyn ran to her and wrapped her arms around her mother in a hug that could express what words couldn't.

Looking down the barrel of a totally new life – one without her husband, a single mother – Kit did what she had to. Picking up the phone she started calling around to break the news.

Then she made a call to start organising a memorial service. The authorities had advised her on the phone that, now the crew were considered dead, it would be best to have a memorial. For the sake of the family. Let them grieve. There were no bodies and there wouldn't be any, so they should hold a service to have some closure. Let people move on.

Robyn's world had morphed into a surreal dream. She walked around on automatic pilot, her body present but her mind somewhere else. People would come around and she'd barely even know they were there, so consumed was she by her grief.

It didn't get much more concrete than the black and white text of the advertisement in the paper for Alf's memorial.

* * *

Monday, 22 October 1973 – Deep Glen Bay, Day 10

Light crept past the towering rocks that stood sentinel over the bay that held the last of the *Blythe Star*'s crew. Opening their eyes, the men saw a grey sky stretching above them. Their first thoughts were of escape and they began to gather their dwindled reserves for another attempt to find a way out. But the mental battle of keeping their bodies going, their muscles moving, of getting up and trying again after the repeated failures of the day before was enough to break the strongest of men.

'Where's Ken?' Mick asked as he tried to breathe some warmth into his frozen and clumsy limbs. Mal McCarroll recalled vaguely that he'd seen Ken get up in the night – presumably for a wee.

Someone looked up and then pointed across to a hunched figure near the water. 'He's over there, on that rock.'

IT'S OVER

Mick's muscles creaked into action as he made his way over. There was Ken, cardigan taken off and folded neatly beside him, sitting on the rock looking out to sea. Except his eyes wouldn't see ever again. His face was turned to the horizon, his skin cool. That wander in the early hours of the morning had been his last. Finally, exhaustion had taken him too.

Mick couldn't compute what he was seeing. This wasn't the way it was meant to go. Ken had been the one always reassuring, encouraging, certain they would make it out. He had been the backbone of the group. His leadership had stopped them from crumbling each time fate dealt them another blow. His sheer force of will had kept them going when all they wanted to do was lie down, give up and let the ocean claim them.

Of all the men in that raft, Ken was the one person Mick would have laid money on to make it out. Seeing him propped there peacefully, as though he had been frozen in the act of sitting and enjoying a morning cuppa as he looked out at the view, Mick was deeply shaken.

If these circumstances could take Ken, then what did that mean for the rest of them?

Ken's words of the day before echoed in his mind. *Make another go, Bucko. Never give up until you're dead.* The words had a new, horrifying reality.

As Mick tried to comprehend this new reality, he noticed the similarity of Ken's and John Eagles' deaths. Both appeared to have stripped down before succumbing to the grasping hands of death that were coming for them. Mick would find out years later that this wasn't as unusual as it seemed. In fact, it had a name – 'paradoxical undressing'. Not entirely understood, it is believed that when the body's core temperature falls so low, the brain makes the fatal error of mistaking extreme cold for heat, and a person's final act is to strip off whatever last protection they have from the cold that is systematically shutting down their body.

Finally, having made land and losing the meagre shelter of the raft canopy, the cold had come for Ken in the night. Added to which, it seems the acute stress of living in the raft may have actually played a role in keeping the men alive. The fight or flight stress response would have raised their blood pressure and heart rate, keeping their bodies primed for any lifesaving action that might be needed.

When they had finally made land and the stimulus for that fight or flight response was removed, the chances are that the men experienced a drop in blood pressure and heart rate. In a person severely dehydrated, fatigued and cold, this is not good. The effects could be so extreme as to send the body into a state of shock, which could be fatal.

When search and rescuers in extreme environments find people who have been fighting for survival for days, sometimes they will keep the person frightened and moving until they can get them to medical help, to stop their body relaxing and falling into that lethal shock.

Standing there on the shore, the one secure thing he'd had to hang onto in this ordeal stripped away, Mick didn't know any of this. He just knew that, after all they'd been through, time had run out for Ken Jones and John Eagles.

The death of Ken reverberated around the group. That this man, their leader, could die, shattered them all. He had 'bullied, sweet-talked, ordered and helped' them all. It was a lonely and frightening feeling to think that they could all die on this isolated little beach and no one might ever know what had happened to them. The cruel joke of letting them make land, only to let them all die.

Just as they had with John Eagles, gentle hands lifted Ken Jones and pulled him further up the shoreline, away from the sea that might come to claim him.

Mick was heartbroken. But that feeling was a luxury for men in less desperate situations. Because, before them all still was the seemingly insurmountable task of getting the hell out of that place, before they all went the same way.

Mick looked at Ken's cardigan, sitting neatly on the rocks. He was sure Ken would have damn well told him to take it. So Mick picked it up and slid his arms into it. Any protection from the elements was vital. Now more than ever.

Ken might have died, but Mick decided he was bloody well going to get out. For Ken. For the crewmates he was looking at who were only days, or hours behind Ken.

That afternoon, Mick forced himself up for another attempt. He set off again to battle the bush and incline that hemmed them in. As he looked back down to their camp, he could see the bright splash of the sliced orange raft that Mal had laid out on the grass earlier to add to the life jackets on the rocks in the hope it would attract the attention of any passing sea traffic or plane.

But the slice of ocean showing at the mouth of the bay was empty and the stretch of sky above them remained silent. The men wondered if anyone was still out there searching for them.

Sometime during the day, George Cruikshank came stumbling back onto the beach. Having been away overnight, he reached the grass and fell to the ground. The others noted his return, but no one had the strength left to ask him where he'd been.

As the day started to close, Mick too returned to the beach. This time the faces he returned to were fewer and sicker than the day before.

They barely spoke before all turning in again for another endless, horrifying night. As they lay there, the cold seeping into them, they couldn't help but wonder who would be left come morning. Would they all be there? Or would they get their escape from this bay the way John Eagles and Ken Jones had? Those who danced with delirium were already speaking to the families they would leave behind. The rest fell into exhausted sleep with their family's faces floating before their eyes.

* * *

Tuesday, 23 October 1973 – Deep Glen Bay, Day 11

As the search ended, Tuesday's skies were free from aircraft scouring the ocean for the missing ship. As families tried

IT'S OVER

to accept and comprehend their new reality, navigating the craters in their life where their men had been, the remaining crew of the *Blythe Star* sheltering in the bay on Tasmania's east coast had no idea that they were believed dead. It was just as well. It might just have pushed them over the edge, an edge they were dancing along as it was.

Instead, they had endured another grim night, the loss of Ken Jones taunting in the darkness, the cold reminding them that they were just a hair trigger away from going the same way.

Alf Simpson woke up just as the sun peeped above the horizon. In those few moments he knew with crystal clarity that if they didn't get out today, they would die in this place. He woke the others, dreading as he did so that they too might have died in the night. Mick woke feeling sombre with the same thought echoing in his head. He and Mal started to talk about their prospects.

'If we don't get out it's over,' Mal said.

'We're going to walk out,' Mick responded. 'And we'll keep going until we either die trying or get help.'

They both knew that doing nothing would be a death sentence.

Alf came over to where they had their heads bent together, discussing. 'What are you two up to?' he asked.

'Alf, we're going to walk out,' Mick said. 'We're going to head out and we're going to keep going until we find someone, or someone finds us, or we fail.'

Alf immediately said he was in. But Mick and Mal were unsure. Alf was a fair bit older than them, and he wasn't a light fellow. Mick knew from his many attempts, that pushing through the bush was hard enough for his frame – let alone the bulk of Alf.

But again he thought, *Who am I to stop him from wanting to save himself?* In any case, Alf wasn't going to accept staying behind. There was no stopping him. He was coming.

'Look, we're not turning back this time,' Mick said, to be crystal clear. 'We'll get out of it one way or another – either by success or failure.' They didn't need to spell out what escaping through failure meant.

So, they took the knife back down to the raft and cut strips off it again, crafting more makeshift shoes and coverings. Prepared as much as they could be, they went back to where the other four were lying on the grass. They told them that they were headed out and would be back with help.

They didn't talk about what would happen if they didn't come back. They didn't have to. Everyone knew it was crunch time. This was their last chance. A chance that was walking away on the backs of Mick, Mal and Alf, their feet wrapped in bright orange raft material and temporary raft ponchos flapping around their shoulders.

Pausing to take stock, Mick felt the responsibility heavily. Mick Power's six-foot-five bulk was like a dead weight strewn across the ground. He was looking seriously unwell and was still bringing up blood. Cliff Langford was barely among the living. Gaunt, he'd lost three stone in weight and his mind was no longer with the others.

There was a calmness to knowing they had come to the end of the line. A simplicity. There were no more choices to be made – just one path forward. All the backup plans had been exhausted. There were only two outcomes now – make it out on this attempt or die.

It was around ten in the morning when the three men turned their backs on the sorry scene and struck out into the bush. They were beyond hope at this stage. All they had was a steely determination that this would be the time they found help.

Not many people face their mortality in such a close and confronting manner, but as 18-year-old Mick stared it down, he didn't flinch. He thought of the four souls relying on him. He thought of Ken Jones. Of Joanie and his family. And he forced himself to keep putting one foot in front of the other.

It's inexplicable why, when people are pushed to extremes of endurance, they will do something selfless to help another, even a stranger. Mick hadn't known these men two weeks ago, and yet now he was prepared to die trying to get them and himself help.

The men headed south, clambering and climbing the sheer rise. Their hands were quickly tender and scratched from grasping at roots and branches as they tried to haul themselves upwards. Each time some plant would give way under them and they fell back, they would pick themselves up, reach up again and zero their thoughts in on one step. Just one step.

One step more.

And one step more.

Hours passed, and they'd progressed just a hundred metres. But slowly, putting one foot in front of the other, they climbed upward. The lip of the cliffs inched closer.

Finally, they managed what had seemed impossible during their relentless efforts the day before. The ground started to level and they realised they had made it to the rim of the bowl that hemmed in the strewn men waiting below. They were out!

Once they reached the top, it wasn't over though. The land simply plunged up and down in savage undulations.

Mick had never before seen bush as thick as this. He had no comprehension that undergrowth so dense could exist. They heaved their tired, battered, aching bodies up onto scrub so thick it was like a mattress under them. Gingerly their weight would rest on the bracken, bauera and a particular scrubby tree, which has been the bane of Tasmanian bushwalkers and explorers across decades. Unable to push through it, they would take a few cautious steps on top of this hostile tangle before their weight sent them plunging through the tenuous mat. As they fell back down, the scrub would rise up to ensnare them, the mauling branches lacerating their skin. And the process would start again, as they dragged their exhausted bodies upward to try to get on top of the scrub so they could move forward. They would try to spread their weight so they could pull themselves out and over rather than plunge through again.

IT'S OVER

Alf, with his additional body weight, had a harder time of it. He fell through more frequently and found it harder to pull himself out. He was forced to push his way through smaller holes that Mick and Mal could duck and weave their way through. But he just gritted his teeth and kept going. The pain at least let them know they were still alive. Each scratch on their exposed and tender skin was a reminder that they were breathing, their heart beating and spirit kicking.

Still, as they battled their way through the scrub, so often unable to see the ground beneath their feet, Mick kept expecting them to plunge off the cliffs that he knew weren't far. He imagined the bush opening and revealing nothing but air beneath them as they took a wrong step.

With no way to know where they were headed, and no knowledge of the landscape around them they pulled themselves forward aimlessly, trying for a rescue they had no idea how to find. But as long as they were still moving, they were in with a chance. They kept the coast to their left the whole time, the sound of the waves crashing their guide and compass.

The three exhausted men barely spoke to each other. All that was in their minds was whether they could help those men lying in the bay. The going was brutal, but they knew that to go back was suicide.

Each metre was hard fought for. They would dedicate hours to their meagre progress only to hit a block, a cliff or drop or impassable section, and they'd have to turn around and battle their way back again, before they could turn around and try again with another route.

By 6 pm they had come to a dense rainforest. Mick had thought forest this impenetrable only existed in the tropics. They knew they didn't have long before the sun would disappear and there was no way they could continue in the dark. They risked plunging off a cliff or walking in circles if they tried.

But when Alf floated the idea of finding somewhere to bed down for the night, Mick and Mal replied, 'We can't sleep here.'

'We can't go any further today,' Alf said firmly.

They were all battered, bloodied and bruised. Their depleted bodies had been sucked dry of any energy. God only knew what fuel their bodies were running on. So Mick and Mal accepted Alf's wisdom and looked for some place they might curl up for the night.

Alf called out shortly after. He had found a hollow tree that would do as well as a tent for them.

With the light fading the three men made themselves ready for another night out in the open. They pulled ferns, gathering armfuls to take with them as they crawled into the hollow of the tree. Curling up together, ferns scattered over them, they tried to hold onto the warmth from each other. Exhaustion sank into them as night settled on the bush around them.

Before sleep overtook them, they couldn't help but think of the four men they'd left behind at the bay. Were they still four? Or had the day claimed another? They knew Cliff Langford and Mick Power were in a very rough way, and the others not too far behind. Was another night going to be one too many? They knew, too, that they didn't have much more left in them. One night the cold would come for them and they would no longer have the energy to fight it.

Huddled together as they were, rain drops whispered through the leaves. The distant sound of the ocean called to them.

The wet clung to everything and seemed to seep up from the very soil they lay on, the accumulated spongy mat of fallen and composted tree. Curling into a tighter ball, Mick again tried to hold every bit of warmth he could.

CHAPTER 16

You're All Dead

Wednesday, 24 October 1973 – Hobart

The morning was cool and fine in New Town, Hobart. Twenty-nine-year-old Rod Smith was up early – you had to be if you worked for yourself. No one else was going to make your money for you. Stocky, with the muscles of a man accustomed to physical labour, Rod was a logging contractor, an old-school Tasmanian. He worked hard for his family – his wife, Heather, and a young son and a daughter just a few months old.

Rod swung himself up into the cab of his red Ford logging truck. The engine rumbled into life, the chugging vibrations reverberating through the cab. Taking hold of the steering wheel, Rob eased the truck onto the road and started the two-hour drive to his logging coupe, where he'd marked up the trees he'd fell that day.

Cruising contentedly, the black road slipping beneath the wheels of his truck, Rod was happy with his own company.

Just as well – the life of a solo logging contractor was a solitary one. There were people who said Rod was crazy for working by himself in remote parts of the Tasmanian bush wielding chainsaws and heavy machinery, but Rod was a pragmatic kind of man. 'Somebody standing beside me isn't going to stop me getting killed. It's as simple as that,' Rod would answer.

Foresting was in Rod's blood. He came from a timber family and had learned from his dad the right way to go about things. 'You do it properly today, you can come back tomorrow and keep doing it,' his dad told him. 'Don't do it right today, don't bother coming back tomorrow.'

It was a lesson that had stuck with Rod, when, as a child, he learned from his grandfather and father to cut timber using a two-ended cross-cut saw, axe and wedges. He learned the technique of how to read a tree, to see where it would fall, control it and read the colour of the sawdust coming from the cut. Long before he ever touched a chainsaw, he knew how to control a tree's fall and knew that if you couldn't do that you might as well walk out of the bush and not come back because you'd be an accident waiting to happen. Rod was proud of his timber pedigree.

Out here in the bush he was comfortable, in a way someone from the city never would be. Much like Mick, who loved sea life for the self-sufficiency, where it was just you and your commonsense to work things out, Rod was used to getting himself out of trouble. Out in the bush it was just you and a very long walk if you needed backup. Rod knew just about every bush repair trick for his truck's engine, all administered alongside some stern talkings-to. The old red Ford had had its fair share of curses and cajoling.

Rod made his way to the Tasman Peninsula, pulled off the main road and headed down to the logging tracks that wove through the bush. Leaving the tarmac behind, the going became rough, the road unsealed, with slick mud and holes that looked like they might swallow a small car in places. Rod's truck grunted and growled as they rumbled along.

It had been wet lately, and Rod had shifted logging coupes to somewhere less prone to bog. He had given up on Yellow Bluff for the moment and gone somewhere that was still accessible in the slick wet. That morning, though, the windscreen wipers were still. It looked like he might be able to eat his lunch out of the truck cab today.

He'd spent enough time out in the bush to welcome the fine weather. He knew more than most how horrendous the landscape could become in the wet. Steep gullies, slick underfoot and soaking, dense scrub you had a job to struggle through. No, best to pick a spot to focus on that was easier to get through until things dried out a bit.

Rod had come across snippets of the news in the paper and on the telly about the missing ship the *Blythe Star*. He'd heard that they were calling off the search. Those poor buggers. But he hadn't thought much more about it. He was up early and home late, working hard all the hours between for six or seven days a week.

A touch after eight, Rod's truck hissed to a stop and he swung down from the cab to stretch his muscles from the drive. He walked over to take a look at the trees he'd picked out the day before. It wasn't long before the whine of the big, heavy chainsaw tearing through the trees cut through the bush around, followed by a crunching crash as each tree hit the deck. Once Rod had a few trees down he started the dozer and warmed it up. Next up, he got a rope around each tree and dragged it back to where it could be loaded into the truck.

Pausing for morning tea, Rod sipped coffee from his Thermos before getting on with cutting the timber to length. Tree by tree, slowly the day's load built up on the truck, which settled lower to the ground under the weight.

As lunch approached his stomach growled. Rod pulled out his Saladas with Vegemite and margarine, a little cup of diced peaches and some mixed cordial. It was peaceful sitting there in the silence of the bush, the odd wren hopping past, hoping one of the crumbs would fall from his lunch. A good day.

Rod was hungry and soon he'd polished off everything. By mid-afternoon, he was finishing and ready for the drive back to the timber yards to unload his haul and head for home. He went through his usual routine before he headed out, checking the bulldozer's diesel, oil and water so he was set for the next day.

Rod screwed off the radiator cap and set it to the side on the dozer. Then he went to get some water out of a drum to top up the radiator. But when he came back, he saw that the cap was no longer where he had left it. Irritated, he realised that the idling dozer must have shaken it off. Thinking that the cap had just dropped down over the side, he got on with filling up the radiator with water. He'd pick the cap up in a moment.

When the radiator was full, Rod looked around for the radiator cap, but couldn't see it. His frustration mounted and he switched the machine off and looked again, poking around in the dirt and looking under the bulldozer. He started the dozer back up and moved it backward, before walking around to check the ground where it had been. For half an hour he cast about for the radiator cap. *It bloody has to be here somewhere*, he thought. *It can't have just disappeared.*

Eventually, seriously ticked off, Rod admitted defeat. He'd just have to get another one to replace it. He packed up the last of his things, swung up into the truck and turned it over. Then he started the long, grinding drive back out of the forest.

Rod's truck might have had all the mod cons, but in the era before power steering he wrestled with the wheel, leveraging his whole body against it as he navigated the rough track. As he drove he kept a keen eye out to make sure he avoided the holes that were big enough to do serious damage and that he didn't slip entirely off the side of the track. At points the truck was waist-deep in mud, the differential dragging through the muck.

When Rod reached a little flow of water called Blackman's Creek, he pulled up and jumped out to check the load. It was a little routine of his from time to time. He'd check all his logs were still secure and then spend a few minutes watching the little mountain trout swimming about in the creek. Some days he'd feed them the crumbs of his lunch. But as he'd polished it all off that day, the fish would have to fend for themselves.

Then the long steep climb out began. The truck was now in low gear, crawling along at about ten kilometres an hour, sometimes dropping to a slow walk in parts. The rocking and rolling and creaking and banging of the truck was almost hypnotic – it could just about rock you to sleep after the day's efforts. Rod knew that wouldn't happen, but when he hit these steep pinches he would always lean over the steering wheel to put his weight forward in the truck so it didn't succumb to gravity and plunge backward with its heavy load.

As he approached the top of the hill he started to ease back into his seat, relaxing as the slope eased off. He started to change up the gears as the truck picked up speed after its slow crawl. Rod drove toward a junction in the road – as he went through there was a slight turn to the right. Easing the truck around he squinted at the unexpected sight before him.

Ripping his foot off the accelerator he pumped the brakes – stopping a logging truck loaded to the hilt wasn't an easy task.

What on earth was going on here?

* * *

Wednesday, 24 October 1973 – In the bush, Day 12

As Rod had been having his breakfast and warming his truck up in the cool air that morning, Mick, Alf and Mal stirred in their damp and cold tree hollow. Their whole bodies ached from the exertions of the day before. They dared not look at the state of their feet beneath the raft wrappings. The throbbing ache was enough to tell them they didn't want to know what was happening under there. Especially when they knew they would have to get up and keep walking again that morning.

The thirst that had dogged them for days in the raft was clawing at their throats again. They lowered their faces to moss that covered the logs and branches around them, sucking off whatever moisture they could from the plants to try to satiate their thirst. Then they picked themselves up and figured they better keep moving. It wasn't like there was breakfast and a cuppa to linger over and enjoy. Just cold and wet ground and foliage dripping on them. It would be better to be moving to try to generate some warmth in their stiff limbs.

Again they forced their way through the seemingly impenetrable rainforest. They kept to their original course, the coast more or less in sight to their left. Slowly, step after step marked their progress through the day. Having at least escaped the basin of the bay, they made better progress that morning than they had the previous day.

At around 11 am, they were looking ahead when they noticed what seemed to be a thinning of the bush. They pushed forward a little faster and found what appeared to be an old logging slide. It was the first indication of human activity they'd seen for days, a reminder that they weren't alone out there. Somewhere, if they could hang on long enough, there were other people, families waiting with warm houses and soft beds.

The slide had been carved through the thick bush, so they took the easy passage it offered and followed it downhill. Finally, they could walk without being dragged back every step by unwilling foliage. Able to move more freely, they made fast time to the bottom. There, at the end of the slide, was what looked to be an old logging trail, rough dirt and gravel carving through the bush. They stared at it. Should they go left or right?

Literally facing a fork in the road with seven lives hanging in the balance, they made a choice. They went right. With only a vague idea about where they were, it was the best guess they could make that it might get them to civilisation. Their guts said right, so they went right.

Alf headed off first to get a head start while the other two caught their breath for a moment. The larger man was a touch slower, so Mick and Mal said they'd catch him up.

Their shadows shortened as the sun passed overhead. By early afternoon they were dragging themselves footstep by footstep along the road. Mick was walking beside Mal, with Alf out of sight around a bend ahead.

Mick paused for a moment, holding his breath. 'Mal, did you just hear what I just heard?' he asked.

'Yeah, I think so.'

'I'm bloody sure it's a truck,' Mick said, excitement flooding through him and animating his tired voice. 'Whatever we do, we don't want to scare this bloke off.'

Mick was already war gaming this moment. They couldn't afford to let it slip past. Blind Freddy could see that they made an unconventional sight. They had a quick conversation and stepped back slightly into the dense undergrowth on either side. They didn't want whoever was coming to have too much notice they were there in case they gunned it at the sight of their odd appearance.

They waited, every nerve in their bodies taut as they listened to the crunching of a truck changing gears, its throaty grumble getting closer. After twelve days without speaking to another human aside from their shipmates, the sound of another human life seemed almost surreal. Their attention was now totally focused on the sound inching toward them.

Inside the truck, Rod was leaning forward over the steering wheel, willing it to keep rolling forward up the hill. When he reached the crest, he eased back into his seat and made his way through the junction. He was coasting around the right-hand bend when he saw the last thing he expected.

Out of the undergrowth sprang two young men. Dirty, scratched, and dressed in what almost looked to be rags, they had jumped from the undergrowth and raced to his truck, jumping onto the side grabbing any purchase they could.

Rod pulled up and tentatively wound his window down – not all the way mind you, just enough to have a conversation.

He was a big-hearted bloke, but still there was something not right about all this and he didn't want anyone forcing their way inside.

'You're not going to believe me. I bet you don't know where we're from,' Mick blurted out.

'You look like you're escaped convicts,' Rod replied.

'We're off the *Blythe Star*,' Mick said, desperate for this logger to know they needed help.

'No you're not,' Rod fired back. 'They're dead. They've shut the search down and everything.'

'We are, we're off the *Blythe Star*,' Mick insisted. 'We've been floating about for a week and only made it to shore a few days ago. There's another bloke just up the road. We need to get the authorities to go and get our mates. There's a few of them down in the bush.'

Rod had a pretty keen sensor for bullshit and there was no mistaking the earnest desperation of Mick and Mal. And Rod had seen their faces sink and their bodies slump slightly when it hit the two men that the search had been called off. So he popped the door and told them to hop in. The two-person bench seat beside him might just have been the most comfortable thing Mick ever sat on as he and Mal slid inside. The big red truck growled as Rod put it into gear and eased forward.

Mal spoke over the engine. 'Mate, who won the Caulfield Cup?' he asked.

Bloody hell, mate, Mick thought. *We've just survived hell and all you want to know is who won the Caulfield Cup?*

As the truck jolted round the next bend, Alf was revealed. He was looking at the red truck like it was Jesus Christ himself. Disbelieving and delighted, he rushed over to see Mick and Mal already ensconced on the front seat. 'I'll get on the back,' he called to Rod.

'You won't get on the back,' Rod replied. There was no way he was having someone riding on the back with a load of logs out there on that rough road. It would be a bad look to rescue the survivors of the *Blythe Star* just to kill them on the drive out under a load of shifting timber.

'Get in the front,' he said.

So Alf heaved his solid bulk up into the cab. Mick and Mal scooted across, squeezing right over to the gearbox. It might have been a two-seater on spec, but they got three in it that day and no one was complaining.

Mal asked if Rod had a cigarette – twelve days was a bloody long time to go without a light, cold turkey, for a smoker.

'I've only got menthol cigarettes, or I've got some rollies,' Rod said.

'A rollie will do.'

Rod handed over a pack of tobacco, and after rolling a light, Mal dragged deeply. With the smoke curling around the cab, Rod fished around in the glovebox for anything else he could give them. He apologised that he didn't have any lunch to share with them and explained that usually he would, but that day it had all gone – not even the brown trout had got a crumb. 'All I've got are these,' he said, pulling some mints out of the glovebox.

It might as well have been a gourmet five-course meal to the starving seafarers, who accepted the mints gratefully and devoured them. As they wrapped their teeth around the lollies, the jolting ride back to civilisation began and they got talking.

Mal said he was from Launceston.

'Whereabouts in Launceston?' Rod asked – as you do in Tasmania, a place that operates on who you know.

When Mal replied that he lived in a suburb called Invermay, Rod shot back, 'You might know my cousin, Ashley Hall.'

'Yeah! I know Ashley well,' Mal exclaimed. 'I live just down the road from him!'

It was a very Tasmanian rescue.

Introductions done, Mick, Mal and Alf shared some of their ordeal with Rod, telling him again about the desperation of the four men waiting on the beach where they'd washed up in a pretty bad way. Their number-one priority was to call the authorities and get someone down there to collect the others before it was too late for them – if it wasn't already.

Listening to them Rod thought to himself, *They're tough bastards this lot.* He told them he'd get them to Dunalley, where they could make calls to whoever they needed. He was thinking of the police station there, which was the closest. That would be the best place to get them to, and quick smart.

'Sorry I can't go any faster,' Rod apologised, 'I dare not otherwise we'll bust something on the truck and then we'll never get out.'

Even so, he pushed the truck to its limits, driving as hard as he could to get these lads out. As he steered the others filled him in on the ordeal since the ship sank. He was open-mouthed at the deaths, the missed opportunities, the Japanese fishing vessel that seemed to have turned away at their distress signal. Rod could barely believe what he was hearing.

It wouldn't hit him until later, when he looked back on it all, that things might have turned out very differently were it not for that radiator cap. The one that disappeared without a trace. The one he'd spent half an hour looking for. Without that cap missing, without that time wasted, he might never have come across those three men. He would have been gone and driving happily back to town when they scrambled out of the bush. And God only knows what would have happened to them then.

Finally, the truck made the slow turn out of the dirt logging track and onto the tarmac road. As they rolled into the small settlement of Murdunna, Rod asked if they wanted to stop there. He recalled a phone box they could use. But the three crew members said they'd rather go through to Dunalley like Rod had said, and make it to the police station.

Ten or fifteen minutes later, the logging truck rumbled into the tiny fishing town. The brakes hissed as Rod pulled up outside the police station. Leaving the engine idling he got out of the cab and went over. He banged on the door and waited. Then he banged again.

Looking around he tried again, with no response. *Well, this is great*, he thought. *What do I do now?*

Deciding the post office was their next best bet, Rod went back to the truck and told the fellas that the copper wasn't home. Then he eased forward just up the road before pulling up outside a little old weatherboard building.

'I've got some survivors from the *Blythe Star* in my truck,' Rod said to the postmistress behind the counter. 'We need to contact some people because the rest of them are down on the shore.'

The postmistress was wide-eyed with surprise. But she jumped into action and was all business, pulling every plug out of the switchboard, entirely shutting down the phones so they were at Rod's disposal 'Who do you want to call?' she asked.

'Well, first of all I need to call the police at Sorell. There's nobody home at Dunalley.'

The postmistress quickly connected the call and passed the receiver to Rod, who gave his name to the desk sergeant on the other end. 'I'm a truck driver, and I was coming out of Murdunna with a load of logs on and I picked up some survivors of the *Blythe Star*.'

'Picked up who?' asked the desk sergeant.

It didn't take long for Rod to realise this desk sergeant didn't have a bloody clue what he was talking about. *There's a police officer and he doesn't know what the* Blythe Star *is? For God's sake!* thought Rod. He took a deep breath. 'Put me onto somebody I can talk to,' Rod said, in a voice that made it clear he wasn't there to mess around.

While Rod was talking Mick, Alf and Mal had made their way inside. The postmistress took one look at them and swung into gear. Dragging up a table and chairs, she ushered them to sit down. Then, in the spirit of true country hospitality, she disappeared to whip up a batch of scones and get them in the oven.

Meanwhile, Rod had been put through to someone who knew the story of the *Blythe Star*. He listened, amazed, understanding the importance of what Rod was telling him. 'Where are you?' the police officer asked. It wasn't every day in a sleepy corner of Tasmania that a story of this magnitude came knocking on a copper's door. Usually, far more mundane things took up their time.

Rod explained where they were, and where he'd picked them up.

'What are they like?' asked the copper.

'Well, they're upright,' Rod said. Which, given the story they'd just told him, seemed like a pretty bloody amazing accomplishment in his books. 'They're having some food now.'

By now, the postmistress had rustled up a few people to help take care of the three men. Tea and coffee was on the table along with the freshly baked scones. Mick had never smelled or seen anything so good in his entire life. Biting into the first scone was a blissful experience.

'Go easy, boys,' Alf cautioned. 'Eat too much and you'll make yourselves crook.' With little more than the odd dry biscuit and some glucose powder for nearly two weeks, their stomachs were shrunk and sensitive.

The postmistress bustled around them, taking down messages and firing off telegrams for each of them. Then she disappeared, returning with some of her husband's clothes for Mick, which he gratefully accepted. Someone found a length of rope to tie through the belt loops of the pants to hold them up.

The postmistress also called in her husband, a local fisherman in the area, to speak with the seafarers. Everyone was asking about the other survivors. How many were there? What condition were they in? Had they all made it? The postmistress's husband asked them where they came ashore. They didn't know, but they described the features they could remember from the little bay. Some paper and pencil appeared and they sketched what they could.

'That's Deep Glen Bay,' the fisherman said straight away with absolute certainty. Clearly, he knew the coast like the back of his hand. At last, Mick had a name for the place that had saved them but also seen off two of their crew.

As they chatted, Mick was dismayed to hear that local fishermen had offered to help in the search but all the smaller boats had been told no. The authorities didn't want them all getting in the way, apparently. Just stay out of the affected areas while the experts do their job was the message.

It was hard not to think of the what-ifs. It seemed crazy, when this man had identified their landing place in a matter of minutes, that knowledge like his hadn't been put to use in the search. These were people who knew the currents and tides better than anyone.

It wasn't going to be the first time Mick was left gobsmacked after hearing what the authorities had done while they had waited to be rescued in that bloody circle of rubber. No wonder they'd had to save themselves.

As the three bedraggled and hungry crew continued to work their way through scones and tea and coffee, Rod, leaning up against the door frame, took it all in. It wasn't his usual day at work, that was for sure.

There was now a small gathering around the men. One of the locals turned to Rod. 'You don't look too bad for what you've been through,' she said.

Rod raised an eyebrow – he'd only been out at work for the day! He told her as much, and her cheeks turned a rosy hue as laughter rippled around the room.

Over the general chatter, Alf heard a helicopter beating the skies overhead. The rescue team for whoever was hanging on at Deep Glen Bay had arrived. The fisherman quickly radioed the position of the remaining survivors to the pilot and the rhythmic thud of the chopper faded away again.

Mick hoped they'd been able to get help in time. Now, having done everything they could to save the waiting men sprawled on the small patch of rough grass in the bay, it was time to make some other calls.

* * *

Wednesday, 24 October 1973 – Hobart

Jennifer Lee was sitting at her desk at the Tasmanian Transport Commission offices when the telephone rang. Now in her second week in the new job, she was getting into the swing of things. She picked up the phone and asked politely how she could help. Her jaw dropped when she heard who was on the end of the line. It was one of the survivors of the *Blythe Star* calling from Dunalley. Jennifer was stunned. Weren't they meant to be dead? Hadn't they just called off the search?

Straight away she put the call through to Crystal, Captain Maddock's secretary. Then she rushed out to the back office to her colleagues. 'They've been found,' she said, choking up. 'The survivors of the *Blythe Star* have been found!'

Everyone stopped work immediately and gathered around. Elation rippled through the office and there were tears of relief as Jennifer relayed the details of the call she'd just taken.

CHAPTER 17

Someone's Playing a Horrible Joke

Wednesday, 24 October 1973 – Doveton

The day started much like any other. Joanie got up, dressed neatly and got ready for work. Breakfast was eaten, teeth brushed. All very mundane. Except for the fact that the search was over. Mick was dead. Her world had fundamentally altered.

She was going back to work at the chemist shop. What else could she do? There was no longer any point waiting for the authorities to send good news. The wait was over. Now, they just had to somehow live with this knowledge as they tried to piece their lives back together around the hole that Mick had left behind.

At work, Joanie went through the motions with little said between her and Basil. When she heard the sound of running footsteps, she looked around. Someone had burst into the

SOMEONE'S PLAYING A HORRIBLE JOKE

chemist – it was the young man from the post office. He rushed over to Joanie, a small slip of paper in hand. He held the paper out to her, an eager look on his face.

Surprised, Joanie looked down. It was a telegram. Joanie stared at it, uncomprehending.

The young post office lad was standing there, looking at her expectantly. Everyone in Doveton knew about the unfolding drama around Mick and he was anxious to know if this telegram held news.

'I think somebody's playing a horrible joke on me,' Joanie said finally.

The young man in front of her didn't know what to say. His face fell. Joanie couldn't believe how someone could be so cruel. What sort of person would send such a heartless telegram pretending to be Mick, pretending to be okay just as everyone was finally facing the anguish that he was really gone?

Joanie turned to Basil. 'Have a look at this,' she said. 'Somebody sent me a telegram saying, "I'm well. I'm heading to Hobart Hospital. I will call you as soon as I can."' Joanie was distraught at the cruelty of the joke. *How could somebody do this?* she wondered. Gutted, she put the telegram aside and returned to work.

About ten minutes later, another sound floated through the open door of the chemist. Joanie went to the door and looked down the street. Past the milk bar and the post office she saw quite a sight racing toward her from the hairdressers. Joanie's mum, Carmen, was flying up the street, hair wet, half of it still in rollers. Seeing Joanie, she screamed. 'Joanie! Have you heard? Have you heard?' She arrived at the chemist, panting and dishevelled.

'Heard what, Mum?' Joanie asked.

'They've found the survivors of the *Blythe Star*! I think Mick's been found,' Carmen blurted out, excitement radiating off her.

'You're joking,' Joanie said. 'Because I've received this telegram and I thought someone was playing a horrible joke on me.'

'No, no, I heard it on the radio in the hairdressers, Joanie! The survivors are headed to Hobart Hospital now.'

Sticking to his no-radio policy in the chemist, Basil hadn't had it on that day so Joanie had missed the news herself. But at the sight of her mum beaming in front of her with her hair half-done, it clicked for Joanie that this wasn't a joke after all. Mick was alive. Somehow, inexplicably, after everyone had given him up for dead, here he was sending telegrams and headed to the hospital.

Hugging, Joanie and her mum laughed with pure relief and joy. Then the phone rang. Basil answered, then held out the phone to Joanie.

It was Mick.

Hearing his familiar voice, a bit tinny but still Mick, Joanie burst into tears.

'It's okay, it's okay. I'm all good. I'm fine,' Mick said down the phone.

'Are you sure you're okay?'

'Yep, I'm fine and I'll be home soon. I'm headed to the hospital in a bit.'

'I received your telegram but I couldn't believe it was from you,' Joanie told him. 'It wasn't until Mum came up from the hairdressers that I realised it was true.'

'No, no, we're here and we're all good and I'll be home soon,' Mick said calmly, reassuring.

A million questions ricocheted around Joanie's mind. 'How did you get found?' she started.

'Look, I'll tell you about it when I see you.'

Joanie would have to wait for her questions to be answered. But who cared? Mick was alive, he was there on the end of the phone and he'd be headed back to her soon. Delighted and still in shock, she placed the receiver back into its cradle. 'Basil, I'm going down to the Dolemans',' she said, not asking permission this time. After that news, she'd be buggered if she'd be kept at work for the rest of the day.

As she raced out the door, Joanie saw people running toward the chemist to tell her the news that was crackling through Doveton. Marree, Mick's sister, ran over and she and Joanie hugged in the street then turned and ran down to Mick's place.

When they reached the front fence, Joanie saw that the press had beaten her to it. They were already there on the lawn, cameras and microphones at the ready. It seemed like half of Doveton was there too, close to a couple of hundred. The feeling was electric. Joanie couldn't wipe the smile off her face. Over and over she told the story of how the telegram had come but she hadn't believed it and thought it was all a horrible joke. Everyone laughed, and just as they'd shared their tears of grief and anguish days before, now they delighted in sharing their tears of joy and relief.

After a few minutes, Joanie looked around. She couldn't see Steve Henwood, Mick's best mate, in the crush of people at the house. But she could easily have missed him in the crowd. 'Do Steve and Mr Henwood know Mick's been found?'

'I don't know,' came the reply. 'They're at the school, working.'

Joanie wanted to make sure the Henwoods knew the incredible news. If they didn't, she wanted to be the one to tell them, so she and one of Mick's brothers, Rosco, raced up to the Holy Family School. Sure enough, there was Steve and his dad with brooms in hand sweeping the school corridor with no idea of the unfolding jubilation.

'Mick's been found! Mick's been found!' Joanie and Rosco screamed out to them.

The Henwoods threw their brooms in the air and barrelled toward Joanie. When he reached her, Steve picked her up and twirled her around.

'You're serious, Joanie?' they checked, hardly daring to believe.

'It's real! It's real, all right! He's on his way to Hobart Hospital and he'll be home in a few days. I've actually spoken to him!'

The Henwoods never went back to work that day, either – the brooms lay where they fell and the corridors of the school remained unswept.

* * *

Wednesday, 24 October 1973 – Crib Point, Mornington Peninsula

Forty minutes away, on Victoria's Mornington Peninsula, the phone rang in the Simpson home. Robyn, who had just arrived home, crossed the room to answer it. It might have been the middle of the day, but she was home early from school. Her family, too, were trying to get back into a normal routine after the devastating news about Robyn's dad, Alf. Well, a new normal. Life had to go on. Robyn's mum, Kit, was back at work, and that morning Robyn had been packed onto the school bus. Alf's memorial was planned for the next day.

Then, in the middle of the day, Robyn had had a feeling that she just had to go home. She didn't know what it was, or why, but it drove her to the headmistress's office. 'I want to go home,' she said.

'What's wrong? Are you unwell?'

'No, I just want to go home.'

Robyn couldn't explain it, but she just knew she needed to be at home. So her older brother was called. He picked her up and dropped her back to the house. Then the phone rang. Robyn answered. 'Hello?'

'Dunalley calling,' the operator said, before putting the call through.

Where's that? Robyn wondered. She'd never heard of the place. Then she heard an old, croaky voice on the line.

'Who's that?' the voice asked.

'It's Robyn.'

'It's Dad. I'm alive.'

There was a pause. 'My dad's dead,' Robyn said. Her guts twisted as she thought of the memorial service planned for the next day. Whoever this was on the phone, the old-sounding croaking voice, it wasn't her dad.

'It's me,' the voice insisted. 'It's me, pet.'

Pet. The nickname Alf had for his youngest daughter. The nickname no stranger would know but that was so familiar to Robyn. She had the same rising realisation Joanie had had. This *was* her dad. Somehow inexplicably, unbelievably, he was alive.

Robyn and her dad chatted for a few moments. 'Please tell Mum I'm alive and I'm going to Hobart Hospital,' Alf said.

Robyn promised she would before telling her dad she loved him. Then they hung up.

Robyn stood there immobile for a moment, unsure what to do next. Then she picked up the phone again and rang her mum's work. 'Mum, Dad's alive!' Robyn said. 'I've just spoken to him on the phone. They've been found!' She heard a clatter and a thud and then silence on the phone as her mum fainted dead away and hit the floor. Someone else came on the line, and Robyn repeated the information.

Message duly delivered, Robyn stood in the family home alone and overwhelmed by emotion. Then she turned and sprinted out the front door and into the street. 'My dad's alive! My dad's alive!' she screamed.

Robyn wanted to scream it to the stars, the moon, wanted to tell the whole world. Alf. Her dad. Alive.

* * *

Wednesday, 24 October 1973 – Dunalley

Alf hung up the phone, grinning from ear to ear. Hearing the voices of their loved ones was an injection of life for all of them.

Rod, still standing in the doorway, was thinking about the job he had to finish and the truck still idling out the front. Figuring he'd done everything he could for the survivors, he wished them luck and headed back out.

Rod began the slow drive back to the timber yard. As he was grinding his way up a hill, he saw the red and blue of the ambulance's flashing lights coming toward him. 'Go for it, guys,' he said as the vehicle passed.

The ambulance pulled up outside the Dunalley post office. As the three crewmen were bundled into it, someone took a photo to immortalise the moment. Then the doors slammed closed and Mick, Mal and Alf were on their way to Hobart Hospital.

The ambulance officers were all ears about what had happened, but Mick and the others didn't speak much.

They might have been safe in an ambulance on their way to medical care, but their minds were down at the bay with the shipmates they'd left behind. The worry needled them. Had the helicopter found them? Were they safe? Was the chopper collecting men or bodies?

The ambulance made a quick 40 minutes of the journey to Hobart Hospital. The three sailors were rushed inside and it was only there, safe at last, that they heard the fate of the four men they'd left behind.

* * *

Wednesday, 24 October 1973 – Hobart

News travelled quickly in the small community of Tasmania. Someone knew someone, who knew someone else and in no time, everyone knew it. So it wasn't long before the news that some survivors of the missing ship had been found made its way to Trevor Sutton in the TVT6 offices. It wasn't out of the ordinary that the media would hear about something before the police. The bush telegraph was nothing if not efficient.

Someone had called in with the unbelievable information that some survivors had walked out of the bush somewhere down near the Tasman Peninsula. Details were scarce, but the story ran like wildfire around the newsroom. The feeling was euphoric – everyone wanted to know what had happened.

Straight away, Trevor was on the phone to the police to try to confirm the report. If it was true, it was going to be big. Other news of the day was shelved and everything was thrown at the incredible story that there were survivors of the *Blythe Star*. Somehow, they had defied the odds and had walked back into being in some remote patch of Tasmanian bush.

Yes, it was true, the police confirmed. There were survivors.

Trevor knew this was the story that was going to lead the bulletin that night. 'Well, how many?' he prompted the police.

'We don't know. We're discussing it with the people down at Dunalley now. We'll get back to you.'

Trevor waited impatiently for the call back with more information. When the phone finally rang, he snatched it up.

'I think we've got three survivors,' the police officer on the end of the line confirmed. 'But we don't know at this stage about the others.'

'Well, look, we're heading down there,' Trevor said. He wanted to get on the ground and get pictures of this, not to mention a clearer idea of what the hell had happened. He'd reported just the day before that they were calling the bloody search off. Honestly, you couldn't write a story this good.

'No, no, no,' came the hurried reply. 'Not yet. We're organising a rescue and you can't go down yet.'

Trevor was told in no uncertain terms that a news crew was not to make its way down yet. Trevor didn't know where exactly they'd be headed, anyway, so he and his crew had to sit and wait patiently for another callback from the police.

After what seemed an age, the phone rang again. 'We're organising a helicopter to get them to Hobart.'

Again, Trevor pushed for more details. Where would the chopper be coming in? Who would be on board? But the information wasn't forthcoming. The police themselves were clearly trying to work out what the hell was going on.

Meanwhile, the afternoon was ticking by and Trevor's deadline was getting closer. He knew they needed the story today. It would be no good in tomorrow night's bulletin – it would have been all over the papers by then. While they were waiting, Trevor and colleagues talked through how they'd approach the story. What their coverage plan would be depended on when they were able to get vision, and what access they had. Everyone was making calls, calling in favours for information to try to find out where the helicopter would be coming in and when.

At some point, the media were given the tip-off that the survivors would be headed to the airport. So they jumped into their cars and started to race over, only to hear that they'd been given a bum steer in an effort to keep the media pack out of the way when the helicopter actually did come in.

Finally, Trevor got the confirmation that the chopper would be coming in to land at the Domain in the centre of the city and a stone's throw from the hospital. The ambulances would be there to transport survivors straight to the hospital. 'What's their condition?' Trevor asked.

No one knew. Whoever was coming in on the helicopter, they would all find out together what state they were in.

Trevor and his camera crew made their way straight to the Domain. About five journalists from the local papers and television stations, stood around, keyed up in anticipation. Nearby, ambulances were ready and waiting.

Trevor chatted to the ambulance officers, trying to glean what they knew. Which, it turned out was about as much as Trevor. They had no information about who the survivors were or what had happened to the others. The ambulance officers were just as in the dark about the condition of the men and what had happened to the *Blythe Star*.

Checking his watch anxiously, as it ticked ever closer to deadline, Trevor and the other journalists were on tenterhooks. Finally, the helicopter appeared, a distant spec over the city horizon. As it came closer, the thunk of its rotors built in volume. When it touched down at last, a police officer held out a finger, warning Trevor and the others to hold back until the rotors had stopped moving. With the skids on the ground and given the all clear, everyone gathered moved forward as one, Trevor with microphone in hand. The ambulances drove closer, ready to whisk away the crew.

The helicopter door swung open. A police officer was right there, speaking to the survivors, but Trevor couldn't hear what was said. Then, as the helicopter door swung wide and the police officer moved aside, Trevor saw a sight that has never left him: four men clearly on a knife's edge between living and dying. Sitting closest to Trevor was Mick Power, clearly very unwell. Grimy, his clothes in tatters, his eyes glazed, he looked shrunken, his skin mottled, blotchy and terribly sunburnt.

The survivors looked out at the crowd of reporters in bewilderment. As the police and ambulance officers tried to help the men out of the helicopter and onto ambulance stretchers, Trevor concentrated on the job he had to do and his field of vision narrowed. Stepping forward he thrust his microphone into Mick Power's face. 'How do you feel?' It was a question that came out of instinct and habit, said without thought because he was entirely focused on doing his job. In the years that followed, though, the moment remained in the recesses of Trevor's mind. He regretted the inane wording and berated himself for asking such a question of a man in such condition. But those were the days, and that was his job, so he did.

Just as Power was about to reply, the ambulance officers lifted him onto a stretcher, and all that came out was a tortured and agonised moan.

As the police called out 'Stand back! Stand back!', other journalists were peppering the survivors with questions.

'Excuse me, Sir. Can you tell us the names of the people surviving?'

'Could you tell us your name?'

'We've been talking to your son the last couple of days.'

'Can you tell us what happened?'

The men, haggard and gaunt with a look in their eyes like they'd just landed in Alice's Wonderland, tried to answer the flying questions as best they could. Confused and bewildered, they were trying to catch up with what, exactly, had happened to land them at the centre of this fray. The four men had hung on in Deep Glen Bay only to be transported in a matter of minutes from a battle to hold death at bay to the centre of a swirling media storm.

Cliff Langford looked old and stooped, his cheekbones protruding from his narrow face. He had lost 19 kilograms since the ship sank. Once he made it to the hospital they told him he wouldn't have survived another night out there.

Mick Power lay back on the stretcher, eyes clouded with pain and his arms crossed protectively over his chest. His face too was thin and drawn.

Tas Leary, hair swept wildly back from his face and salt and pepper stubble on his chin, lay on a stretcher with a blanket pulled up to his chest. Of all of them, he seemed the most open and coherent, though still with dark, heavy bags under his eyes. Hands tucked behind his head, he looked as though he chatted to the media any old day of the week. As he answered their urgent questions, a wry smile hovered at the corners of his mouth.

George Cruikshank, with enough strength left to disembark the helicopter unaided, looked cautious and, perhaps, a little guarded.

'We were beginning to think you wouldn't make it,' a reporter said to him.

'We were beginning to think that ourselves,' the captain shot back.

An overwhelmed George Cruikshank, just moments after the helicopter that had rescued them from Deep Glen Bay landed in Hobart, looking out at the waiting press pack. *(Reproduced by permission of the Australian Broadcasting Corporation – Library Sales © 1973 ABC)*

In just a few minutes, the men were out and into the waiting ambulances. The doors were pulled closed in the face of the media, microphones still extended, shutting out the questions still being called out in the hope of one final grab for the telly or papers.

As soon as the ambulances rolled away, Trevor was on the phone to call the hospital to see if he could get access to the survivors. He had a big breaking news slot to fill, and those few seconds of footage weren't going to do it alone.

'You can't come in yet. Give us your number and we'll call you back,' the hospital staffer said.

Again, Trevor had no choice but to hurry up and wait. But there was footage that needed processing and quickly. They'd be cutting it bloody fine to get it to air. Already the afternoon was closing in, the chill air that heralded evening settling over the city. And the news went to air at six.

They rushed their film through to the processors to develop, everyone working quickly. Still, they could only get part of the interview processed before it had to be ripped out of the processing chemicals and fed onto the telecine chain and put to air.

The news of the miraculous survival had by now captured the nation, so Melbourne and Sydney stations were taking the TVT6 coverage. The raw, unedited footage of the moment went to air around the country, with Trevor presenting. People in living rooms and kitchens around Australia were glued to the news, which is how some families realised with anguish that their husbands, fathers and sons were not among the survivors. On the 6 pm news. The media had beat the authorities to it. The police visits that were to come would be too late. Families had already received the worst news, delivered in the worst way.

* * *

By now, Rod had unloaded his haul of timber for the day. Back home, freshened up and fed, he headed out again. He thought those tough buggers he'd picked up would probably be due for a fair stay in hospital so he'd decided to drop over some supplies to keep them occupied. He made the short drive to the hospital.

'Where are the *Blythe Star* guys?' he asked at hospital reception.

He was given directions to find them and made his way through the corridors. When he reached the large ward, he poked his head around the door. Mick and the others were sitting up in bed under crisp white sheets. Washed and tidied up, a bit of proper food under their now tightened belts, they had warm smiles of welcome for him.

Walking in, he held out the supplies he'd brought, a collection of books he thought would interest them, including the odd western. Looking around, Rod realised not all the survivors were there. He asked what had happened to the others and was told that all four men waiting in the bay had made it out and had been choppered to hospital ahead of Mick, Mal and Alf. But as they were worse for wear, they were in another ward receiving a higher level of care.

Rod sat and chatted for a while. They shared more details of their story, but they also talked about books and Rod's work. Seafarers are never short of stories to share, and the time passed quickly.

* * *

Trevor's story had aired and he'd stepped away from the camera, but his day wasn't over. The call he'd been waiting for from the hospital came through at about 7.30. He was given the all clear to head in to the bedsides of the survivors.

Once again, with camera crew in tow, Trevor headed out – this time to the hospital. When he reached the ward where Mick and the others were propped up in bed, he found the young forester who had driven the men to safety ensconced in a chair, chatting away.

When Rod saw Trevor and his crew, he took it as his cue to leave and stood up.

'Come out into the hallway for a minute,' Trevor said.

Rod said goodbye to the crew and followed Trevor out.

Trevor got the cameraman to frame up Rod, then asked, 'Can you just look how you looked when you first saw them?'

Rod's expression didn't change as he deadpanned Trevor and the camera.

Finished with Rod, Trevor headed into the ward and introduced himself to the men. Mick might only have been

18, but he was a chirpy young man, coherent and persuasive. Trevor gravitated to him, finally getting his first proper interview with a *Blythe Star* survivor.

Dressed in a white hospital gown, Mick looked like he'd just come out of the shower. He was prepared to have a chat, but still, he was reserved. Trevor tried to draw out as much as he could, but Mick was guarded.

Mick told Trevor how their ship had sunk, and where. That they'd buried a man at sea and two more had died at Deep Glen Bay. He told him about the Japanese fishing ship that appeared to have turned tail and sailed away at their distress signal. It was a story Trevor could barely have believed had the genuine young man, arms scratched and face thin, not been sitting there in front of him.

Trevor tried to get to the details of what had happened to cause the ship to up and roll over. But Mick, his emotion raw and immediate, was more concerned about the three men he'd farewelled. Sensing Mick's sadness, Trevor chose his words carefully, still feeling guilty for his question to the seafarer earlier that afternoon.

Listening to the torrid tale, Trevor had a gut-wrenching realisation as Mick described the course of their drift. If Trevor had gone up with Vern on their planned search – called harebrained by his news editor – they would have flown right over the top of the men in the raft. There were nine of them at that stage. Back at the station, Trevor shared the information, upset by the sliding-doors moment that had gone another way. But from then on, he kept it to himself. For

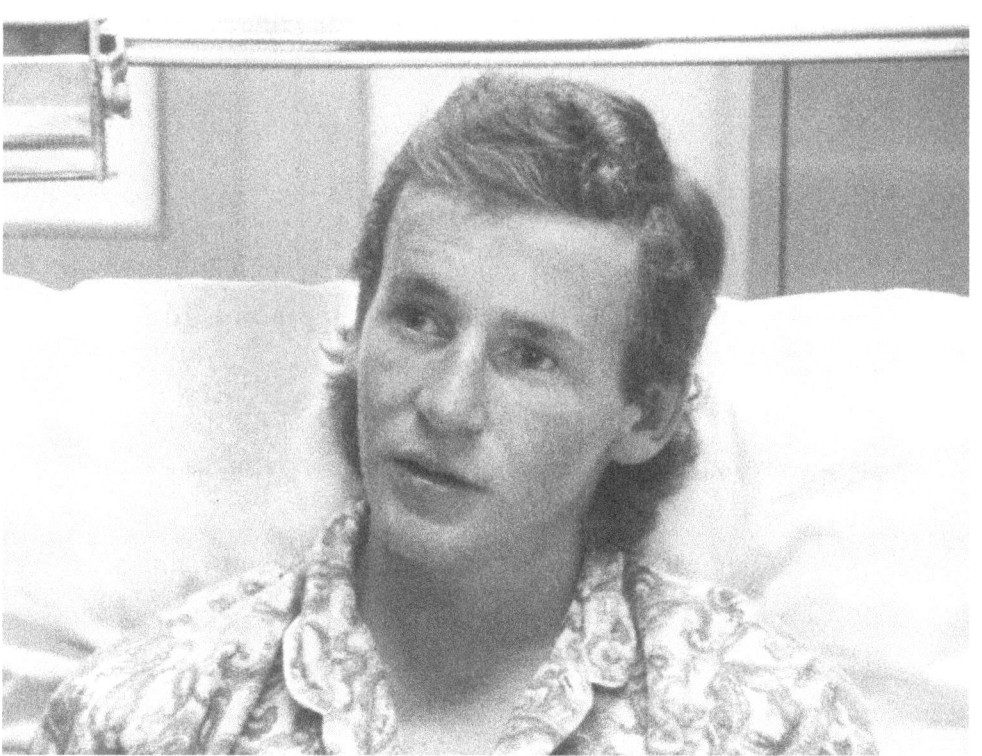

Mick Doleman told the outline of what the men had endured from his hospital bed in the Royal Hobart Hospital after the surviving crew were rescued.
(Reproduced by permission of the Australian Broadcasting Corporation – Library Sales © 1973 ABC)

the next 50 years, Trevor would play out the what-ifs. It was a private guilt he carried, that maybe, if he'd gone above his boss's head, if he'd pushed harder, two lives would have been saved.

That night Trevor put another TV special together with Mick's interview, which went to air at 9 pm. Finally, coverage complete, Trevor went home exhausted.

* * *

The men might have been found, but there were still many questions unanswered. 'Just what did happen aboard her?' mused news reporters around the country.

While the men were being brought back into the realm of the living, the media descended on the families of the survivors.

'Oh, I'm just dying to get down there, you know, and see how he is and everything,' Cliff Langford's wife, Mary, said. The fact of the matter was, Cliff was being spoonfed by a nurse because he was too weak to lift a spoon to his mouth.

'How could he have managed all those days on a raft?' the reporter asked.

'He has a strong will. Very strong will,' Mary replied. 'You know, he sort of doesn't crack up at anything. He never does.'

Mick Power's wife, Christine, shared the depths of her anguish when she had thought Mick, who she called Mike, was lost to her. 'I thought Mike had gone on to better things, yes,' she said. 'A neighbour of mine come rushing in and said that there had been people found on the rocks. I thought she meant dead bodies.'

'And what did you do as soon as you learned?' the reporter asked.

'I did everything. I jumped in the air, I cried.'

That night the remaining seven crew of the *Blythe Star* slept in warm, soft beds with full bellies, water on the table beside them and help just a call away. They slept without cold eating away at them and knowing that in a few days they would see their loved ones.

Each man made sense of the experience his own way. Cliff Langford thought perhaps it was a message from God, a warning to give up the sea and spend more time with his family. All of them were dreaming of wrapping their arms around the loved ones they'd been thinking of for two weeks, and feeling their solid reality in the flesh.

George Cruikshank didn't have to wait long. His wife was in Hobart and was able to rush to the hospital that day. But what she found left her confused and concerned.

The media caught her not long after. 'Now you've seen your husband, how do you think he looks?'

'Terrible,' she said. 'I mean, I've never seen him with a beard before.'

'How does he feel? Has he told you that he—'

Mrs Cruikshank jumped in. 'Well, uh, he seems shocked, you know what I mean? He doesn't seem to know what he's doing, you know what I mean?' She tried to grapple with the changes she'd found in the man she knew so well. She explained to the reporter that when she was talking to George Cruikshank about the rest of the crew he didn't seem to know what she was talking about. 'He said, "Who do you mean?" I'm trying to tell him all this, but it doesn't seem as if it's sinking in.'

It's hard to know what was happening in George Cruikshank's mind. Maybe he was broken by circumstances too big for him. Maybe he was thinking ahead to the inquiry. Maybe he was barely lucid after hunger and dehydration and exposure. Maybe all of those things were true.

While the media frenzy surrounding the rescue gave rise to headlines screaming survival, it hadn't been a survival story for everyone. Three men had lost their lives. John Sloan's love, Joan, would never see his body. Ken Jones and John Eagles remained on the beach at Deep Glen Bay, the police returning the following day to recover them so they could be returned to their families.

Children, wives, siblings and friends watched the coverage knowing that one's survival story was also their story of loss. The sinking of the *Blythe Star* had blown their families apart, leaving a hole with shredded, weeping edges where their men used to be.

Still, the widows of the dead men were gracious. Ken's de facto partner, Francis, sent flowers to the survivors in hospital.

The thought that Ken's family would be without that giant of a man was crushing for Mick. Out of everything that had happened, the loss of his mentor tore at him most. Mick wanted the world to know what kind of man Ken was and that he shouldn't have died, that without him none of them would be there.

A psychologist from the University of Tasmania came to the hospital to sit by the survivors' bedsides and record their experiences and responses. Mick had a few questions of his own. He wanted to know why Ken Jones and John Eagles had taken their clothes off at the end, and how they could all have had that collective dream of delirium in the raft.

He didn't get the answers he was looking for. But it seemed likely that the delirium was born of the stress their brains and bodies had endured after days with little food or water. It was likely the cold and exhaustion also made their minds sluggish, then the moral injury of losing John Sloan pushed them right to the brink. The pitch dark and the constant movement and never-ending white noise of the waves may have been a form of sensory deprivation. So their struggling minds tried to make sense of the lack of sensory stimuli and fabricated a delusion that each of them, in their highly susceptible state, picked up from each other, which in turn fed and heightened the fantasy.

CHAPTER 18

Welcome Home

Thursday, 25 October 1973 – Hobart

The day after Mick staggered out of the bush and flagged down Rod in his big rumbling red logging truck, he was lounging in hospital when his parents walked through the door. The Tasmanian Transport Commission had stumped up for their fares, along with those of the other survivors' families. Not so for the families of John Sloan, John Eagles and Ken Jones.

Mick was itching to be out of the hospital. He'd spent two weeks confined to a tiny raft, and now he wanted to be out and free. He wanted to head home, to see his family and friends … and Joanie. But the doctors were keeping him for a few days to monitor his condition after all he'd been through and bring his health up to speed.

After a few days, he was finally given a leave pass from hospital and let loose in a department store to purchase some new clothes, everything save his jocks having gone down with the ship. Given he was shopping on the Tasmanian Transport Commission's dollar Mick chose a suit. He'd never owned a suit in his life. He picked it up and put it on, feeling like a million bucks. With some shoes and a few other odds and ends he was set.

Then it was time to head back to Victoria and back to the life he thought he might never see again. On the way back to Doveton from the airport, Mick and his folks stopped in at his Aunty Rita's. He was greeted with tearful hugs from his cousins and grandfather. It was just a glimmer of the celebrations to come.

Finally, he stepped into another taxi, this one would take him home. Hair pushed back from his face and suit on, Mick was ready.

In Doveton, Joanie was waiting impatiently for Mick's arrival with a growing crowd. The buzz of excited chatter bounced around every room of Mick's family home, as Joanie did the math to work out Mick's estimated time of arrival. TV crews were on standby to capture the returning hero, and it seemed as though just about everyone else in Doveton had turned up to welcome one of their own back from the clutches of death.

Standing there in the driveway waiting, time seemed to slow to a crawl. The last couple of weeks since Mick had left might have passed in the blink of an eye, but this moment felt interminable now Joanie knew she was going to see him again.

Then she spotted Mick's taxi cruising up the street. It pulled up outside his house to a roar of cheering. People around Joanie were jumping up and down, tears spilled down happy cheeks. Joanie ran over – nothing and no one was going to hold her back and no one tried.

The door popped open and swung wide. With the help of his parents, Mick leveraged himself out of the back seat. Joanie flew toward him, her eyes drinking him in. She was shocked by how much weight he'd lost in so short a time. He looked skinny, almost frail. His feet were clearly hurting him – the deep lacerations would take time to heal – and he had a hobbling, unsteady gait as he stumbled toward her. Then he wrapped her in his arms.

Barely able to believe the feeling of his arms around her, the sound of his voice and the sight of his face so close to hers, Joanie was so happy she could have lifted up and floated away. Mick's appearance might have shocked her, but he was still the same old Mick with the same smile, the same warmth. After a few long moments, she let him go, knowing she had to share him with everyone else there that day.

Mick looked past her and saw the crowd there to welcome him. Hundreds were gathered, crowded into every available space. The television cameras were rolling, capturing everything. Real-life fairytales don't come by any old day of the week and the media were lapping it up. Audiences couldn't get enough.

For the benefit of the media, Mick's sister threw the journos a line. 'Mick's gonna marry Joanie!' she jokingly shouted to them as if she was feeding a lump of chicken to hungry dogs.

Delighted, they seized on it, even though it was news to Mick. Joanie's colour rose, shy and embarrassed.

It seemed like everyone was walking on air. Everything was funnier, more colourful. The light was brighter, the music louder and the food more flavoursome. People spilled out of Mick's place and onto the street, drinking, eating, talking and celebrating.

At one point, Mick came across his cousin, Tommy. A close friend, Mick had always ribbed Tommy for his preference for a good cup of tea over a beer. But this day was one to be celebrated and Tommy had cracked his first beer to drink to Mick's health. Mick noted the beer in his hand, laughed and congratulated him.

Finally, after hours that seemed like days Mick's mum started to move everyone out. 'We need to give this boy some rest,' she said.

Slowly the place cleared and Mick was able to take a moment to breathe and appreciate all the things of home that he thought he would never see again.

Mick lay in bed that night exhausted but happy. The soft familiarity of his bed, his home seemed like a dream – or the past two weeks did. Which one was the real world? It was as though each experience belonged to a different place and time. It was hard to reconcile the world of losing Ken and battling fear and cold and the thought of sharks with the warm embrace of home.

It was hard to think of home without thinking of Ken, who would never feel that again. Of Ken's love, Francis, and their four-year-old, Susan, who would never see him walking up the driveway or feel his arms sweep them up into a hug. Mick thought of how the little girl's world had just shattered as she realised that Daddy wouldn't be coming home. That the world could be unsafe and cruel. It was a hard lesson for anyone, let alone a child of four.

The next evening, Mick managed to sneak Joanie away so they could spend a few hours together, just the two of them. They went to a Chinese restaurant in nearby Dandenong. Looking over the menu, Mick's stomach couldn't believe what his eyes were seeing and he ordered enough to feed ten men. After so long with so little he reckoned he'd earned it.

The waiter brought out the food and arranged it carefully on the table so it would all fit. Stomach growling and mouth salivating, Mick picked up his fork and dived in. But after a few mouthfuls, he stopped, put his fork down and called the waiter over. 'You can take it back mate,' he said. 'I'm sorry, I'll pay for it but I can't eat it. My stomach just won't absorb it.'

His shrunken stomach couldn't ingest any more.

* * *

At Crib Point, Robyn Simpson had been anticipating the moment her dad, Alf, made it home. Waiting in the lounge, a bundle of excited energy, she looked out through the curtains at every sound of a passing car. Robyn couldn't wait to see the bear-like bulk of her dad walking back up to their front door – the same door he'd farewelled her from just a couple of weeks earlier, when he'd told her to look after Mum.

Robyn saw the car pull up and she flew outside, her heart racing. When Alf Simpson stepped out of the car, she gave him a hug that said all the things she couldn't say to him the past few weeks, a hug that told him of her fear and her anguish, her relief and her love.

'It's good to see you, sweetheart,' he said into the top of her head.

'Oh, Dad,' she said, dissolving into happy tears.

The moment seemed to be playing out like Robyn was in a Hollywood movie brought to life. It didn't seem real and she found herself swirling in this strange reality. She just couldn't fathom what had happened. All that anguish and then here was her dad again.

And he was the same old dad. Although, as Robyn pulled back and walked beside him up to the house, she noticed the looseness of his skin. His bulk had diminished and, now she looked at him, she thought he seemed like skin and bones.

Looking up into his face, Robyn saw the weight of what he'd been through in the lines around his eyes and mouth. A haunted look lingered in his eyes. It looked like he'd been through hell. But now he was home, and they could heal him, make it better. Whatever he had seen, whatever he had experienced, Robyn knew he was in the best place to bring him back into himself and cast the shadows of those two weeks far behind him.

Alf walked slowly with painful, stumbling steps, his feet heavily bandaged. Still, much like the welcome waiting for Mick, Alf's return wasn't going to pass without fanfare. A couch was dragged out onto the street, and an impromptu party of sorts got underway. Alf was plonked in a chair, like a regent overseeing his court. Unable to move without assistance due to the state of his feet, he didn't care – he was happily ensconced, surrounded by loved ones. A handful of friends came to see him, delighted to have their mate back. One of them held out a fistful of small slips of paper.

'What's this?' Alf asked.

'It's the bloody receipts for our suits,' they replied. 'We had to have them cleaned for your memorial!'

Ever the good sport, Alf laughed and took the receipts to pay.

It would be a few months later, when Alf had regained some of his strength, that he strode into the offices of the *Herald Sun*. 'I'm here to pay for a death notice,' he said.

'Who's it for?'

'Me!' he answered, his wicked sense of humour pulling the corners of his mouth into a smile. Not many people could say they'd walked in and paid for their own death notice, and he was pretty chuffed to have made it back from the dead to do so.

Across papers and magazines and televisions the reporting was jubilant. But, while the country celebrated this incredible survival story, the families of the three men who died were shattered. They had to try to find a way to hold together the pieces that were left in the midst of a media storm celebrating the survival of seven. Suddenly, wives were looking at how on earth to keep their families afloat financially, wondering how they would keep hold of businesses and houses and how they could help their children grieve. Losing a dad sent fracture lines through the lives of children, which they carried into adulthood.

Once Mick had basked in the love and relief of his family and community, he and Mick Power had something very important to do. They travelled to a house in St Kilda, where four-year-old Susan Jones was trying to understand what forever meant. She would never see her dad, Ken Jones, again. Mick and Power visited to pay their respects to a man who had changed them immeasurably, and to let Susan and Ken's partner, Francis, know just how pivotal a role he had played in their survival. How Mick wished he'd been going there to visit Ken.

CHAPTER 19

Who's to Answer?

In the weeks after making it home, Mick revelled in the simple delights of being able to get a drink from the tap at any time of the day and night, and the sturdiness and warmth of his bed at night. Luckily, summer was biting the heels of spring, because he couldn't stand even the whisper of cold.

Mick's body was recovering. He was putting weight back on and his feet were gradually healing – although he wouldn't be playing footy for a while.

Mick knew an inquiry was coming – the Federal Minister for Transport, Charles Jones, had announced it when he announced that the search was being called off, two days before Mick, Mal and Alf had stumbled out of the bush in front of Rod's clanking truck.

Then a letter arrived. Mick was being summoned to

appear as a witness in the Marine Court of Inquiry into the sinking of the *Blythe Star*.

On the morning of Monday, 3 December 1973, the first day of the inquiry, Mick thought of Ken Jones, John Eagles and John Sloan. The thought that they had died when the whole fiasco might well have been avoided had been simmering since he'd made it home.

Mick slipped on his yellow cardigan with white stripes and combed his hair, checking that his wavy mullet was sitting neatly down his neck. Then he left the house and caught a train into the city. He was hoping the whole thing wouldn't take long. He didn't have much time for things like legal proceedings. He was going to make sure there was a voice for the three men who couldn't speak for themselves, but he didn't need to ponce around a court any more than was necessary.

Melbourne was busy as people made their way to work, totally oblivious to the significance of the day to seven men wanting to know how they were left for dead. This would be their chance to find out what the hell went wrong. They were in for a hell of a ride.

Arriving at court, Mick was met by crowds of hungry media, all looking for a sound bite. The rescue of the *Blythe Star* crew had been a bloody big story; now the sequel promised to be just as gripping for the journalists jostling outside court.

Mick headed inside and was shepherded into a sterile, white holding room. As a witness he would have to sit there with the others waiting to be called, unable to hear what was unfolding until after he had said his piece. He had been given strict instructions not to speak about the case to the other men inside. Mick thought they must be joking. He'd just spent almost two weeks holed up in a life raft with these blokes and now they were telling them not to talk?

In the courtroom, proceedings got underway. In addition to the lawyers assisting the court, nine barristers were lined up, all acting for the various players. There were union barristers, Tasmanian government barristers, a barrister for George Cruikshank – everyone had lawyered up.

Evidence was being laid out about the *Blythe Star* and its final fatal voyage. Barristers' questions drew out details that made it clear the *Blythe Star* had not been seaworthy on the day it sailed.

The federal department of transport naval architect who had approved the ship for sea said in his testimony that he had been misled by the Tasmanian Transport Commission about the ship's specifications, which had not included details of repairs and modifications undertaken in the past 14 years. Had he known the real information? He would never have signed off on it.

The inquiry heard about the unfitness of the emergency provisions – the flares that burned too hot to hold. Several of those flares in the raft had been marked unserviceable or were out of date, but still they were packed for use by ten desperate men when their ship sank. Then there was the absence of space blankets to keep the men from freezing to death, the expired rations, the brackish and murky tinned water and, crucially, no radar reflector that might have helped them get rescued days earlier.

It became clear that George Cruikshank had been hired even though he didn't hold all the necessary qualifications for the job. He didn't have a certificate to operate the emergency radio. Which, in an emergency, is a problem.

It also became very clear that the bookkeeping and organisation of the Transport Commission was woeful, at best. At one point, the state of the ship's papers were described as having been 'tied up by a cowboy'.

At the end of each day, Mick and Mal McCarroll met with the union barrister to find out what had happened and how things were playing out. Given they couldn't sit in the courtroom until after their evidence was heard, this meeting was their chance to know how the inquiry was unfolding. As details of the authorities' responses came out, they painted a picture of neglect, ineptitude and callousness. Mick was gobsmacked by the authorities' downright disregard for the ten lives that had been on that ship. How could they have waited days before starting the search?

Each new morsel of information inflamed Mick's anger more. While they'd been battling to keep themselves alive, enduring the unendurable, giving John Sloan a sea burial and saying goodbye to two more, the authorities had been bickering and trying to cover their tracks. The Tasmanian Transport Commission had been cagey about the information it handed over to Marine Operations in Canberra, which was coordinating the search, in an effort to avoid embarrassment that they'd somehow lost a ship.

Embarrassment? What was the weight of their lives worth?

Mick was seething that, as he saw it, his life and his mates' lives had been put at risk to prioritise profits and reputations. And yet, as the inquiry continued, it seemed as though those in charge were still at it, covering their tracks and defending themselves by refusing to acknowledge that those in head office had any culpability for the ship's stability, even though Tas Leary had raised concerns about the amount of deck cargo. Responsibility was pushed back onto the crew.

As man after man stood in the wooden dock to give their evidence, it became clear that there *was* too much deck cargo on the ship, which had made it unstable. This should have been a concern in itself, but even more so given, just a few months earlier, the ship had almost rolled after being overloaded to a similar degree. Quick action on the bridge had righted the ship on that occasion and it had sailed on. Despite this recent history, there had been pressure to move as much cargo as quickly as possible: get it on those decks and get it up to King Island pronto.

All this was rattling around in Mick's head as the long, boring hours ticked by in that white, clinical room, as he waited to say his piece. Each day he would head home with a shattering headache.

Mick came from a seafaring family, and he knew the unofficial rule. You never dob on anyone. You never give anyone up. But he also knew that three men's lives had been lost and they deserved to have someone speak for them.

One afternoon, Mick and Mal met their barrister for the daily debrief on what had happened in court that day. What Mick heard decided it for him. His barrister reported that George Cruikshank's lawyer was trying to shift blame for the sinking onto first mate Ken Jones and chief engineer John Eagles. He was creating a case that it was Ken's responsibility to check the stability of the loaded cargo and that he should have protested the ship's overloading, and that John Eagles had mismanaged the ballast, further adding to the ship's instability.

Like hell they were going to make scapegoats of two dead men, men who had both acted with incredible fortitude in different moments. This was the chief engineer who had gone back down into the depths of the *Blythe Star* to switch off the engine, suffering a serious burn in the process, so the crew could abandon ship without being minced by the propeller. And Ken Jones, without whose encouragement everyone knew they would have lain down and waited for the waves to take them during those endless godforsaken hours in the raft.

Mick chewed all this over as he waited for the knock on the door that would signal his turn in the dock. Finally, his name was called. It was time to give his evidence. He walked into the austere and imposing room and he took his place in the dock. It was an intimidating scene for an 18-year-old. A pack of barristers was lined up before him, and the court was standing room only, packed with media, interested parties and members of the public.

Mick could see the press, pens and pads at the ready. The judge had already given the clamouring media mob a stern warning: they were to leave the witnesses in peace as they entered and left the inquiry. He'd also cautioned Mick and the other witnesses not to speak to them, or their testimony might be struck off. Mick had no intention of talking to the press.

'Your full name is Michael Thomas Doleman?'

'Correct.'

The transcript of a statement Mick had given about the whole affair was then read to the court.

'Is there anything else you wish to add?' the barrister enquired before concluding.

'I was quite disappointed in the captain, who did absolutely nothing during the whole time we were in the life raft.'

Then, starting at the right end of the line of lawyers, the questioning began.

As the questions continued, Mick tried to hold his own and give his testimony professionally and honestly. He held his tongue trying to keep his seething anger in check, and to remain calm and deliberate, not an easy thing to do with the injustice unfolding around him. But he was determined to give an honest account.

Under examination from John Winneke, the counsel assisting the court, Mick came to the evening the ship sailed down the calm waters of the Derwent and out into the ocean. He ran them through the bizarre dispute where the chief engineer had accused the bosun of putting water down the funnel, and the captain's apparent raving that had followed.

'From your observations you made of the captain at that time, did you form any opinion about him?' Winneke asked.

'Yes, I did. My opinion was he was under the influence of alcohol.'

'What observations did you make apart from this conversation you had that helped you to form that opinion?' Winneke pressed. 'First of all, did you see him walking about the bridge?'

'Yes, he was walking from the wing of the bridge into the bridge, occasionally just going out and checking.'

'How was he walking? Did he appear to you to be walking okay, unsteady, or what?'

'It was a wobble, not a stagger. But a wobble more than anything.'

'Nothing else about his appearance?'

'His face was really red and his eyes were pretty red,' Mick recounted.

'Had you actually seen him drinking before the ship set sail?'

'Yes'

'When?'

'When I went up to sign on.'

It went on and on as lawyer after lawyer dissected Mick's evidence. But, standing in the dock, this slim young man held firm against the innuendo and derision that the barristers used to try to needle him. He was a lone voice giving evidence that

George Cruikshank had been under the influence of alcohol when they sailed. Everyone else held the seafarer's line and kept quiet.

On the train home that night, Mick's head was swimming with what he'd said, what he hadn't said, what he should have said. He knew by speaking up he would have to answer to people who thought he was breaking an incontrovertible rule of maritime life.

It didn't take long for the criticism to start flowing from his fellow union members as he got back into life – at the pub or union offices or at sea. But he wasn't going to cop criticism for doing the right thing without a response. 'Captains have been sacking us, hanging us, flogging us for a hundred years,' he fired up in response. 'And when people die and ships are sunk why the fuck shouldn't they be brought to account?'

Mick was his father's son in this regard. Doing what was right, not what was easy, even if it meant not conforming. It was a lesson he'd learned the day his dad had marched the family out of Father Fitzpatrick's church. Mick wasn't going to cop shit for standing up for one of the best men he had ever had the privilege of knowing, a man who had died because of failure, neglect and incompetence. Ken Jones was not going to have this sinking hung around his neck.

In the face of Mick's fierce and staunch defence, the criticism soon died away.

The next day, Mick was back on the stand. Brian Treyvaud, representing George Cruikshank, wasn't going to let Mick go lightly. His cross-examination was cutting and dripping with condescension, as he referred to Mick's 'very refreshing evidence'. His line of questioning stressed time and again Mick's young age and his inexperience at sea.

'Your statement yesterday that the captain was under the influence of liquor,' he fired across the court, 'you told us was based on the fact that you had seen him in a hotel, the fact his face and eyes were red, that you thought he wobbled as he walked, and you have these two incidents of there being nobody at the helm and the ship allegedly off course. What other matter do you want to say caused you to come to that conclusion at the age of eighteen?'

'And the lecture he gave me, just raving on and repeating himself,' Mick responded, once again holding his anger in check.

Treyvaud lined up his questions, laying the groundwork for a trap by which he would discredit Mick.

Did Mick admit the captain was giving instructions to guide the ship down the river?

Did Mick admit there was no significance to the captain's unexplained and unannounced departures from the bridge?

Look at him now across the court: the captain just has a very weatherbeaten face, doesn't he? Surely nothing could be made of the fact it was red that day?

'If you take all those matters into account, that the concessions you have made this morning, it makes the basis upon which, at your age, you formed an impression that this man was to some extent affected by liquor doubtful to say the least, doesn't it?'

'Not to me it doesn't.'

'If every other member of the crew says the captain was not affected by liquor at all or says he noticed nothing in relation to the captain's sobriety at all, would you say they are all wrong and you are the only one in step?'

'No, I would not, but I would still believe I am right.'

'And they would all be wrong?'

'Not necessarily, no.'

'It would be pretty hard to reconcile the two attitudes, wouldn't it?' Treyvaud badgered. 'Yours on the one hand and theirs on the other. They would seem, wouldn't they, to be at cross-purposes?'

'I think I spent more time with him on the bridge than anyone else.'

He might have been young, and easy to dismiss for his age, but Mick stood firm, looking the barristers in the eye and telling his story truthfully and undiluted. Enduring the shredding they levelled at him in that stand would serve well to toughen him up for what was to come.

* * *

It took months, but once all the evidence was heard, weighed and written up in a report the inquiry's work was done. The results were in.

George Cruikshank came under scathing fire, the court 'satisfied beyond all reasonable doubt he failed in his duty'.

But the assertion he was drunk was thrown out. Mick's evidence was discounted, probably due to his age.

Mick was angry to be dismissed. And more angry when it became clear to him where the blame for the ship's sinking was going to be laid. The final report stated: 'Jones was solely responsible for the supervising of the loading of cargo and assessing the effects of that loading on the stability of the *Blythe Star*.'

Essentially, the unstable load was being thrown onto Ken Jones's grave.

And then, the final nail, that a key contributing factor in the sinking was down to mismanagement of the ballast, or as the final report alluded 'an operational error in the engine room' which had been overseen by chief engineer John Eagles.

While the Tasmanian Transport Commission was criticised for the delay in initiating a search, and the ineptitude that search entailed, they dodged responsibility for the actual sinking of the ship.

As Mick saw it, two things that likely led to the ship's sinking were being laid at the feet of two dead men, Ken Jones and John Eagles. The disregard with which their lives had been treated, the nonchalant attitude of the Transport Commission, lit a fire in Mick. Be buggered if he would let some other 18-year-old somewhere go through what he had.

Fighting for improved maritime safety became a burning passion of Mick's for the next 50 years. He was fearless, refusing to be cowed by rich men in suits pushing profits.

Despite all this, there was good to come from the inquiry and the disaster preceding it. A recommendation of the inquiry was that all ships carry an EPIRB (emergency position indicating radio beacon), which can immediately send out an emergency distress signal triggering a rescue. This would have been lifesaving for the crew of the *Blythe Star* had one been on the life raft.

Shortly after the disappearance of the *Blythe Star*, the Commonwealth Department of Transport made it mandatory for all ships to report their position to the Australian Maritime and Safety Authority (the Marine Operations Centre prior to 1991). Failure to do so will instigate an established chain of events, which if not satisfied will automatically fire off a search and rescue operation.

Given the confusion that reigned as authorities tried to ascertain which way around Tasmania the ship had sailed, it also became mandatory for all masters to lodge their intended route with authorities before sailing. Added to which, there is now a requirement they include stability and loading calculations.

All significant advances in maritime safety in Australia, they were too late for the three men who lost their lives after the *Blythe Star* sank. But who knows how many other lives those safety reforms have saved since.

* * *

Not long after the inquiry, Jennifer Lee, the young telephonist at the Tasmanian Transport Commission who had started her new job on the day they realised they'd lost a ship, was walking back to the office at lunchtime when a Kingswood pulled up to the kerb beside her.

Looking through the car window, Jennifer saw the craggy weatherbeaten face of George Cruikshank. He was offering her a lift.

Jennifer climbed in, glad to rest her feet. Until they pulled back out into the traffic, that is. For the next five minutes, Jennifer was scared for her life as the car careered all over the road. Cruikshank was driving like he was three sheets to the wind, and it occurred to her that his nerves were shot to pieces. A less generous person might have assumed he was drunk. Cruikshank had been cleared to go back to sea after the incident, and he seemed nice enough but, looking at him, Jennifer saw a broken man.

* * *

All the survivors of the *Blythe Star* carried the legacy of those two weeks of extreme duress and endurance. Some never went back to sea again.

For the families of John Sloan, John Eagles and Ken Jones the decision of the Marine Court of Inquiry wasn't the end, it just shepherded in a long battle with authorities for compensation for the loss of their men's lives while in the employ of the Tasmanian Transport Commission. As the ship owners, insurers and the Transport Commission tried to shift liability an insurance payout wasn't forthcoming and no compensation flowed.

John Eagles' family had to sell up their banana plantation, and John's beloved Land Rover, to make ends meet while the process for fair recompense played out. Meanwhile, Ken Jones's partner, Francis, was vocal in calling for some provision to be made for her and Ken's daughter, Susan. But authorities seemed unsure how to handle compensation, as Ken was still legally married to his wife in New Zealand. The same conundrum appears to be behind the lack of action on a recommendation for a medal of bravery that would have recognised what Ken did for the crew – many who credited their survival to him.

John Sloan's wife, Joan, grew increasingly frustrated by the tardiness and buck-passing she saw as she struggled to get by on a widow's pension of $40 a week, supplemented by a little cleaning work. All three families were tied up in legal battles with the Transport Commission until 1978. Five long years of financial struggle on top of the grief of losing their loved ones.

As the dust settled on the whole affair, young Robyn Simpson noticed her dad, Alf Simpson, was different. He was more irritable than he had been, and little things annoyed him. He started to drink more. But this was the 1970s, when talk of something like post-traumatic stress disorder was still a long way off, especially in the hyper-masculine world of seafaring.

Alf would wake in the middle of the night with flashbacks of the *Blythe Star* sinking. Back at sea, instant panic would wash over him if the engine noise dropped as his body remembered what that might mean. He threw himself into his family and garden, finding healing in the beauty of his flowers. Flowers that won him awards. But there were other things that didn't change. Alf still gave the best hugs. Hugs that would suck the oxygen out of you. Having come so close to losing everything, he held tight to those things he loved all the more.

Mick went back to sea a few months later, sure he was ready to face it again. Joanie was in disbelief and dreaded the thought of more hours wondering where Mick was. But she realised that seafaring was in his blood. She loved Mick, and he wasn't him without that. So, she took him as he was and held herself together as he farewelled her to return to sea. She would be there waiting for him when he came home again.

The first vessel he sailed on after the disaster was almost a copy of the *Blythe Star*. A small ship, it would practically roll on grass, and in the ocean it bobbed and tossed. Every night, the ship would roll – port, starboard, port. In the darkness Mick's brain would be screaming each time. *Come back up! Straighten back up!*

He only managed three weeks before he called it quits. He couldn't go back to that kind of ship. From then on, he was very selective about the kind of ship he would go to sea on.

Each man handled their trauma in their own way. Mal McCarroll never talked of what happened with his family, returning to sea for 16 years until cardiomyopathy put an end to his seafaring career and life prematurely. Once he had recovered from his injuries, Mick Power also returned to seafaring, retiring in 2002. Much like Mick Doleman, he was a committed union man. Meanwhile, Cliff Langford took his narrow escape as a sign that he shouldn't return to sea.

Tas Leary put together a big scrapbook of press clippings, letters and photos related to the *Blythe Star*, carrying it with him through several house moves until he handed it to his son when he died. A year after the sinking, he was driven to write a heartbreaking letter seeking help in reply to the psychological researcher who had visited them in hospital.

> Dear Professor Henderson,
> Thank you for your letter received a few days ago.
>
> I feel it important, from my own point of view, that I do see you. I may need your advice.
>
> Following the Inquiry I returned to sea … In general terms I was not greatly disturbed except when the ship's engines were stopped at sea (which did happen) or when the ship rolled heavily. My feeling then was one of anxiety bordering on panic. I then decided it might be best if I gave up the sea to work ashore.
>
> Since July 17th I have been working as a truck driver. During recent weeks I have had considerable trouble with nightmares.
>
> Without going into fine detail (which can wait until you see me) my wife tells me that I have often cried out in my sleep. Although she has been unable to understand much of what I have been saying she says I have frequently spoken of not being able to let go of the

paddle, being wet and cold and of having no room to move. Once recently she said I cried out for water.

From my own point of view, and from my own recollection, I know that the hours when I have had the greatest difficulty in sleeping and the greatest sense of worry have been just before sunrise.

In my wakeful hours at work I have found myself being greatly upset by trivial incidents, usually involving people and unkind statements which, previous to the sinking, I would have laughed off.

Yours sincerely,

Stan [Tas] Leary

While the crew familiarised themselves with a new normal, trying somehow to integrate their traumatic experience into their lives, they didn't speak about it. There were no great tales told over a beer at the pub. Wives and children and parents never heard just what had happened and its impact upon them. They just put it aside and tried to keep living good, honest normal lives. There were some things that were beyond words, that couldn't be conveyed in the safety of a living room. They were things that were best forgotten.

The experience was a weight they all carried and shared together, but they held it close. After the frenzied media storm immediately following their rescue, they didn't try to explain an event that was beyond words. How could they?

Barely a man when he set sail on the *Blythe Star*, Mick had watched his ship disappear beneath the hungry waves of the ocean just 12 hours into a routine shipping leg, seemingly taking with it his dreams, his hopes, his future. Mick would hold the story of what happened out there close to his chest for more than 40 years.

It is hard not to wonder what the long-term impact of events were on the bodies and minds of the seven crew who survived. Mick Doleman, who at 18 was the youngest by a number of years when they sailed, is the only crew member to have lived beyond his 60s.

Fifty years after the *Blythe Star* disaster, Ken Jones' daughter Susan McKenna started reaching out to the other family members of the crew, and Mick as the only surviving crewman, to organise a 50th commemoration. When it was held, exactly 50 years on, relatives of almost all the crew came together and were able to swap memories of their men – to share what they knew of the story.

* * *

In the months following the sinking, Mick and Joanie got serious. Their relationship changed from the heady and carefree stirring of new love into something solid and intense.

There must have been something in that pizza they had on their first date, because 50 years on they are still together. They have a couple of children, and a sprinkling of grandchildren.

On a Friday night you will still find them on the couch, a drink in hand, listening to music and chatting and cackling away together.

CHAPTER 20

Not Just a Shipwreck Survivor

Mick endured the unimaginable and had somehow walked away. Those 12 days did not define him, but they certainly shaped him. Growing up with his fierce sense of morality, Mick had always done what he thought was right – regardless of whether it would land him in a punch-up or getting the strap. His experience with the *Blythe Star* stoked that burning for justice in his belly.

Once it was all over, he thought back on the promise he had made himself in those long hours after John Sloan's death. That he would be a better man should he make it through, the sort of man who deserved to survive the unthinkable.

Even though he didn't comment publicly again about what happened in 1973 for four decades, it shaped his working life. He couldn't go back in time and save Ken Jones, John Sloan and John Eagles, but he could sure as hell make sure the same didn't happen to anyone else. Always a union man, after the sinking of the *Blythe Star*, he became more involved and was a regular face in the union offices.

Mick watched the union delegates around him – educated men who were tough, knowledgeable and respected. He wanted to become a man in their image, so spent hours volunteering for the Seamen's Union of Australia. In the union he revelled in the solidarity of the workers – it was the same camaraderie that had drawn him to seafaring.

Over the years, Mick moved up the ranks, finally working as a bosun, before he started to consider leaving seafaring to move into the union world full time, to a place where he could have broader influence over the decisions that could prevent a ship like the *Blythe Star* going down. It wasn't an easy decision – he loved life at sea.

He had been regularly filling in for union officials when they had to travel or take a break, and running for election as an official himself seemed the next step. So, Mick put his hat in the ring to run for the role of Assistant Victorian Branch Secretary. He had the encouragement of two much-respected mentors, Bert Nolan, the Victorian Branch Secretary of the Seamen's Union of Australia, and Pat Geraghty, the General Secretary.

During the lead-up to voting, Mick arrived at the union offices one morning to find Bert Nolan busily throwing documents into a Gladstone bag.

'You're nicking off!' Mick said. 'I'm not sure I can handle all this trouble while you're gone, I need you close at hand.'

'Mick,' Bert replied, pausing his packing. 'The sun will always come up the next day and believe me, mate, you're not smart enough to make a fuck up I can't fix.'

'Thanks for the vote of confidence, mate,' Mick replied.

Shortly after this encounter, Mick was elected as the Assistant Victorian Branch Secretary of the Seamen's Union of Australia. It was 1984, just over a decade since he battled his way out of the thick Tasmanian scrub. In just three years he would be heading up the branch.

The charisma that had always drawn people to him, be it on the footy field in Doveton or at sea, and his refusal to back down from a fight he believed was worth having soon distinguished Mick as a union official. By the early 1990s, Mick had a reputation as an honest, hardworking and respected union man.

In the year prior to taking on the role in a permanent capacity, Mick had already been working closely with others, like Pat Geraghty, on the amalgamation of the separate unions for seafarers, cooks, marine stewards and waterside workers into a single, powerful, united body – the Maritime Union of Australia. Part of this project meant envisioning what a new union could look like and then fleshing out the rules that would govern it. He also paved the way for a Tasmanian branch of the union in years to come.

In the late 1990s, Mick moved into a national role as National Organiser of the Maritime Union of Australia. Taking on the role in 1997 meant moving his family to Sydney, but it was worth it. Just a year later he became the

Assistant National Secretary. It was in this role that he took on the 1998 Australian waterfront dispute. The dispute was described by John Howard in his memoir as the 'most bitterly fought domestic issue of my whole time as prime minister'.

In April 1998, Patrick Stevedores dismissed and locked out its entire union workforce – around 1700 workers. It was all done with the backing of the Howard government and involved secretive plans to recruit and train an alternative workforce who would be ready to step in and work as soon as the union members were let go. To get around legally binding agreements between Patrick Stevedores and the Maritime Union of Australia, a new company was set up: P&C Stevedores. It had no such agreement with the union and could happily go on to hire a non-union workforce.

This decision kicked off months of industrial action on a scale not seen for a long time, and Mick was right there in the middle of it.

The response from the union and the workers brought home for Mick the importance of communication, relationships and trust. The union immediately reached out to every worker who had been dismissed and asked them not to cash their redundancy cheque, which would be taken as an acceptance of redundancy, or sign any paperwork. Instead, they suggested the cheques be placed in union safes until the dispute was resolved. The workers complied and did not break ranks. The trust that the union had built, which people like Mick had contributed to in the preceding years, paid off and made the large-scale industrial action that followed possible.

The organisation and precision of the protest action was impressive. Each official was allocated a port and workplace to oversee throughout the dispute. Mick's domain was Port Botany in Sydney. Each day Mick would check in with the other ports to see what was happening and then meet with other officials and workplace union delegates to strategise.

Their networks were vast. Every day they could rally thousands of people – workers, community, church groups, footy clubs and more – to turn up at short notice to protest and support the workers who had been locked out. Tension was high, and some of the 'scabs' (non-union workers who had taken on the jobs) would wear balaclavas to protect their identities as they arrived to work. Standing behind a wire fence outside the terminal at Port Botany, Mick observed on more than one occasion a 'scab' getting into a dispute with the company after arriving, not realising they had been signed up to work in jobs that union members had been locked out of. On occasion, they would refuse to work and leave, and Mick and other union officials would ensure they were safely escorted through the crowd of protesters. They had a hard line against violence, although some protests did escalate, like when a protest camp in Fremantle was broken up by riot police in the middle of the night. At times, workers faced off against hundreds of police who were trying to break the picket line.

Eventually, the company was forced to negotiate with the Maritime Union of Australia and toward the end of 1998 an agreement was reached. While there were still redundancies, what had happened had a significant impact on unions and the trade movement and Mick had seen firsthand the power of united workers.

* * *

Mick was conscious of fighting for the safety of all seafarers and was aware that safety was harder to come by for some than others. He had always been uncomfortable with the way some at sea had treated their female coworkers and had always stepped in whenever he saw disrespect. When a story broke in the media on 9 September 1993 that a female sailor in the navy had been sexually assaulted in Malaysia on HMAS *Swan*, Mick felt sick. He wasn't the only one.

Initial attempts by the Minister for Defence Science and Personnel to downplay the issue and assure the public it wasn't a widespread problem were soon swept aside by a rising tide. Within months a full-blown Senate inquiry into sexual harassment in the Australian Defence Force was launched. The stories that emerged about female seafarers in the navy were harrowing. Mick watched as these horrific stories came to light and felt compelled to do something.

He started making calls with two objectives in mind: to find out what exactly was happening to female seafarers in the merchant navy, and then to fix it. No ifs, no buts. He made it clear that the merchant navy shouldn't wait until they were forced to address the issues, they needed to get on the front foot. He engaged a women's shipping advocate to guide the process and they embarked on a program to change the industry.

A few weeks later a seminar was assembled. The Australian Shipowners Association, every maritime union, industry leaders and crew had all gathered to the rallying cry.

The scrape of plastic chairs and tables as people took their seats died away and the keynote speakers stepped up to the lectern. When Mick's turn came to speak, he addressed those gathered with passion about the need to hear hard truths and tackle them head on.

'If we take anything from this, we've got a job ahead of us and I'd rather get in front of the argument than have to deal with it after there has been poor treatment of women in the maritime industry,' he said.

Afterwards, they opened up the floor to hear from those gathered. Mick saw a slight, young dark-haired woman stand up. As she started speaking the room fell silent. Her voice carried across the heads of everyone gathered. The words that reached Mick broke his heart.

'I have to go to bed with one man, to protect me from other crew members,' she said.

The room was silent. Horrified. Mick was shattered to hear it. He knew that what this woman bravely shared had to be a line in the sand. Walking out of that room he thought, *I'll knock heads together if I have to, this has to be fixed.*

Mick worked tirelessly with the women's advocate and the industry to create a document that laid out what had come from the seminar, the expectations of seafarer behaviour and mechanisms for complaints moving forward. Then, Mick himself called, visited and persuaded every employer in the shipping industry to sign the document, not to mention all three maritime unions.

The maritime industry when Mick first went to sea in the 1970s was male-dominated and misogynistic. Mick was doing everything he could to make sure that wasn't still the case when he left it. His experience with the *Blythe Star* had shown him what it meant to be vulnerable to powerful people and, while not at all the same as what female seafarers faced, he couldn't stomach the thought of anyone feeling a similar sense of powerlessness or suffering.

Over the years, Mick continued to champion the reforms he helped put in place and was always a loud voice, protesting violence against women in his industry and outside of it. He would walk into a room to give a talk, looking down at the front rows of burly seafarers, with their arms crossed and looking unimpressed. Not infrequently he left to standing applause. He believed in dedicating real service and putting in the hard yards, changing minds and wearing down the shoe leather for the cause.

His work and advocacy was recognised in 2012 when Mick was named the White Ribbon Ambassador of the year. White Ribbon, which exists to eradicate violence against women, honoured Mick's years of work to extend the message throughout the union.

He was proud to be leading change in his industry, acknowledging that men were the problem and should be part of the solution. Before Mick started his campaign to bring these issues into the light, very few had heard this kind of discussion from the maritime industry.

* * *

By the 2010s Mick was well regarded for his union achievements. As a high-profile figure he was asked in 2012 what he most wanted in the world. His answer says a lot about the man that 18-year-old shipwreck survivor grew into.

'I want the wealth of the world to be redistributed,' he responded. 'I can't believe the wealth that exists in such a few hands, while people starve, while the environment is being destroyed, while kids are uneducated, while there are illnesses and diseases that could be cured. The world is becoming less tolerant, less prepared to share, less prepared to help.'

Mick was never one to sit and talk about the change he wanted to see in the world, he went out there and took hold of the future – the same way he had when he said he would get help or die trying.

Just as Mick's concern for his fellow seafarers wasn't hampered along gender lines, so too it wasn't bound by borders on a map. In 2002, just as Timor Leste gained independence from Indonesia, Mick got on a plane to make sure that as the country rebuilt itself the workers weren't forgotten.

When he arrived, Mick found that Dili, the capital of Timor Leste, was basic. Dogs roamed the rubbish-strewn streets and tension hung in the air. The country might have had independence, but there was still violence and Mick felt the clinging fear.

Mick and 50 others gathered in a hot, stifling room. He was there on behalf of the Maritime Union of Australia and was speaking to gathered Timorese alongside representatives from APHEDA (the Australian Council of Trade Unions Aid Abroad) and the New Zealand Seafarers Union.

Mick and the other union officials spoke to the Timorese about the power they could harness to demand conditions as a formalised group. The Timorese didn't know what a union was, or what a union did. The idea of speaking up and demanding better treatment went against the fear from years of oppressive and violent rule. The meeting's proceedings were shambolic at times, with interruptions and people arguing, the translators working hard to keep up with the flow of conversation. Then, a buzz went through the room as people turned to look at a newcomer who had entered.

Mick turned and saw Xanana Gusmão, the man who had stepped in to become the first president of the newly independent nation of Timor Leste. He had been a resistance leader during Indonesian rule and was sent to prison for it. He was revered. Mick had spoken with Gusmão the day before, and laid out the importance of protecting the workers that would rebuild Timor Leste, known then as East Timor. He was surprised but delighted to hear Gusmão now repeating much of what Mick had imparted to the room at large. Here was the president of Timor taking Mick's advice on the development of trade unions. People hung on Gusmão's words.

It might have been slow-going, but it seemed as though Timor Leste would unionise. A rally was organised for the coming days. Students gathered to gain support and momentum for a union movement, to make their voices heard for the first time. Thousands marched through the unsealed roads of Dili, chanting and holding banners made earlier in the day.

The nation would need ships, and the workers on those ships would need protecting. It didn't matter to Mick whether it was a seafarer in Timor or Australia, a worker's life was a worker's life, and that was worth fighting to protect. His work didn't end with the goodwill and promises that first trip had garnered. He kept going back to Timor Leste for years, working with the Timorese to empower them to demand the same basic rights that workers in nations like Australia would take for granted.

Just as he was a voice for those who couldn't speak at the *Blythe Star* inquiry, so too has he been a voice for those who have felt they can't speak in the industry. He announced his retirement as Deputy National Secretary of the Maritime Union of Australia in 2015 and continued to work as a rank and file advocate in the areas of Timor Leste, Papua New Guinea, as well as for domestic violence issues. He still won't walk away from a fight for what he sees as right.

That will never change.

Epilogue

2023

On 12 April 2023, the RV *Investigator* rose and fell gently on the swell of the Southern Ocean. Sitting off South West Cape, the ship had taken a detour on the way home from an Antarctic voyage following a request from a researcher. If they had time, the researcher asked, could they do a sweep with their equipment over the area and see what they could find? It was called a 'piggyback project', and the scientists aboard had agreed to try.

With the ship holding its position, the scientists lowered their camera equipment into the water below. On a screen on board, the murky swirling depths of the ocean mist were slowly revealed.

A kaleidoscopic mass of darting yellow filled the screen as the camera moved through a shoal of fish. As the camera descended, the deep aquamarine was marred only by occasional floating white flecks.

The camera sank still deeper. Then, from the blurred gloom ahead, something loomed, and a large mass took shape. Eventually, the mass coalesced into the profile of a ship's bow.

The camera moved closer, scanning along the length of the ship. Silent and still, the ship was sitting upright. It was encrusted in jewel-like corals. The front railing was broken at the bow. A lone fish darted across, then a seal gracefully twirled past, dancing around the wreck.

The camera shifted, and there, on the hull, some letters could just be deciphered.

The *Blythe Star*.

Here it was on the sandy ocean bed. Fifty years on from sinking, it was exactly where the crew said it would be. The ship looked almost perfect, as though it were sailing, were it not for the fact it was 150 metres below the surface. The camera was able to confirm that the locking bars, which kept the hatches closed to stop water pouring in should the ship list, were missing. A receipt had been discovered after the inquiry, suggesting the locking bars had been put into storage to allow more deck cargo to be loaded. Which meant that when the cargo shifted and the ship tilted, the water poured in.

When Mick got a message to let him know they had located the ship, it had just three words: 'They found it.'

He was blown away. It had been 50 years since he'd sat huddled against his crewmates, trying to keep the cold and demons at bay. Now, he was the only person alive of the ten men who'd sailed out of Hobart that fateful Friday. He sat down with the researchers a few weeks later and saw the ship sitting there, intact, at the bottom of the ocean.

* * *

Mick never looked for fame. He never spoke of what happened after the ship left Prince of Wales Bay until every other survivor had died. Out of respect for his fellow crew and for their families, he held his tongue for decades. Until, finally, he realised that if he didn't tell his story, it would be lost to history. Other people – people who weren't there – would tell the story from their own point of view.

Mick had seen that happen once before at the inquiry, and he couldn't let that be the only version. So he put down his own version. The version from the point of view of an 18-year-old boy who went to sea and returned a man, someone who stared death in the face and fought back.

Mick's story is one of endurance. It equals the great odysseys of literature. But it's true.

Acknowledgements

The first acknowledgement of this book belongs with Mick Doleman, without whom the story of the *Blythe Star* and her shipwrecked crew may have remained a little-known obscurity of history. As the last remaining survivor, his willingness to tell the story and bring the memory to life has given a voice to the crewmen who are no longer able to.

Thanks also go to all the families of the *Blythe Star* crew who have helped me understand these men and their story, with particular mention to Joanie Doleman and Susan McKenna who have been beyond helpful in fleshing out details and chasing down information. Michael Stoddart has also been incredibly generous with his knowledge of events, and his book is a valuable resource.

Thank you to Blythe Moore, without you seeing that this story needed to be told and your tireless advocacy of it none of this would have happened. Thank you to Grant Wolter for endlessly entertaining chats about the story, and for being a sounding board always up for an only-vaguely-related tangent. Liz Gwynn and Helen Shield, thank you for your enthusiasm and work as we started researching this story all that time ago.

To our publisher Roberta Ivers, I am so glad the podcast made you cry on a train and you reached out about how to tell this story another way. Thank you for your boundless energy, optimism and encouragement. Thank you to our in-house editor Rachel Cramp and copy editor Jude McGee for the care and attention you have both brought to helping us tell the most powerful story we could. Pam Dunne, thank you for your forensic eye as our proofreader, your attention to detail is incredible. Lisa Hunter from ABC Commercial, thank you for making the connections and facilitating the process by which the book has been possible.

There are some incredible photos included in this book, thank you to the following for supplying us with them; Susan McKenna, Stephen Leary, Jason Power, Donna McCarroll, Michael Stoddart, Nick Dare, CSIRO, ABC Archives and Archives Tasmania. Thank you to Gaylene Quitadamo for administrative support of Mick, getting him where he needs to be and helping us move information around.

Finally, a heartfelt and big thank you to our families who have been there while we brought this story to life and supported us through that process.

Timeline

Thursday, 11 October 1973: Mick Doleman flew to Hobart to join the crew of the *Blythe Star*.

Friday, 12 October: The *Blythe Star* sets sail, bound for King Island loaded with fertiliser and beer.

Saturday, 13 October: The *Blythe Star* sinks off Tasmania's South West Cape. All crew members escape in a life raft.

Sunday, 14 October: The *Blythe Star* fails to show up on King Island, and it is assumed it will arrive the next day. No radio contact can be made with the ship, captained by George Cruikshank. The crew manage to keep the life raft free from the dangerous rocks of Pedra Branca, but lose the drogue that has been slowing their southerly drift.

Monday, 15 October: When the *Blythe Star* fails to turn up on King Island, the Transport Minister and officials from the Tasmanian Transport Commission take a flight along the coast to see what they can find before deciding they will need to notify the Marine Operations Centre in Canberra that there is a ship unaccounted for.

Tuesday, 16 October: An air search for the *Blythe Star* begins.

Wednesday, 17 October: The men endure punishing weather in the life raft.

Thursday, 18 October: The men have the first sign that someone is searching for them, sighting a plane overhead. Ken Jones sets off a flare, but the plane doesn't see them. That night they see a Japanese fishing trawler, that seemingly ignores their distress signal and turns away.

Friday, 19 October: John Sloan is discovered dead early in the morning. After a day hoping for rescue, the men give him a sea burial.

Saturday, 20 October: The men float off Eaglehawk Neck, able to see the Lufra Hotel but unable to make land.

Sunday, 21 October: The remaining crew wash ashore at Deep Glen Bay, where John Eagles dies from exposure and exhaustion. The Commonwealth Minister for Transport,

Charles Jones, announces that the next day will be the final day of the search.

Monday, 22 October: The search for the *Blythe Star* and its crew ends. At Deep Glen Bay the crew make the discovery that Ken Jones has died overnight.

Tuesday, 23 October: Mick Doleman, Alf Simpson and Mal McCarroll decide to walk out of Deep Glen Bay or die trying. They manage to make it out into thick bush, pushing through until dark forces them to sleep in a hollowed-out tree.

Wednesday, 24 October: Mick Doleman, Alf Simpson and Mal McCarroll come across forester Rod Smith and are rescued.

Monday, 3 December: Marine Inquiry into the sinking of the *Blythe Star* begins.

Monday, 15 July 1974: Marine Court of Inquiry's decision into the *Blythe Star* is handed down.

Glossary

Able Seaman	A seafarer with at least three years' experience at sea
Aft	The rear of a ship
Bosun	A ship's officer in charge of equipment and the crew
Bow	The front part of a ship
Bridge	A room where a ship is steered and navigated from
Bucko	A seafarer with at least a year's experience at sea (*see also*: Ordinary seaman)
Bulkhead	A wall in the ship's superstructure
Deck boy	A seafarer in training, with less than 12 months' experience at sea
Drogue	Something that trails in the water behind a vessel to slow it down

First mate	The officer who is second in command of a ship
Galley	A ship's kitchen
Gangway	A walkway or ramp connecting the ship to land or other vessels
Mess	The dining area of a ship
Ordinary Seaman	A seafarer with at least a year's experience at sea
Poop deck	A raised deck at the back of the ship over a cabin
Port	The left side of a ship when facing forward
Porthole	A window in the ship's hull
Ringbolt	A stowaway on board a ship
Starboard	The right side of a ship when facing forward
Stevedore	A worker who oversees the loading and unloading of a ship's cargo
Superstructure	The part of a ship that stands above the main deck, usually comprising the bridge, cabins, etc.
Wheelhouse	See 'bridge'

Having dreamed of a life at sea since he was a young boy, 16-year-old Mick Doleman (second from left) began his seafaring career at a deckboy school in Newcastle.
(Courtesy of Mick Doleman)

When he started working at sea, Mick couldn't believe his luck – he had a cabin of his own, plenty of food and the camaraderie of a crew. Here he sits aboard the *Tri Ellis*, taking in the view.
(Courtesy of Mick Doleman)

Built in 1955, the *Blythe Star* was retained by the Tasmanian Transport Commission to carry cargo to the islands in Bass Strait. Mick joined the ship when he was 18 years old, for a supply voyage to King Island.
(Courtesy of the Tasmanian Archives: LPIC33/1/132)

Above left: The last photo taken of Ken Jones, with his daughter, Susan, when she was three years old. He sailed on the *Blythe Star* just a month later. *(Courtesy of Susan McKenna)*

Above right: Alf Simpson had given up work as a chef to rejoin the merchant navy as a cook, a decision that saw him aboard the *Blythe Star* in October 1973. *(Courtesy of Robyn Butcher)*

Left: A simulation of the sinking of the *Blythe Star*.
1. The ship listing.
2. The capsized ship, showing the stern from where the men leapt to the life raft just before the ship disappeared.
3. The ship sinking. Mick couldn't believe a ship could sink so easily, with so little noise and fanfare. *(Nicholas Dare)*

Within the first 24 hours adrift, the shipwrecked crew of the *Blythe Star* sighted the imposing rocks of Maatsuyker Island, one of the windiest places in the world, but couldn't draw the attention of the lighthouse keeper. *(Courtesy of the Tasmanian Archives: AA193/1/1463)*

With their minds and bodies deteriorating in the savage conditions, the crew drifted in and out of sight of the daunting coastline for days. Making land was more dangerous than staying afloat. *(Reproduced by permission of the Australian Broadcasting Corporation – Library Sales © 1973 ABC)*

Twelve days after the *Blythe Star* sank, the remaining crew washed ashore at Deep Glen Bay on Tasmania's east coast, only to find themselves hemmed in by steep cliffs and ocean. *(Piia Wirsu)*

After battling through the thick Tasmanian bush for two days, three battered and weary crewmen flagged down a red logging truck driven by Rod Smith, who finally took them to safety.
(Courtesy of Rod Smith)

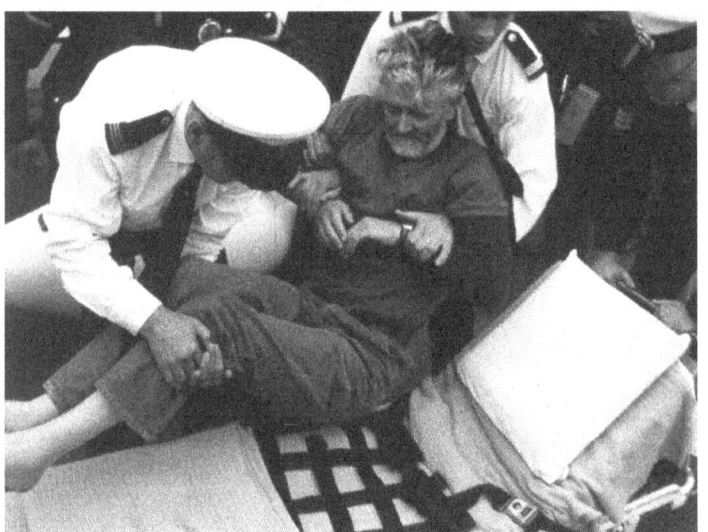

Stan 'Tas' Leary, one of the four crew who were unable to hike out of Deep Glen Bay, being lifted from the helicopter that rescued them onto a stretcher before being rushed to hospital.
(Reproduced by permission of the Australian Broadcasting Corporation – Library Sales © 1973 ABC)

According to news reports at the time, able seaman Cliff Langford wouldn't have survived another night out in the elements. He answered questions from the press as he was wheeled to a waiting ambulance.
(Reproduced by permission of the Australian Broadcasting Corporation – Library Sales © 1973 ABC)

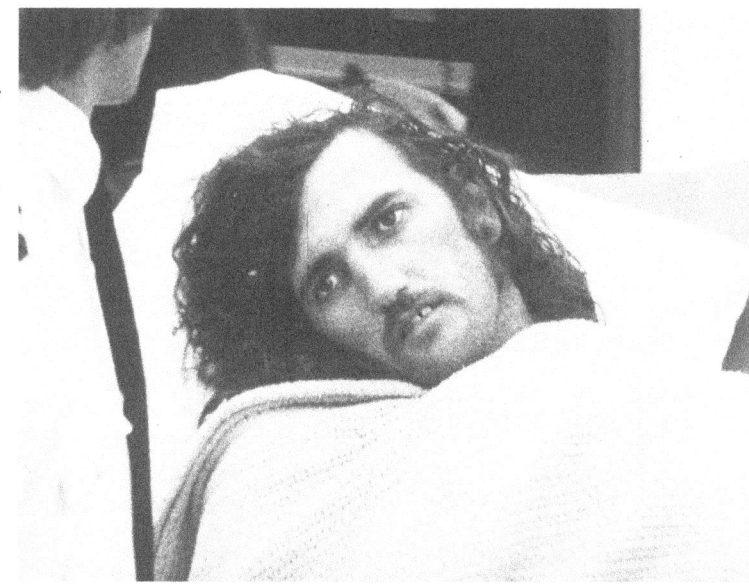

A haunted Mick Power was in poor shape when rescued, having fallen when trying to escape from Deep Glen Bay. *(Reproduced by permission of the Australian Broadcasting Corporation – Library Sales © 1973 ABC)*

Barefoot to rest his swollen and battered feet, Alf (left) relaxes in a lounge chair back at home while his family and friends celebrated his return. His daughter noticed changes in her dad after the ordeal, as if he was carrying a weight. *(Courtesy of Robyn Butcher)*

A Marine Court of Inquiry was left to get to the bottom of the *Blythe Star*'s sinking and the resulting loss of life. Here, members of the inquiry examine a life raft alongside Tas (left), who shows them the cramped conditions the men endured. *(Courtesy of Stephen Leary)*

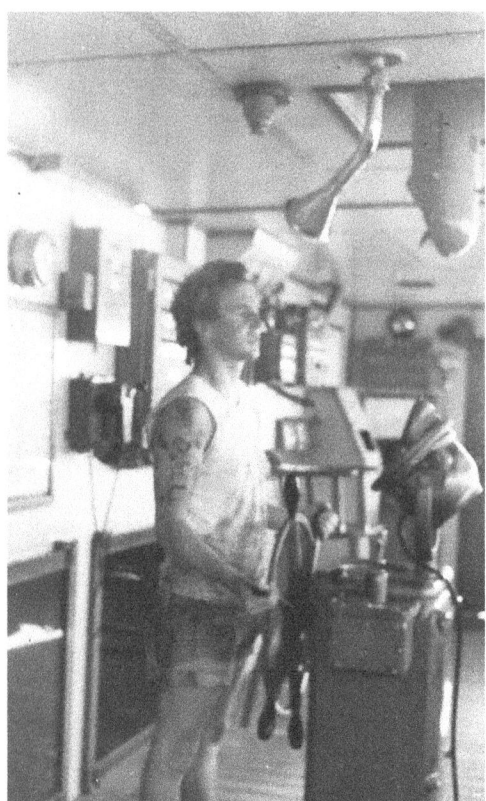

Left: After the ordeal, most of the surviving crewmen returned to work at sea. At 19 years old, Mick stands at the bridge of the *Tri Ellis*. *(Courtesy of Mick Doleman)*

Above: Mick's experience of the *Blythe Star* disaster and the following Marine Court of Inquiry shaped his working life. Mick became heavily involved in the union and went on to fight for improved maritime safety for the next 50 years. Here Mick (centre) leads a Victorian Trades Hall Council rally. *(Courtesy of Mick Doleman)*

When Timor Leste achieved independence from Indonesia, Mick (centre) travelled there as part of a union delegation to help guide the establishment of unions, ensuring workers' rights while the country rebuilt. *(Courtesy of Mick Doleman)*

Mick addresses the crowd at a rally in Hobart in the early 1990s to support Bass Strait Shipping. (Courtesy of Mick Doleman)

Following his return from the *Blythe Star* disaster, Mick resumed his relationship with Joanie, who went on to become his wife and the mother of his two children, Diesel and Stacey. *(Courtesy of Mick Doleman)*

Mick and Joanie are still together more than 50 years after the sinking of the *Blythe Star*. *(Mikaela Ortolan)*